A Basic Guide to International Business Law

H. Wevers, LLM

Fourth Edition

Noordhoff Uitgevers Groningen/Houten

Cover design: G2K (Groningen-Amsterdam)
Cover illustration: Stocksy - Edward Adios - 89961

Any comments about this publication or others may be addressed to:
Noordhoff Uitgevers bv, Afdeling Hoger Onderwijs, Antwoordnummer 13, 9700 VB Groningen, e-mail: info@noordhoff.nl

MIX
Papier van verantwoorde herkomst
FSC® C118189

0 / 16

ISBN 978-90-01-86273-2
NUR 820

Preface

The author would like to thank those who have contributed in one way or the other to this, the fourth edition of the Basic Guide to International Business Law, and those who have supported me in the writing of it.

Special thanks are due to Mr Willem van Oosterom LLM and Mr Ivar Hageman Msc, lecturers at the Saxion University of Applied Sciences in Enschede for their friendship, their kind co-operation and their valuable comments on the third edition of the Basic Guide.

I thank my good friend Mr Jeremy Duncan of Perth (Scotland) for his friendship and for his valuable help in refining the use of English in the text of the Basic Guide.

I dedicate this book to my children, Dirk and Sterre, and to my darling, Esther. Thank you for your support, encouragement and love.

As with the third edition, the author bears sole responsibility for any mistake made in this book.

Enschede/Deventer,
August 2015

Harm Wevers

Contents

1 Introduction to International Private Law and European Law

International law is laid down in rules referred to as Conventions, Treaties, Regulations and Declarations. Even though such terms might imply that their importance is limited, the international law, which they create, is indeed a part of the national law of many states, or at least those states that adhere to the rule of international law. It is also a part of everyday life for the nationals of those states who enjoy additional rights deriving from international law. The importance of international law is explained with particular regard to the fields of International Private Law, International Business Law and International Public Law. The structure and institutions of the European Union as well as the fundamentals of EU law are also explained in this chapter.

1

International Private Law in action

Mulder, a Dutch national living in Arnhem (The Netherlands), buys a new kitchen for his home at Küchen Wunder GmbH, a company established in Oberhausen (Germany). On 1 April 2012, he signs a contract of sale in Oberhausen. The kitchen thus ordered will be delivered and installed on 1 June 2012 in Arnhem. Mulder makes a down payment of 50% of the total selling price of €20.000,–. Klaus Wunder, the owner of the company, explains that a down payment like this is customary in Germany. The terms of sale in the contract – handed to Mulder by Wunder – state that the contract of sale will be governed by German law. In case of litigation, a German court of law will have jurisdiction. On 1 May 2012, Küchen Wunder GmbH files for bankruptcy. Mulder will never see the new kitchen arrive at his home. He wants his money back, but his claims are rejected by both Küchen Wunder GmbH and its owner. Mulder hires a German lawyer to try to get some of his money back. Mr. Schmitt informs Mulder that the EU has issued a Directive in order to protect consumers from a seller's bankruptcy. Mulder wonders what a Directive is and whether he or his lawyer can rely on this Directive in a German court of law. Mulder has heard a colleague of his mention the Convention on the International Sale of Goods (CISG). He wonders, the Directive apart, if this Convention can do him any good.

In this case a German court of law has jurisdiction. German law will govern the contract unless Dutch law offers a more favourable outcome to Mulder. If the Directive has direct effect, Mulder can rely on the Directive in a German court of law. If not, Mulder has to look for a different solution. As Mulder is a consumer, he cannot rely on the provisions of the CISG. The reason for this is that, though The Netherlands and Germany are Contracting States of the CISG, the convention refers to places of business rather than consumers and therefore does not apply. The German court of law must therefore apply either Dutch or German law. Either way it should be possible to nullify Mulder's contract with Küchen Wunder GmbH and uphold his claim. Whether Mulder will get his money back, though, depends on the provisions of the Directive. This verdict of the German court of law is enforceable in Germany.

1.1 Introduction to International Private Law

International law is law agreed by two or more states and is applicable to those states and in most cases their nationals. It is laid down in rules referred to as Treaties, Conventions, Regulations and Declarations. Most states around the world have signed up to several thousand of these rules, each state being referred to as a Contracting State of this Treaty or that Convention. The effects of signing a Treaty or Convention can vary. States that sign a Treaty or Convention agree to be bound by its rules. Sometimes states reserve the right to determine at a later date to what extent a treaty or convention will affect the state or its nationals.

International Public Law

International law can be divided into International Public Law and International Private Law. International Public Law is concerned with such issues as the set-up of international institutions (the United Nations, the European Community, and the European Court of Human Rights), human rights (European Convention on Human Rights) and the extradition of nationals from another country to their home country.

International Private Law

The aim of International Private Law is to solve problems in international legal relationships which arise from different legal systems. As every country has its own legal system, a legal relationship e.g. arising out of a contract of sale may involve at least two national legal systems. If the legal conflict only involves two parties living in the same country, there can be no choice over which legal system to use. International Private Law provides a set of rules either to decide the matter, or to refer the litigating parties to a national legal system where the answer lies. Basically every country has its own International Private Law. However, over the years several Treaties and Regulations have been set up to deal internationally with these legal problems. International Private Law deals with three main issues: jurisdiction in cases of litigation between two parties from different states (including the possibility of executing the verdict given by the court of law that has jurisdiction, in the countries of the litigating parties), the law to be applied in cases of international litigation between two private parties, and solutions to legal problems arising out of an international legal relationship.

Apart from the developments in the field of International Private Law, the law applying to the Member States of the European Union (EU) has become more voluminous and more important over the years. EU law means: the Treaty on the Functioning of the EU and all legislation which is based on it, binding for all Member States of the EU. EU law deals with several aspects of International Private Law.

International Business Law

International Business Law as a part of International Private Law is a specific field in itself. Until recently every country had its own 'international private law'. Various treaties covering wider areas of International Private Law were drawn up to offer guidance to the use and development of International Private Law.

First, here are some examples of topics with which International Private Law is concerned. Every act or conflict under national private law can have an international dimension and give rise to several questions, as demonstrated in the examples below.

EXAMPLE 1.1

A car driver living in Germany causes a traffic accident with a driver living in France in a car park in Amsterdam (The Netherlands). The accident results in unbearable psychological damage to the Irish setter owned by the German driver, a crushed box of very valuable Cuban cigars and a broken bottle of Scotch whisky. The questions are:

- Does a Dutch court of law have jurisdiction in this case? Or should the parties turn to an English, German, Irish, Cuban, Scottish, UK or French court of law?
- What law must be applied to this case?

As we shall find out, the answer to which court of law has jurisdiction depends on the places where the two parties involved live and where the accident occurred. The law and law courts of Ireland, Cuba, Scotland and the UK obviously have no part to play in this problem.

EXAMPLE 1.2

A Dutch national living in Enschede (The Netherlands) works for a German employer established in Gronau (Germany). At the end of his first year, there his employer decides to fire him for no apparent reason. The relevant questions in this situation are:

- Can a Dutch court of law rule on this conflict between a German employer and a Dutch employee?
- Does Dutch law apply to the individual employment contract?

This legal conflict involves two parties, living in different countries. As we shall find out, in a situation like this the employee is in a better position than his employer, as he is seen as the weaker side in this legal conflict.

EXAMPLE 1.3

A seller, established in the UK, delivers 1,500 pair of ladies' shoes to a buyer who is established in Italy. However, the buyer, despite several reminders, does not pay the price they agreed on. The English seller starts litigation against the Italian buyer, in an attempt to cancel the sales contract and to get back the shoes he delivered. The questions in this case are:

- What court of law has jurisdiction?
- Is English law applicable to the sales contract?
- Is there an international treaty dealing with matters such as these?
- If there is a treaty, does it supersede English law or not?
- Is it possible for the seller – in one way or another – to declare the sales contract null and void, and if so, what would be the effects of such an act? Would the shoes be returned by the buyer?

Again, the two parties to the contract of sale are living in different countries. This enables them to choose which court of law will have jurisdiction over their conflict. They can also choose which law will apply to their contract. As the Convention on the International Sale of Goods (CISG) is applicable to this case, this law only applies to situations to which the CISG does not provide an answer. Either the CISG or the law chosen by the parties provides the solution to the conflict and the answers to the abovementioned questions.

The rules of International Private Law provide answers to such cases by focussing on aspects such as the place of residence of the defendant, the place where the employee usually works, or the place of business of the seller and (sometimes) the nationality of one of the parties.
Most of the questions mentioned in the examples given in this paragraph will be dealt with in Chapters 2 to 5 inclusive, which examine the contents of three relevant international Treaties and Regulations.

Three main issues of International Private Law

Three main issues of International Private Law can be deduced from the above-mentioned examples. These main issues are also referred to as the three 'pillars' of international private law. Hereafter, the three questions raised will have to be linked with the words 'main issues'.

Question 1: What court of law has jurisdiction in a case of litigation? How is the verdict of a court of law that has jurisdiction executed?

EXAMPLE 1.4

A seller established in The Netherlands supplies 1,500 kilos of cheese to a buyer established in Germany. The buyer however, despite several reminders, does not pay the price they agreed on.

What court of law has jurisdiction in this case? A Dutch or a German court of law? If a Dutch court of law has jurisdiction and gives a verdict, how is the verdict going to be effected i.e. executed in (both Holland and) Germany?

To answer questions like these we are going to use the European Communities Regulation on Jurisdiction and Enforcement of Judgements in Commercial and Civil matters, hereafter referred to as the 'Brussels I Regulation'. The Brussels I Regulation will be dealt with in Chapter 3.

Question 2: What law is to be applied in order to resolve the conflict between the – contracting – parties i.e. the parties to the contract?

EXAMPLE 1.5

A man with Dutch nationality, whose home address is in Groningen (The Netherlands), works in Nigeria for his employer Shell Petroleum. At the end of his first year there his employer decides to fire him due to the fact that the employee has accepted bribes.

Does Dutch law apply to this individual employment contract? Or would it still be possible to apply Nigerian law, should this prove to be more favourable to the Dutch employee?

The regulation to be used here is the European Communities Regulation on the Applicable Law on Contractual Obligations, referred to as Rome I Regulation and is dealt with in Chapter 4.

Question 3: Is there a specific treaty that provides an immediate solution to a conflict between contracting parties? As this is the contract used most often in the world, this question will be dealt with by using the contract of sale.

1

EXAMPLE 1.6

A seller established in Germany delivers 500 barrels of beer to a buyer established in Belgium. The buyer refuses to pay the price they agreed on, because the beer has gone bad during transport from Offenburg (Germany) to Bruges (Belgium). The Belgian buyer wants to cancel the sales contract and get back the down payment he made. Is it possible for the buyer to declare the sales contract null and void, and if so, what effect will this have?

As the conditions of an international sales contract have been fulfilled, the treaty to use here is the United Nations Convention on the International Sale of Goods, referred to as 'CISG'. The CISG is dealt with in Chapter 5.

Bear in mind that, in this particular case, if the answer to Question 1 is that a Dutch court of law has jurisdiction, this does *not* automatically mean that Dutch law should be applied. It might very well be that a Dutch court of law should apply Belgian, French, English or any law other than Dutch law, according to the regulation mentioned in Question 2. Question 1 and Question 2 are concerned with different topics and are to be found in different international treaties or conventions. Ultimately these two questions are not related. The same applies to Question 3, i.e. another international treaty with its own topics, contracting states and issues. The answer to a problem arising from Question 3 does not provide answers to problems arising from the first two Questions.

1.2 Introduction to European Law

EU law

European Law (or: EU law) in itself is also International Law. One of the main differences is the fact that all EU law is based on one Treaty, the Treaty on the Functioning of the European Union (TFEU), instead of numerous Treaties on various subjects. Another difference is that several institutions and types of legislation are based on this TFEU, and this is unusual in the field of International Private Law.

European i.e. EU Law is more important than we often realise as it takes precedence over the national laws of countries that have signed the Treaty on the Functioning of the European Union (TFEU). However, European Law does not cover every aspect of business competition between Member States or between undertakings that are or are not of the same Member State. So other national and international rules and regulations still have a role to play. The EU, for example, has been working on a European civil code for several years, but until it comes into effect, the Dutch 'Burgerlijk Wetboek' will remain the law for Dutch nationals just as the 'Bundesgesetzbuch' or the 'Code Civil' will remain the law for German or French nationals. To examine the effect EU law has over national laws see the case of Costa vs. ENEL.

EXAMPLE 1.7

The case of Costa v. ENEL exemplifies the relationship between national and European Law and the effect of European Law on (Italian) nationals. In this case the nationalisation of an electricity company was legal under Italian law, but in conflict with EU law. According to the European Court of Justice, Italian law had to be overruled in this case. The text of the case of Costa vs. ENEL can be found in paragraph 1.3.

Undertakings operating within one Member State of the EU, or within several EU countries, have to be aware of the rules of EU Law. They have to operate within the legal bounds set by the Treaty on the Functioning of the European Union (TFEU). The European Commission investigates and decides whether or not the conduct of such an undertaking is, for example, in conflict with the rules of Art. 101 TFEU. Is there an agreement that restricts competition within the EU, or does the undertaking abuse the dominant position (Art. 102 TFEU)? If so the European Commission is known to have imposed heavy fines on several undertakings for breaking the rules on competition law issued by the EU.

The main objective of the EU is to achieve economic integration through the use of a common market where goods, persons, capital and services can circulate freely. A very important condition to make it work is that Member States should give up their sovereignty in those areas governed by the EU Treaty. As a result of this the EU becomes a so-called supranational organisation, a 'State above the Member States', which has the authority to make rules that bind the Member States of the EU, without their specific and prior consent.

Supranational organisation

The starting point here is the supremacy of EU law: EU law takes precedence over national law and is thus applied uniformly throughout the EU. In EU law we can distinguish between directly applicable EU law and directly effective EU law.
EU law that is directly applicable means that the provisions of EU law apply directly within the legal systems of the Member States, without the need for further acts by the governments of these Member States. Member States have no control over what EU law is directly applicable – the Treaty on the Functioning of the EU (TFEU) determines what EU law is to be directly applicable. Article 288 TFEU states that Regulations of the EU are always directly applicable and that a Regulation shall have general application. Direct applicability is therefore a highly relevant issue for Member States. Note that the direct applicability of EU law has no connection with the principle of direct effect of EU law, despite the apparent similarities.

The provisions of directly effective EU law give rights to nationals of the EU who can rely on them in a court in their own country e.g. in a lawsuit against another person or their own national government. Directly effective EU law is therefore only of interest to nationals as it does not in itself affect the Member States. Any provision, such as, for example, a Treaty Article, only has a direct effect if the ECJ has said it does. Only the ECJ can decide if EU law has direct effect, a question on which neither Member States nor their nationals are competent to pronounce. If the ECJ decides a

Treaty Article should have direct effect, then a national can rely on this Article before a national court of law.
In the case of Van Gend & Loos, the European Court of Justice laid down the conditions for a Treaty Article to have direct effect. In this case Van Gend & Loos, a transport company established in Holland, entered into a lawsuit against the Dutch customs authorities. Van Gend & Loos claimed that, in their view, Dutch customs acted in conflict with Art. 12 of the EC Treaty (now Article 112 TFEU).

Art. 12 EC Treaty (now Article 112 TFEU) prohibits Member States from introducing new taxes between Member States. Van Gend & Loos can only rely on Art. 12 (now Article 112 TFEU) if it is directly effective. Therefore, the Dutch court of law asks the ECJ to give a preliminary ruling under Art. 234 EU Treaty (now Article 267 TFEU) to determine whether or not this Article has a direct effect. Can Van Gend & Loos rely on Art. 12 EC Treaty (now Article 112 TFEU) before a Dutch court of law? In this particular case, the ECJ listed the requirements a Treaty Article must meet in order to have a direct effect:
- The provision must be clear and unambiguous (depending on the interpretation of the text of the provision).
- The provision must be unconditional (there are no additional national measures necessary in order for the provision to be effective).
- The provision must take effect without further acts of the EU or Member States.

These criteria have been interpreted quite liberally in the cases which followed that of Van Gend & Loos. The final conclusion of the ECJ was that Art. 12 (now Article 112 TFEU) was directly effective, so:
- Van Gend & Loos were able to rely on this Article before a Dutch court of law, and
- Van Gend & Loos did not have to pay taxes that were contrary to this Article.

From this moment, therefore, Art. 12 came directly into effect in all Member States of the EU. Other examples of Articles of the TFEU which the ECJ has decided have a direct effect include:
- Free movement of persons (Article 45 TFEU),
- Free movement of goods (Articles 34, 35, 36 TFEU),
- Right to equal pay for men and women (Article 157 TFEU),
- Competition law (Articles 101, 102 TFEU).

All EU nationals can enforce these Articles in a national court.

Through the years the membership of the EU has grown to 28 Member States: Germany, France, Italy, The Netherlands, Belgium, Luxembourg, United Kingdom of Great Britain and Northern Ireland, Ireland, Denmark, Greece, Spain, Portugal, Austria, Finland, Sweden, Poland, Lithuania, Latvia, Estonia, Czech Republic, Slovenia, Malta, Hungary, Cyprus, Slovakia, Bulgaria, Romania and Croatia.

1.2.1 The Institutions of the EU

EU institutions are unique. They do not correspond to any other institutions at either national or international level nor do they have any connection with Treaties other than the Treaty on the Functioning of the European Union (TFEU). The institutions of the EU are:

- European Parliament (Articles 223 – 234 TFEU),
- Council of the EU (Articles 235, 236 TFEU),
- Council of Ministers (Articles 237 – 243 TFEU),
- European Commission (Articles 244 – 250 TFEU),
- European Court of Justice (Articles 251 – 281 TFEU).

The European Parliament
Members of the European Parliament (EP) are directly elected by European citizens. The number of representatives from each country varies according to the size of the country.
The elected members take part in Parliamentary Committees dealing with specific aspects of EU policy such as agriculture, international trade and transport.
The European Parliament has a role in approving the budget of the EU which is submitted in draft form by the Council of Ministers.
The European Parliament also has a role in the legislative process of the EU. Until the Maastricht Treaty, it had been a largely consultative role. However, consulting the European Parliament is compulsory in specific areas such as the implementation of competition rules. If the European Parliament is not consulted, the legislation is annulled.
Under the Lisbon Treaty (2007) the EP is to have a more influential position than ever before. The powers of the Parliament will be strengthened in terms of legislation, budget and also political control, which will mean a real step forwards in terms of the democratisation of the European Union. Under the Lisbon Treaty, a more fundamental role has been given to the EP in order to bring about a more democratic Europe and to bring Europeans closer to the EU.

The European Council of the EU
The moment the TFEU came into effect, the European Council became a new institution of the EU. The European Council supervises certain aspects of the legislative procedures of Member States, such as criminal procedures (Articles 48, 68, 82, 83, 86 and 140 TFEU). The European Council has several other areas of responsibility, ranging from employment in the EU (Article 148 TFEU) to terrorist threats (Article 222 TFEU).

Council of Ministers
The Council of Ministers is also referred to as the Council of the European Union and has a rotating membership of representatives at ministerial level. Each representative is authorised to speak and act for his own government. Membership of the Council therefore depends on the issue under discussion.

EXAMPLE 1.8

The BSE crisis: the Council of Ministers consists of the Ministers of Agriculture of every Member State.

EXAMPLE 1.9

Admission of new Member States to the EU: the Council of Ministers consists of the Prime Ministers of every Member State.

1

The functions of the Council are:
- making EU policy in all areas;
- making decisions, based on proposals from the Commission.

Much of the work of the Council is done by COREPER, a permanent body of representatives from the Member States. The function of the COREPER is to examine the Commission's proposals before the Council makes a final decision. Under the Lisbon Treaty the Council will adopt a new decision-making process referred to as the "double majority". This means that a majority of votes (55% of all votes i.e. 15 of 27 Member States) will lead to a decision only if it reflects both the will of the majority of European citizens (i.e. at least 65% of all European citizens) and also the relative weight of Union Member States (the number of votes of each Member State depending on its "importance" within the EU).

The European Commission
The European Commission currently has 28 Members appointed by the agreement of the governments of the Member States. The Commission operates independently of any government, body or person. Every Commissioner has his or her own portfolio, such as cartel issues, defence, international trade, agriculture.
The functions of the Commission are that of:
- Initiator: it initiates EU legislation. All EU laws start with the European Commission.
- Guardian of the Treaties: to investigate whether Member States or undertakings abide by the obligations of the TFEU or those imposed on them by EU institutions. If not, they have to prevent these Member States or undertakings from infringing EU law and they also have the right to take legal action against that Member State or undertaking.
- Executive: implementing the policies decided by the Council.

The European Court of Justice
The European Court of Justice of the EU has jurisdiction in only those cases specifically prescribed by a provision in the TFEU. If the conditions of a Treaty Article dealing with matters of jurisdiction are met, then the European Court of Justice has jurisdiction. As verdicts of the European Court of Justice are very important, it is necessary to know which Articles give jurisdiction to the European Court of Justice most often. This chapter therefore pays special attention to Art. 263 (concerning the action for annulment of decisions of e.g. the Commission) and Art. 267 (preliminary rulings of the European Court of Justice, a ruling requested from the European Court of Justice by a court of law of a Member State on e.g. the interpretation of a Treaty Article relevant to a national lawsuit pending in that court of law).

1.2.2 Sources of EU law
Apart from the TFEU, there are several other types of legislation: Regulations, Directives and Decisions.

Regulations

Regulations are general rules that apply uniformly throughout the EU, and no further acts of Member States are necessary. There are Regulations on numerous topics. A Member State can change neither the effect of a Regulation nor the way it applies in its own territory or to its nationals. **Regulations**

Directives

Directives require each Member State to implement the legislation in a Directive within a certain period of time. They grant Member States discretionary powers as to the means of implementation. Note that a Member State can be penalized if it does not implement the Directive within the prescribed period. In the Francovich case (paragraph 1.3), the Italian government was held liable for damages to a private person. This person sued his own state because he suffered financial loss as a result of the Italian government not implementing a Directive in time. It is therefore important that Member States incorporate Directives into their own national legal systems within the prescribed time limits. Sometimes a Directive is used as a means of legislation if the EU is convinced that a Regulation will not receive sufficient support by Member States for it to be issued. **Directives**

EXAMPLE 1.10

Rules on product liability have to be incorporated in the national legal system of every EU Member State. This is according to a Directive issued by the European Commission. If the Dutch government does not do so in time, it must pay a heavy fine to the EU. As The Netherlands is a Member State of this supranational organisation, it must implement this Directive in time. As such, it can neither object to nor change these rules and this includes their effect on Dutch nationals.

Decisions

Decisions are individual acts, binding on a Member State or an individual or a group of individuals. An example of this is the fine imposed by the Commission in a cartel case. **Decisions**

1.2.3 European Court of Justice and preliminary rulings under Art. 267 TFEU

According to Art. 267 (1) TFEU the ECJ shall have the legal right to give preliminary rulings concerning: (a) the interpretation of this Treaty; and (b) (...) the validity and interpretation of acts of the institutions of the Community (...). **Preliminary rulings**

Most of the major verdicts given by the European Court of Justice have been made with reference to Art. 267. Furthermore, most of the cases in this book result from preliminary rulings under Art. 267. As explained earlier, by giving a preliminary ruling the ECJ gives its interpretation of a Treaty Article i.e. what exactly does this Article mean in relation to a particular case? Does the Article have a direct effect or not? Art. 267 enables the European Court of Justice to add new law to already existing EU law. A preliminary ruling given by the European Court of Justice can therefore be regarded as a (fourth) source of EU law.

A national court is entitled to put questions concerning the validity and interpretation of EU law to the ECJ. Proceedings in national courts are suspended during the period of time required by the ECJ to answer their questions. Art. 267 therefore ensures a uniform interpretation of the Articles of the TFEU and uniformity in the application of EU law throughout the EU.

The ECJ does not apply the law in national proceedings. This is still the task of the national court of law. The national court of law will give a verdict in the light of the preliminary ruling given by the ECJ under Art. 267 TFEU. The ECJ does not rule on the conflict between two litigating parties.

Conditions for a preliminary ruling under Art. 267 TFEU

1 'Courts and tribunals' have the right to request a preliminary ruling

Under Art. 267 *'every court or tribunal of a Member State'* may request a preliminary ruling of the ECJ. The type of court or tribunal is irrelevant.
Any body, therefore, that exercises a judicial function, makes legally binding decisions on the rights and obligations of individuals and is subject to the control of public authorities is considered to be a court or tribunal under Art. 267.

EXAMPLE 1.11

A normal Dutch court of law such as the 'Rechtbank' or the Dutch Supreme Court (Hoge Raad) meets the above-mentioned conditions concerning a court or tribunal and is therefore entitled to refer the matter to the ECJ under Art. 267.

EXAMPLE 1.12

A privately appointed arbitrator is not a court or tribunal under Art. 267 as no public authority can exercise any control. It is not possible for a case to be referred to the ECJ under Art. 267 if it is subject to arbitration (paragraph 3.5).

2 The necessity of the preliminary ruling

Another condition mentioned in Art. 267 (2) is that a decision by the European Court of Justice on a question raised by a national court is necessary to enable it (i.e. the national court) to give judgement.
In the Cilfit case (paragraph 1.3) the ECJ held that a reference under Art. 267 is unnecessary if:

- the question regarding EU law is irrelevant, or
- the question regarding EU law has already been decided by the ECJ (= a deed clair), or
- the correct interpretation of EU law is so obvious that there is no room for any doubt (= also a deed clair).

These three conditions can be decided by the national courts of law themselves. If a party claims that the national court of law should refer to the European Court of Justice, it is basically up to the national court to come to a decision – based on the criteria from the Cilfit case – on whether or not a reference should be made. It is not up to the parties that are litigating.

3 No judicial remedy under national law

Art. 267, 3 TFEU states that in a case pending before a court or tribunal of a Member State against whose decisions there is no judicial remedy (i.e. no further appeal) under national law, that court or tribunal *shall* bring the matter before the Court of Justice.

What Art. 267, 3 TFEU covers is not clear and has given rise to controversy as to the exact interpretation of the word 'shall' and where it leaves the criteria established by the Cilfit case? There are two issues here:

- Does this section only concern those national courts which are courts of final appeal, such as the House of Lords, the Conseil d'Etat and the Hoge Raad?
  In general, the answer is yes: a court of final appeal shall refer the matter to the ECJ. Moreover, the ECJ has taken the view – when reviewing the case of Costa vs. ENEL –, that lower national courts *must* refer the matter to the ECJ when there is no right of appeal or other judicial remedy under national law.
- Where does the word 'shall' leave the national courts of final appeal?
  A national court of final appeal need not make a reference under Art. 267 where one of the three criteria of the Cilfit case has been satisfied. The national court of final appeal therefore still has the right to decide for itself whether a reference under Art. 267 should be made. However, the lower national court whose decisions offer no right of appeal must make the reference under Art. 267, regardless of the criteria in the Cilfit case.

The relationship between the national court system of a Member State and the ECJ, with reference to Art. 267, is explained in schedule 1.1. The schedule shows that if the conditions of Art. 267 are fulfilled, the national court of law must refer to the ECJ. This can be any national court of law, at any level within the national legal system.

SCHEDULE 1.1 Relationship between the preliminary ruling of the ECJ and national legal proceedings of a Member State

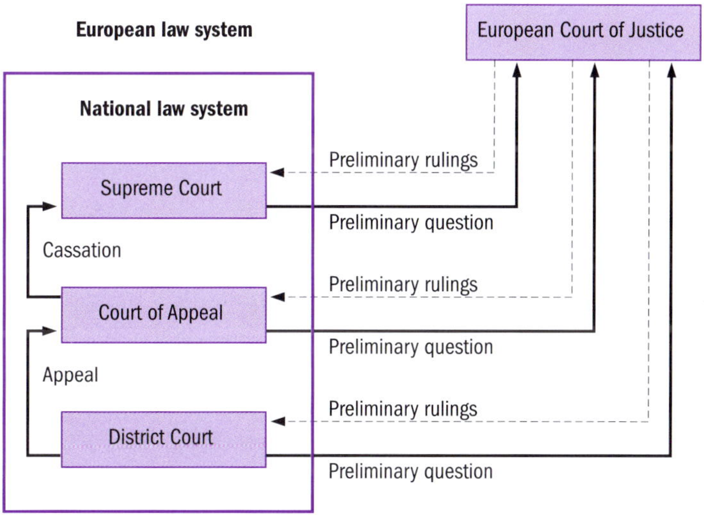

EXAMPLE 1.13

In The Netherlands, in a civil lawsuit, there is no right of appeal against a decision of the Rechtbank (district court) when the plaintiff's claim does not exceed €1,750. If the plaintiff, a private party claiming payment of €1,500, were to ask the Rechtbank to refer the case to the ECJ under Art. 267, then the lower court must do so.

4 Questions put before the European Court of Justice must involve genuine issues of EU law
A question raised by a court or tribunal must involve a genuine issue of EU law raised in that national court. It is not the job of the ECJ to give advisory opinions on general or hypothetical questions. The preliminary ruling has to be applied to a real dispute. This condition is not found in Art. 267 TFEU, but rather derives from the case of Foglia v. Novello (paragraph 1.3).

However, in contemporary case law of the European Court of Justice, it is difficult to establish whether this requirement of Art. 267 is still relevant. Looking at recent ECJ preliminary rulings, one cannot determine whether a legal remedy was available or not and for that reason one cannot determine whether the national court was required to go to the ECJ for a preliminary ruling. Every time a national court of law voluntarily addresses the ECJ it is safe to assume that the fourth condition of Art. 267 is not relevant.

Effects of an Art. 267 TFEU preliminary ruling
A preliminary ruling under Art. 267 binds the national court in that particular case. As we have seen earlier the national court of law decides on this case. It is its duty to give a verdict. Another court could ask the European Court of Justice for a fresh interpretation of the matter under Art. 267 in another case, if all the conditions mentioned above are fulfilled. It is not possible for the European Court of Justice to declare any of the acts of the institutions invalid by means of this preliminary ruling. In order for this to be done, one must follow the correct procedure under Art. 263 TFEU.

Action for annulment under Art. 263 TFEU

Action for annulment

Under Art. 263 TFEU when an action for annulment is raised the ECJ reviews the legality of acts of the institutions of the EU, such as the Commission.

Revisable acts
Under Art. 263 Regulations, Directives and Decisions are revisable acts.

Right to challenge
Under Art. 263 (2) and (4) the right to challenge these acts is given to Member States, the Council, the Commission and to natural or legal persons. The decision must be addressed to this person or if this is not the case, be of direct and individual concern to this person.

Grounds for challenge
The grounds for challenge are mentioned in Art. 263 (2):
- Lack of competence (no legal authority according to the TFEU),
- Infringement of an essential procedural requirement,
- Infringement of this Treaty, or
- Misuse of powers.

Time limits
Under Art. 263 (5) the proceedings referred to under this Article must be instituted within two months of the publication of the measure.

Effects of annulment under Art. 263
Art. 264 states that acts will be nullified as a result of this procedure. The institutions of the EU must take appropriate measures to compensate plaintiffs and produce legislation to replace any act nullified under Art. 263.

EXAMPLE 1.14

The Commission imposes a heavy fine on the Dutch company Tetra for infringing European cartel law as referred to in Art. 101 and 102. If Tetra wants to contest the fine, they should go to the European Court of Justice and have this act of the Commission reviewed under Art. 263. This is a new procedure by Tetra against the Commission brought before the ECJ. It is not a preliminary ruling under Art. 267 as there is no ongoing national legal procedure requiring an explanation of the TFEU by the ECJ.

1.3 Cases of the European Court of Justice

The following cases of Costa vs ENEL, Van Gend vs Loos, Francovich, Foglia vs Novello and Cilfit relate to the topics discussed in this Chapter. Note that the most important parts of the case are printed in bold. At the very least, a thorough study of these parts of the case should be made as they contain the most relevant information. A short summary of these issues is given under Notes.

Notes:

The nationalisation act was in order according to Italian law, but Costa claimed that the nationalisation was in conflict with the EEC-Treaty

Case Costa vs. ENEL

European Court of Justice, Case 6/64, 15 July 1964

Facts

By an act of law, on 6 December 1962 the Italian Republic nationalised electricity production and supply and set up an organisation, named E.N.E.L., to which the assets of the electricity corporation were transferred. Flaminio Costa, solicitor and shareholder of the enterprise Edison Volta, felt badly done by the nationalisation of the electricity production and distribution in his country. He refused to settle a bill for several hundred liras from the new nationalised company ENEL. Summoned to appear in court, he defended himself with the proposition that the nationalisation act was in violation of the EEC-Treaty. Hence, the Italian judge applied to the Court of Justice with a request for an explanation. Meanwhile the Italian constitutional court had passed judgment on the law for founding ENEL. According to this court, the situation at hand was quite simple: the EEC-Treaty had been ratified by common law and therefore the Regulations of a later and conflicting law overruled those of the EEC-Treaty. The Court of Justice was of a different opinion.

Grounds

...

9. In contrast to ordinary international treaties, The EEC-Treaty has created its own legal system which, when the Treaty entered into force, became an integral part of the legal systems of Member States and which their courts are required to apply.

The EEC has a legal system of its own and this legal system is binding on Member States and its nationals as these States have transferred their sovereignty in this field to the EEC

10. By creating a Community of unlimited duration, having its own institutions, its own personality, its own legal capacity and capacity of representation at international level and, more particularly, having real powers stemming from a limitation of sovereignty or a transfer of powers from the States to the Community, the Member States have limited their sovereign rights, albeit within limited areas, and have thus created a body of law which binds both their nationals and themselves.

11. The integration into the laws of each Member State of provisions which derive from the Community, and more generally the terms and the spirit of the Treaty, make it impossible for the States, as a corollary, to accord precedence to a unilateral and subsequent measure over a legal system accepted by them on a basis of reciprocity. Such a measure cannot therefore be inconsistent with that legal system.

12. The executive force of community law cannot vary from one State to another in deference to subsequent domestic laws, without jeopardising the attainment of the objectives of the Treaty set out in Art. 5 (2) and giving rise to the discrimination prohibited by Art. 7 (now Articles 2 up to and including 6 TFEU).

16. The precedence of community law is confirmed by Art. 189 (now Article 288 TFEU), whereby a Regulation 'shall be binding' and 'directly applicable in all Member States'.

17. This provision, which is not subject to any reservation, would be quite meaningless if a State could unilaterally nullify its effects by means of a legislative measure, which could prevail over community law.

18. It follows from all these observations that the law stemming from the Treaty, as an independent source of law, could not, owing to its special and original nature, be overridden by domestic legal provisions, no matter how they have been framed, without being deprived of its character as community law and without the legal basis of the Community itself being called into question.

EU law takes precedence over national (Italian) law

19. The transfer by the States of the rights and obligations arising under the Treaty from their domestic legal system to the Community legal system carries with it a permanent limitation of their sovereign rights, against which a subsequent unilateral act incompatible with the concept of the community cannot prevail. Consequently Art. 234 (now Article 267 TFEU) is to be applied regardless of any domestic law, whenever questions relating to the interpretation of the treaty arise.

Notes:

Case Van Gend & Loos

Court of Justice, Case 26/62, 5 February 1963

Facts

Van Gend & Loos, an importer, alleged that an increase in Dutch import duties was contrary to Art. 12 of the Treaty of Rome (now Article 18 TFEU). The Dutch court referred to the Court of Justice (under Art. 234 of the Treaty (now Article 267 TFEU)) the question as to whether a litigant before a national court could rely directly on the Treaty, in particular on Art. 12 (now Article 18 TFEU).

Grounds

Art. 12 EEC-Treaty (now Article 18

... Community law therefore not only imposes obligations on individuals but is also intended to confer upon them rights that become part of their legal heritage. These rights arise not only

TFEU) has a direct effect: it gives Van Gend & Loos the right to rely on its provisions before a national court of law

where they are expressly granted by the Treaty, but also by reason of obligations which the Treaty imposes in a clearly defined way upon individuals as well as upon the Member States and upon the institutions of the Community.

...

It follows from the foregoing considerations that, according to the spirit, the general scheme and the wording of the Treaty, Art. 12 (now Article 18 TFEU) must be interpreted as having direct effect and creating individual rights that national courts must protect.

Notes:

Case Francovich

Court of Justice, cases C-6/90 and C-9/90, 19 November 1991

Facts

Directive of the Council of Ministers

In Holland: no further acts needed; already been taken care of by the Unemployment Act

In Italy: too late

In 1980, the Council of Ministers of the European Community passed Directive 80/987, concerning the mutual adjustment of the legislation of the Member Countries with regard to the protection of employees in the event of their employer becoming insolvent. This directive protects employees when the enterprise in which they are employed goes bankrupt. This directive leaves a certain measure of choice up to the Member Countries as to the period covered by the security fund as well as to the organisation, financing and functioning of the guarantee funds. The Netherlands did nothing about this as the matter had already been sorted out in the Unemployment Act. The Member Countries were supposed to have had this directive incorporated into their national legislation no later than 23 October 1983. On 2 February 1989, Italy was condemned by the Court for the non-execution of this directive. Some Italian employees - including Francovich -, who had not been paid for several months due to the insolvency of their employers, thereupon decided to lodge their claim for wages with the Italian State and to hold the Italian State responsible for the fact that a security fund to meet their costs had not yet been established. The Italian judge remitted the case to the Court of Justice of the European communities in Luxembourg.

Grounds

Art. 234 (now Article 267 TFEU)

10. The first part of the first question submitted by the national courts seeks to determine whether the provisions of the directive which determine the rights of employees must be interpreted as meaning that the persons concerned can enforce those rights against the State in the national courts, the State having failed to adopt implementing measures within the prescribed period.

11. As the Court has consistently held, a Member State which has not adopted the implementing measures required by a directive within the prescribed period may not plead its own failure to perform the obligations which the directive entails against individuals. Thus wherever the provisions of a directive appear, as far as their subject matter is concerned, to be unconditional and sufficiently precise, those provisions may, in the absence of implementing measures adopted within the prescribed period, be relied upon as opposed to any national provision which is incompatible with the directive or in so far as the provisions of the directive define rights which individuals are able to assert against the State. (judgment in Case 8/81 Becker v Finanzamt Muenster-Innenstadt [1982] ECR 53).

A directive did not have a (horizontal) direct effect until now.

26. Accordingly, even though the provisions of the directive in question are sufficiently precise and unconditional as regards identifying those persons entitled to the guarantee and as regards the content of that guarantee, those elements are not sufficient to enable individuals to rely on those provisions before the national courts. Those provisions do not identify the

1

person liable to provide the guarantee, and the State cannot be considered liable on the sole ground that it has failed to incorporate the directive within the prescribed period.

Liability of the State for loss and damage resulting from breach of its obligations under Community law

...
30. That issue must be considered in light of the general system of the Treaty and its fundamental principles.

(a) The existence of State liability as a matter of principle

Cases Van Gend & Loos and Costa vs. ENEL

31. It should be borne in mind at the outset that the EEC-Treaty has created its own legal system, which is integrated into the legal systems of the Member States and which their courts are required to apply. The subjects of that legal system are not only the Member States but also their nationals. Just as it imposes burdens on individuals, Community law is also intended to give rise to rights, which become part of their legal patrimony. Those rights arise not only where they are expressly granted by the Treaty but also by virtue of obligations which the Treaty imposes in a clearly defined manner both on individuals and on the Member States and the Community institutions (see the judgements in Case 26/62 Van Gend & Loos [1963] ECR 1 and Case 6/64 Costa v ENEL [1964] ECR 585).

If a Member State breaks EU law, an individual has a right to put in a claim against his Member State

32. Furthermore, it has been consistently held that the national courts whose task it is to apply the provisions of Community law in areas within their jurisdiction must ensure that those rules take full effect and must protect the rights which they confer on individuals (see in particular the judgements in Case 106/77 Amministrazione delle Finanze dello Stato v Simmenthal [1978] ECR 629, paragraph 16, and Case C-213/89 Factortame [1990] ECR I-2433, paragraph 19).

33. The full effectiveness of Community law would be impaired and the protection of the rights, which they grant, would be weakened if individuals were unable to obtain redress when their rights are infringed by a breach of Community law for which a Member State can be held responsible.

This is especially the case when an individual suffers loss or damage

34. The possibility of obtaining redress from the Member State is particularly important where, as in this case, the full effectiveness of Community rules is subject to prior action on the part of the State and where, consequently, in the absence of such action, individuals cannot enforce the rights conferred upon them by Community law before the national courts.

35. It follows that the principle whereby a State must be liable for loss and damage caused to individuals as a result of breaches of Community law for which the State can be held responsible is inherent in the system of the Treaty.

Conditions under which for a Member State may be held liable by an individual

36. A further basis for the obligation of Member States to make good such loss and damage is to be found in Art. 5 of the Treaty, under which the Member States are required to take all appropriate measures, whether general or particular, to ensure fulfilment of their obligations under Community law. Among these is the obligation to nullify the unlawful consequences of a breach of Community law (see, in relation to the analogous provision of Art. 82 of the ECSC Treaty, the judgement in Case 6/60 Humblet v Belgium [1960] ECR 559).

37. It follows from all of the above that it is a principle of Community law that the Member States are obliged to make good loss and damage caused to individuals by breaches of Community law for which they can be held responsible.

(b) The conditions for State liability

38. Although State liability is thus required by Community law, the conditions under which that liability gives rise to a right to reparation depend on the nature of the breach of Community law giving rise to the loss and damage.

39. Where, as in this case, a Member State fails to fulfil its obligation under the third paragraph of Art. 189 of the Treaty to take all the measures necessary to achieve the result prescribed by a directive, the full effectiveness of that rule of Community law requires that there should be a right to reparation provided that three conditions are fulfilled.

First condition:
Second condition:
Third condition:

40 The first of those conditions is that the result prescribed by the directive should entail the grant of rights to individuals. The second condition is that it should be possible to identify the content of those rights on the basis of the provisions of the directive. Finally, the third condition is the existence of a causal link between the breach of the State's obligation and the loss and damage suffered by the injured parties.

41. Those conditions are sufficient to give rise to a right on the part of individuals to obtain reparation, a right founded directly on Community law.

42. Subject to that reservation, it is on the basis of the rules of national law on liability that the State must make reparation for the consequences of the loss and damage caused. In the absence of Community legislation, it is left to the internal legal system of each Member State to designate the competent courts and lay down the detailed procedural rules for legal proceedings that are fully intended to safeguard the rights which individuals derive from Community law (see the judgements in Case 60/75 Russo v AIMA [1976] ECR 45, Case 33/76 Rewe v Landwirstschaftskammer Saarland [1976] ECR 1989 and Case 158/80 Rewe v Hauptzollamt Kiel [1981] ECR 1805).

Do the conditions apply to this case?
1 = right given by the directive to employees,
2 = to a guarantee of payment
3 = as there is a causal link the national court must uphold the claims of the employees against their own State

43. Further, the substantive and procedural conditions for reparation of loss and damage laid down by the national law of the Member States must not be less favourable than those relating to similar domestic claims and must not be so framed as to make it virtually impossible or excessively difficult to obtain reparation (see, in relation to the analogous issue of the repayment of taxes levied in breach of Community law, inter alia the judgement in Case 199/82 Amministrazione delle Finanze dello Stato v San Giorgio [1983] ECR 3595).

44. In this case, the breach of Community law by a Member State by virtue of its failure to incorporate Directive 80/987 within the prescribed period has been confirmed by a judgement of the Court. The result required by that directive entails granting employees a right to a guarantee of payment of their unpaid wage claims. As is clear from the examination of the first part of the first question, the content of that right can be identified on the basis of the provisions of the directive.

45. Consequently, the national court must, in accordance with the national rules on liability, uphold the right of employees to obtain reparation for loss and damage caused to them as a result of failure to incorporate the directive.

Notes:

1

Italian wines are taxed at a much higher rate than other wines

French tax law could be in violation of Art. 95 EC-Treaty, but the issue was never put before a French tax court

Contract between Novello and Foglia: 'no payment of unlawful taxes'

Contract between Foglia and Danzas (same provision)

Danzas pays taxes at French border; Foglia pays Danzas the full amount, but Novello refuses to pay taxes = lawsuit Foglia vs Novello

Case of Foglia vs. Novello

Court of Justice, Case 104/79, 11 March 1980

Facts

The French tax department distinguishes three categories of liqueur wines. The first category consists of 'vins doux naturels'. The excise payable is They are taxed with an excise of FRF 22.5 per hectolitre of wine plus a consumer tax of FRF 1790 per hectolitre of added alcohol. With regard to this, the French government, has declared it is prepared to discuss the possibility of Italian liqueur wines also being regarded as 'vin doux naturel'. However, prior to this judgment no such negotiations had ever taken place. The second category is of no importance in this case. The third category includes all other liqueur wines and more particularly, those liqueur wines that are imported into France from Italy. Not only is a consumer tax of FRF 4270 per hectolitre payable but also a production tax of FRF 710 per hectolitre. What it all boils down to is that the tax in this category is considerably higher than in the first category, a fact that the Italians do not exactly appreciate. It is not a matter of import duty but of a national tax, which is (at least in theory) levied equally on all products consumed in France, whether they have been imported or not. Art. 95 of the EEC-Treaty stipulates that Member States are not allowed to levy higher domestic taxes on products from other Member States than on similar national products. By categorising liqueur wines in such a way that Italian wines are, in fact, taxed at a higher rate than French wines the French wine tax could be in violation of this article. The usual way of determining this in a juridical way would be to refuse to pay the French tax or to claim back tax already paid. This would lead to a case before a French administrative judge, who could request a pre-judicial decision from the Court of Justice (under Art. 234 EEC-Treaty (now Article 267 TFEU)) as to whether Art. 95 allows the classification of wines into different categories if this leads to an actual difference in taxation. On the basis of the decision of the Court of Justice the French judge would be able to declare whether or not the French Regulation was void. Not a single Italian exporter or French importer had taken this course of action prior to the judgment.

On 1 February 1979, the Italian Mrs. M. Novello ordered a number of cases of Italian liqueur wines from the Italian wine merchant P. Foglia which were to be sent to Mrs. A. Cerutti, a Frenchwoman, as a present. In the agreement between Mrs. Novello and Mr. Foglia a price was agreed upon and it was explicitly stated that the buyer would not be asked to pay any illegal tax 'in violation of the free movement of goods between both countries, or any other unlawful tax'. Mr. Foglia entrusted the transport company Danzas with the shipment of the wine. In the agreement he concluded with Danzas, he made the same stipulation about unlawful levies. Danzas delivered the wine to Mrs. Cerutti and sent a bill for transportation and other costs to Foglia. The bill included entry for 148,300 lira in taxes, which Danzas had had to pay to import the wine into France. Foglia paid the whole amount to Danzas and claimed the same sum back from Mrs. Novello. Mrs. Novello paid the bill less the 148,300 lira, which was, according to her, illegally collected by the French customs and which she therefore did not intend to pay, according to the agreement she had with Mr. Foglia. This presented the Italian judge with a somewhat peculiar disagreement between Foglia and Novello. On the one hand there was Novello, who was of the opinion that the French levy was unlawful and that she therefore should not have to pay the 148.300 lira to Foglia; on the other hand there was Foglia, who was also of the opinion that the 148,300 lira had been wrongly levied and who wanted to have this officially accepted by a judge. Such a conclusion would be very useful for him as a wine merchant and would also allow him to claim the tax back from the carrier Danzas. The judge asked the Court of Justice for a preliminary decision about the legitimacy of the French tax. The French government would make use of the right of all Member States to put forward their point of view in preliminary procedures.

Grounds

1. By an order of 6 June 1979, that was received at the Court on 29 June 1979, the *Pretura di Bra* referred to the Court pursuant to Art. 234 of the EEC-Treaty five questions on the interpretation of Art. 92, 95 and 234 (now Article 267 TFEU) of the Treaty.

Plaintiff = Foglia
Defendant = Novello

2. The proceedings before the *Pretura di Bra* concern the costs incurred by the plaintiff, Mr. Foglia a wine-dealer having his place of business at Santa Vittoria d'Alba, in the province of Cuneo, Piedmont, Italy in the dispatch to Menton, France of some cases of Italian liqueur wines which he sold to the defendant, Mrs. Novello.

Contents of the contracts between Novello and Foglia, and between Foglia and Danzas

3. The case file shows that the contract of sale between Foglia and Novello stipulated that Novello should not be held liable for any duty claimed by the Italian or French authorities contrary to the provisions on the free movement of goods between the two countries or any other charge she was not required to pay. Foglia inserted a similar clause in his contract with the Danzas transport company to which he had entrusted the shipment of the cases of liqueur wine to Menton; that clause stipulated that Foglia should not be held liable for any unlawful charges or charges he was not required to pay.

Danzas paid taxes without protest or complaint; the payment made by Foglia included taxes. Only Novello refuses to pay taxes, in accordance with her contract with Foglia

4. The order, with the referral to the ECJ, finds that the subject matter of the dispute is restricted exclusively to the sum paid as a consumption tax when the liqueur wines were imported into French territory. The file and the oral argument before the court of justice have established that that tax was paid by Danzas to the French authorities, without protest or complaint; that the bill for transport which Danzas submitted to Foglia and which was settled included the amount of that tax and that Mrs. Novello refused to reimburse Foglia with the sum paid in tax in accordance with the clause on unlawful duty or charges which were not due which she had expressly included in the contract of sale.

5. In the view of the *Pretura*, the defence put forward by Novello would result in doubts over the validity of French legislation concerning the consumption tax on liqueur wines in relation to Art. 95 of the EEC-Treaty.

6. Foglia's attitude during the proceedings before the Pretura may be described as neutral. Foglia has in fact maintained that, in any event, he could not be held liable for the amount corresponding to the French consumption tax since, if it was lawfully charged, it should have been borne by Novello whilst Danzas would be liable if it were unlawful.

7. This point of view prompted Foglia to request the national court to widen the scope of the proceedings and to summon Danzas as a third party having an interest in the action. The court nevertheless considered that before it could give a ruling on that request it was necessary to settle the problem of whether the imposition of the consumption tax paid by Danzas was in accordance with the provisions of the EEC-Treaty or not.

Foglia has no real interest in the outcome of the lawsuit against Novello, but wants a statement from the ECJ concerning the disputed French tax in future

8. The parties to the main action submitted documents to the *Pretura*, which enabled it to examine the French legislation concerning the taxation of liqueur wines and other comparable products. The court concluded that such legislation resulted in 'serious discrimination' against Italian liqueur wines and natural wines with a high degree of alcoholic content. This was because of special arrangements made for those French liqueur wines termed 'natural sweet wines' and the preferential tax treatment accorded certain French natural wines with a high degree of alcoholic content and bearing a designation of origin. On the basis of that conclusion, the court formulated its questions, which it submitted to the Court of Justice.

9. In their written observations submitted to the Court of Justice the two parties to the main action provided an essentially identical description of the tax discrimination which is a feature

1

of the French legislation concerning the taxation of liqueur wines; the two parties consider that that legislation is incompatible with community law. In the course of the oral procedure before the Court Foglia stated that he was participating in court proceedings because of his own business interests and those of the wider community of Italian wine traders who had a stake as an undertaking belonging to a certain category of Italian traders in the outcome of the legal issues involved in the dispute.

Foglia and Novello do not have a real conflict upon examination of their contract

10. It thus appears that the parties to the main action were intent on obtaining a ruling that the French tax on liqueur wines was unlawful. This was achieved by the expedient of proceedings before an Italian court between two private individuals who were in agreement over the intended result and who inserted a clause in their contract in order to induce the Italian court to give a ruling on the point. The artificial nature of this expedient is underlined by the fact that Danzas did not exercise its rights under French law to institute proceedings over the consumption tax, although it undoubtedly had an interest in doing so in view of the clause in the contract by which it was also bound. It is further underlined by the fact that Foglia paid Danzas' bill, which included a sum paid in respect of that tax, without protest.

If there had been a real conflict over the legitimacy of the French tax, then a French tax court should have been addressed instead of the ECJ

11. The duty of the Court of Justice under Art. 234 of the EEC-Treaty (now Article 267 TFEU) is to supply all courts in the Community with information on the interpretation of community law which is necessary for them to settle genuine disputes which are brought before them. A situation in which the Court was obliged to give a ruling by the expedient of arrangements such as those described above would jeopardise the whole system of legal remedies available to private individuals to enable them to protect themselves against tax provisions which are contrary to the Treaty.

Function of Art. 234 (now Article 267 TFEU); ruling is denied by the ECJ

12. This means that the questions asked by the national court, regarding the circumstances of this case, do not fall within the competence of the Court of Justice under Art. 234 of the Treaty (now Article 267 TFEU).

13. The Court of Justice accordingly has no jurisdiction to give a ruling on the questions asked by the national court.

Notes:

Case of Cilfit

Court of Justice, case 283/81, 6 October 1982

Facts

Payment for an inspection of wool

In September 1974, a group of Italian businesses in the wool trade, which included the Cilfit company, summoned the Italian Public Health Department before the Tribunal in Rome and demanded repayment of the duties on for the sanitary inspection of imported wool, which they felt they had been unjustly forced to pay. These duties were due according to Act no 30 dated 30 January 1968.
Proved to be wrong in the first instance and then on appeal, the plaintiffs finally appealed to the court of cassation. One of the points they made was that the duty on inspection should not have been collected, as it was said to be contrary to Regulation no 827/68 of the Committee of 28 June 1968 which creates a common market for certain products mentioned in annexe II of the Agreement. These products, listed at heading 05.15 of the common customs tariff, included any products animal origin'. The Public Health Department argued that wool was not mentioned in annexe II of the EEC-Treaty and that wool was therefore not covered by the above-mentioned tariff. According to the Department, the scope of Regulation no 827/68 was perfectly clear and so a preliminary referral to the Court of Justice was entirely unnecessary.

The Italian court of law is of the opinion that if the solution to the problem is obvious then it should not refer the case make a reference to the ECJ

The *Corte di Cassazione* was of the opinion that the Public Health Department's defence raised a question about the interpretation of Art. 234 of the EEC-Treaty (now Article 267 TFEU). The Department argued that this arrangement could be understood in this manner, that the Corte – whose decisions are not subject to appeal – was not obliged to refer to The Court of Justice of the EU if the answer to the question concerning the explanation of proceedings of the institutions of the Community was so evident, that even the possibility of doubt concerning the explanation was out of the question.
The Corte di Cassazione therefore decided to postpone its judgement, and to ask the Court of Justice for a preliminary decision as to whether a highest judge should be relieved of his/her obligation to refer a case if he/she thinks the community law is perfectly clear.

1

Grounds

1. By order of 27 March 1981, which was received at the Court on 31 October 1981, the Corte Suprema di Cassazione (Supreme Court of Cassation) referred to the Court of Justice for a preliminary ruling under Art. 234 of the EEC-Treaty (now Article 267 TFEU) a question on the interpretation of the third paragraph of Article 234 EEC-Treaty (now Article 267 TFEU).

2. That question followed a dispute between wool importers and the Italian Ministry of Health concerning the payment of a fixed health inspection levy on wool imported from outside the Community. The firms concerned based their argument on Regulation (EEC) no 827/68 of 28 June 1968 concerning the common market for certain products listed in annex II to the treaty (official journal, English special edition 1968 (i) p. 209). Art. 2 (2) of that Regulation prohibits Member States from levying any charge having an effect equivalent to a customs duty on imported 'animal products', not specified or included elsewhere, classified under heading 05.15 of the common customs tariff. Against that argument the Ministry for Health contended that wool is not included in annex II to the Treaty and is therefore not included in the common market for agricultural products.

3. The Ministry of Health infers from those circumstances that the answer to the question concerning the interpretation of the measure adopted by the community institutions is so obvious as to rule out the possibility of there being any interpretative doubt and thus obviates the need to refer the matter to the Court of Justice for a preliminary ruling. However, the companies concerned maintain that since a question concerning the interpretation of a Regulation has been raised before the Corte Suprema di Cassazione, against whose decision there is no judicial remedy under national law, that Court cannot, according to the terms of the third paragraph of Art. 234 (now Article 267 TFEU), escape the obligation to bring the matter before the Court of Justice.

4. Faced with those conflicting arguments, the Corte Suprema di Cassazione referred to the Court the following question for a preliminary ruling:

Content of the question brought before the ECJ by the Italian court of law

> 'Does the third paragraph of Art. 234 of the EEC-Treaty (now Article 267 TFEU) – which provides that where any question of the same kind as those listed in the first paragraph of that article is raised in a case pending before a national court or tribunal against whose decisions there is no judicial remedy under national law that that court or tribunal must bring the matter before the Court of Justice – therefore lay down an obligation to submit the case which precludes the national court from determining whether the question raised is justified or does it, and if so within what limits, make that obligation conditional on the prior finding of a reasonable interpretative doubt?'

5. In order to answer that question it is necessary to take into account the system established by Art. 234 (now Article 267 TFEU), which confers jurisdiction on the Court of Justice to give

1

preliminary rulings on, inter alia, the interpretation of the Treaty and the measures adopted by the institutions of the Community.

6. The second paragraph of that article provides that any court or tribunal of a Member State *may*, if it considers that a decision on a question of interpretation is necessary to enable it to give judgment, request the Court of Justice to give a ruling thereon. The third paragraph of that article provides that, where a question of interpretation is raised in a case pending before a court or tribunal of a Member State against whose decisions there is no judicial remedy under national law, that court or tribunal *shall*, bring the matter before the Court of Justice.

7. That obligation to refer a matter to the Court of Justice is based on co-operation, established with a view to ensuring the proper application and uniform interpretation of community law in all the Member States, between national courts, in their capacity as courts responsible for the application of community law, and the Court of Justice. More particularly, the third paragraph of Art. 234 (now Article 267 TFEU) seeks to prevent the occurrence within the Community of divergences in judicial decisions on questions of community law. The scope of that obligation must therefore be assessed, in view of those objectives, by reference to the powers of the national courts, on the one hand, and those of the Court of Justice, on the other, where such a question of interpretation is raised within the meaning of Art. 234 (now Article 267 TFEU).

8. In this connection, it is necessary to define the meaning of the expression 'where any such question is raised' for the purposes of community law in order to determine the circumstances in which a national court or tribunal against whose decisions there is no judicial remedy under national law is obliged to bring a matter before the Court of Justice.

If a question on the interpretation of EU law has been raised, then this does not automatically mean that Art. 234 should be used

9. First of all, in this regard, it must be pointed out that Art. 234 (now Article 267 TFEU) does not constitute a means of redress available to the parties in a case pending before a national court or tribunal. Therefore the mere fact that a party contends that the dispute gives rise to a question concerning the interpretation of community law does not mean that the court or tribunal concerned is compelled to consider that a question has been raised within the meaning of Art. 234 (now Article 267 TFEU). On the other hand, a national court or tribunal may, in an appropriate case, refer a matter to the Court of Justice of its own motion.

10. Secondly, it follows from the relationship between the second and third paragraphs of Art. 234 (now Article 267 TFEU) that the courts or tribunals referred to in the third paragraph have the same discretion as any other national court or tribunal to ascertain whether a decision on a question of community law is necessary to enable them to give judgment. Accordingly, those courts or tribunals are not obliged to refer to the Court of Justice a question concerning the interpretation of community law raised before them if that question is not relevant, that is to say, if the answer to that question, regardless of what it may be, can in no way affect the outcome of the case.

'Necessary or not' (part I)

11. If, however, those courts or tribunals consider that recourse to community law is necessary to enable them to decide a case, Art. 234 (now Article 267 TFEU) imposes an obligation on them to refer to the Court of Justice any question of interpretation which may arise.

12. The question submitted by the *Corte di Cassazione* seeks to ascertain whether, under certain circumstances, the obligation laid down by the third paragraph of Art. 234 (now Article 267 TFEU) might nonetheless be subject to certain restrictions.

13. It must be remembered in this connection that in its judgment of 27 March 1963 in joined cases 28 to 30/62 (da Costa vs *Nederlandse belastingadministratie* (Dutch tax authority) (1963) ECR 31) the Court ruled that: 'although the third paragraph of Art. 234 (now

Article 267 TFEU) unreservedly requires courts or tribunals of a Member State against whose decisions there is no judicial remedy under national law ... to refer to the Court every question of interpretation raised before them, the authority of an interpretation under Art. 234 (now Article 267 TFEU) already given by the Court may deprive the obligation of its purpose and thus empty it of its substance. Such is the case especially when the question raised is materially identical to a question which has already been the subject of a preliminary ruling in a similar case.'

'Necessary or not' (part II)

14. The same effect, as regards the limits set to the obligation laid down by the third paragraph of Art. 234 (now Article 267 TFEU) may be produced where previous decisions of the Court have already dealt with the point of law in question, irrespective of the nature of the proceedings which led to those decisions, even though the questions at issue are not strictly identical.

15. However, it must not be forgotten that in all such circumstances national courts and tribunals, including those referred to in the third paragraph of Art. 234 (now Article 267 TFEU), remain entirely at liberty to bring a matter before the Court of Justice if they consider it appropriate to do so.

'Necessary or not' (part III)

16. Finally, the correct application of community law may be so obvious as to leave no scope for any reasonable doubt as to the manner in which the question raised is to be resolved. Before it comes to the conclusion that such is the case, the national court or tribunal must be convinced that the matter is equally obvious to the courts of the other Member States and to the Court of Justice. Only if those conditions are satisfied, may the national court or tribunal refrain from submitting the question to the Court of Justice and take upon itself the responsibility for resolving it.

17. However, the existence of such a possibility must be assessed on the basis of the characteristic features of community law and the particular difficulties to which its interpretation gives rise.

18. To begin with, it must be borne in mind that community legislation is drafted in several languages and that the different language versions are all equally authentic. An interpretation of a provision of community law thus involves a comparison of the different language versions.

19. It must also be borne in mind, even where the different language versions are entirely in accord with one another, that community law uses terminology, which is peculiar to it. Furthermore, it must be emphasised that legal concepts do not necessarily have the same meaning in community law and in the law of the various Member States.

20. Finally, every provision of community law must be placed in its context and interpreted in light of the provisions of community law as a whole, regard being had to the objectives thereof and to its state of evolution at the date on which the provision in question is to be applied.

Summary of the verdict given by the ECJ

21. In light of all those considerations, the answer to the question submitted by the *Corte Suprema di Cassazione* must be that the third paragraph of Art. 234 of the EEC-Treaty (now Article 267 TFEU) is to be interpreted as meaning, that a court or tribunal against whose decisions there is no judicial remedy under national law, is required, where a question of community law is raised before it, to comply with its obligation to bring the matter before the Court of Justice, unless it has established that the question raised is irrelevant or that the community provision in question has already been interpreted by the Court or that the correct application of community law is so obvious as to leave no scope for any reasonable doubt. The existence of such a possibility must be assessed in light of the specific characteristics of community law, the particular difficulties to which its interpretation gives rise and the risk of divergences in judicial decisions within the Community.

Summary

1

- International Law consists of International Public Law, International Private Law and International Business Law.
- EU law is the legal system of the EU. It consists of the TFEU and all the Regulations, Directives and Decisions based on that Treaty together with the case law of the European Court of Justice.
- The EU Member States have transferred a part of their sovereignty in legal jurisdiction and the passing of legislation to the EU, making the EU an organisation close to a supranational organisation: the EU is a State above its Member States.
- EU law takes precedence over the laws of the Member States. Depending on the type of legislation, EU law can be directly applicable in the Member States.
  If EU law has direct effect, it is possible for nationals of Member States to use EU law in their own national court of law.
- The EU has several, unique institutions: the European Parliament, the Council of Ministers, the European Commission and the European Court of Justice (ECJ).
- Under Art. 267 TFEU the ECJ is competent to give preliminary rulings.
- Under Art. 263 TFEU the ECJ is competent to annul acts and decisions of institutions of the EU.
- In the case of Costa vs. ENEL, it has been established that EU law takes precedence over the laws of the Member States.
- In the case of Van Gend & Loos it has been shown that if the ECJ decides that a Treaty Article has direct effect, it is possible for a national of a Member State to use EU law in a national court of law.
- The details of the Francovich case show how a national can hold his own Member State liable for a breach of EU law.
- The case of Foglia vs. Novello states that the litigating parties should have a genuine interest in the outcome of the preliminary ruling of the ECJ.
  This case thus imposes a further condition on a national court of law before asking for a preliminary ruling under Art. 267 TFEU.
- The case of Cilfit shows how it may be established if a preliminary ruling under Art. 267 TFEU of the ECJ is necessary before a national court can give judgment.

Glossary

Action for annulment	Legal option under Art. 263 TFEU to challenge a decision of an EU institution before the ECJ.
Convention	A written agreement between two or more states, or between states and international organisations.
Decision	Act of an EU institution that affects only the party to which the decision is addressed.
Direct applicability	EU law is directly applicable when it takes effect in the Member States without any further action by these States.
Direct effect	EU law has direct effect when the ECJ decides that a national is allowed to use EU law in a national court of law.
Directive	EU law binding on Member States: the content of the Directive has to be incorporated into national legislation within a prescribed period of time.
EU law	The TFEU, together with all the Regulations, Directives and Decisions based on the TFEU and, in addition, the case law of the European Court of Justice should be regarded as EU law.
International Business Law	International private law concerning the activities and organisation of multi-national businesses.
International Private Law	Law which deals with legal problems arising from legal relationships between parties domiciled in different countries to which different legal systems apply.
International Public Law	Public law is enforceable by states only and deals with legal problems of citizens domiciled in different states and involving the laws of different states.

1

Preliminary ruling	A court of law of a Member State has the option of asking for advice on the interpretation of a point of EU law under Art. 267 TFEU. If the conditions of Art. 267 TFEU are the court of law may address the European Court of Justice. The advice given by the European Court of Justice has to be taken by the court of law of the Member State (the advice is referred to as a 'ruling'). The court of law of the Member State is responsible for the final verdict (for that reason the 'advice' i.e. ruling of the European Court of Justice is referred to as being 'preliminary' i.e. prior to the final verdict).
Regulation	A type of EU legislation which takes effect in the Member States, without the States being able to change its effect on their national legal systems
Supremacy of EU law	Resulting from case law of the European Court of Justice, EU law is higher than the laws of Member States.
Supranational	The EU is the only example in the world of what could be referred to as a supranational organisation, i.e. an organisation that is higher than the states that created it, due to the voluntary transfer of sovereignty to that organisation.
Treaty	A written agreement between two or more states, or between states and international organisations.
Three main issues	The three main issues of international private law concern jurisdiction, applicable law and specific treaties for specific cases.

Exercises

Exercise 1.1

In 2004 the EU issued a Directive concerning the position of workers who work under a fixed term contract. The objective of Directive 04/123 was to improve the position of these workers. For instance, the Directive prohibits the employer from terminating the fixed term contract unilaterally, unless employer and employee agreed to this option when they concluded the contract of employment. The Directive was supposed to be incorporated into the national laws of the Member States before 1 January 2006.

Mr Hellenberg works as an employee of Porsche A.G. in Stuttgart. He received an employment contract for one year as a computer engineer. However, Porsche A.G. terminates his employment contract after 6 months on 1 July 2006, as they are allowed to do under the rules of the Bundesgesetzbuch (BGB i.e. the German Civil Code). At this time the BGB makes no distinction between contracts of an indefinite period and fixed term contracts, such as the one Hellenberg has. Both contracts can be terminated unilaterally by the employer, without a provision on this point being necessary in the employment contract.

It is obvious that the BGB is in conflict with the Directive 04/123 over this point. It is also clear that the German authorities did not incorporate the Directive into German law in time. Hellenberg's contract could not have been terminated like this had Directive 04/123 been brought into the German legal system in time. Hellenberg starts litigation against Porsche AG and the German State in the German court of first resort, the Labour Court of Stuttgart.

1 Is Directive 04/123 directly applicable, according to the TFEU?
2 What issue has to be settled first before Hellenberg can rely on the provisions of Directive 04/123 in a German court of law? Use relevant case law in your answer to this question!
3 In what case did the European Court of Justice first point out that EU law takes precedence over the laws of the Member States?
4 Is it possible for Hellenberg to claim damages from the German State because of the fact that it did not implement Directive 04/123 in time? Use relevant case law in your answer to this question!

Exercise 1.2

Basketball is organised at international level by the International Basketball Federation (FIBA). The FIBA rules govern international transfers of players; the national federations must follow its guidelines when drawing up their own transfer rules. FIBA rules prohibit clubs in the European zone from fielding foreign players in national championships who have played in another country in the European zone and have been transferred after 28 February. After that date it is still possible, however, for players from non-European clubs to be transferred and to play.

Mr Lehtonen is a Finnish basketball player. At the end of the 2009/2010 season he was engaged by Castors Braine, a Belgian basketball club, to take part in the final stage of the Belgian championship. Mr Lehtonen concluded a contract of employment as a professional sportsman with that Belgian basketball club on 3 April 2010. After that Castors Braine were twice penalised by the Belgian basketball association because they had fielded Mr Lehtonen. By a decision of the Federation Royale Belge des Sociétés de Basketball (FRBSB) both matches played by Castors Braine were declared lost. The opposing teams objected to Castors Braine fielding Lehtonen, as he had been transferred after 28 February, and they complained to the Belgian basketball association that this was a breach of the FIBA rules concerning the transfer of players within the European zone.

Lehtonen started legal proceedings against the FRBSB before the Court of First Instance in Brussels demanding that the penalties imposed on the basketball club Castors Braine be lifted and that Lehtonen himself be allowed to play in the Belgian championship. The Court of First Instance in Brussels decided to ask the European Court of Justice whether the FIBA rules on the transfer of players within the European zone were in conflict with the principle of free movement for workers as described in article 45 TFEU.

1 What matter must first be investigated, prior to Lehtonen being able to rely on the Article of the TFEU concerning the free movement of workers, in a Belgian court of law? Mention relevant case law in your answer to this question.
2 What conditions have to be met to allow the Belgian court of law to ask for a preliminary ruling from the European Court of Justice? Mention relevant case law in your answer to this question.
3 Suppose that there is an EU directive on the free movement of professional sportsmen and women, but this Directive was not incorporated into national legislation by the Belgian government in time and as a result Lehtonen suffers financial loss. Can Lehtonen hold the Belgian state liable for this loss? Mention relevant case law in your answer to this question.

2 Negotiations

In general, agreements are made following negotiations between contracting parties. The same principle applies to international contracts. This chapter is concerned with the legal aspects of negotiations between future contracting parties. What is the legal relationship between negotiating parties during the stage prior to an agreement becoming final? What are their options at the moment negotiations end? This chapter also provides guidelines on safeguarding legal positions and interests while negotiating a business contract with a foreign party.

2

Reaching an agreement or not?

On 5 March 2012 Smit B.V., a company from The Netherlands, enters into negotiations with Dumbreck GmbH, a company from Germany. The negotiations are over the sale, delivery and installation of a computer network to Smit. On 1 April 2012, Dumbreck offers Smit such a computer network at a price of €40.000,-, but Smit does not accept. In the course of several meetings after 1 April 2012, it turns out that Smit's requirements are quite detailed. Dumbreck must invest more time and money than usual in making a new offer to Smit. Smit remains hesitant and demands that Dumbreck make a more detailed offer than the one put forward by Dumbreck on 1 April 2012. In a letter of intent, both parties agree that Dumbreck should make a final proposition to Smit before 1 January 2013. However, on 5 December 2012, Smit informs Dumbreck that the deal is off as far as it is concerned. Dumbreck ask themselves questions like: what is an offer, what is the legal status of a letter of intent, what are the rights and obligations of the negotiating parties and what are Dumbreck's options in this case regarding any kind of compensation?

2.1 Reaching an agreement

There cannot be any doubt as to the legal status of agreements. Numerous laws and international treaties concern themselves with equally numerous agreements. It follows then, in the next section on reaching an agreement, that the content of such an agreement can be derived either from national law or an international Treaty such as the Convention on the International Sale of Goods, both of which look quite similar in this respect. There is no specific written law or treaty on negotiations during the period in which the 'contracting parties to be' conduct talks on, for instance, conditions of sale.

Preliminary stage

This stage of negotiations is henceforth referred to as the preliminary stage, this being the stage prior to the final agreement between the two parties. This chapter will provide answers to questions on the rights and obligations of the negotiating parties during this preliminary stage.

An agreement between two parties is reached when one party accepts the offer of the other. An agreement therefore consists of an offer and the acceptance of that offer. Before an agreement is reached parties negotiate – often for weeks, months or even years – over the content of their final agreement. In reaching an agreement, the parties have to go through several distinct procedures. In schedule 2.1, A and B are the negotiating parties, who reach an agreement in the end.

1 A draws up an offer and sends it to B.
2 The offer is delivered to B.
3 B takes time to think things over.
4 B comes to a decision and sends his acceptance to A.
5 B's acceptance reaches A: at the very moment B's acceptance reaches A the agreement becomes final.
6 This moment is just after the moment when an agreement becomes final.

Schedule 2.1 shows the sequence of offer, acceptance and conclusion of an agreement. A more detailed explanation, with examples, follows.

SCHEDULE 2.1 Stages of making an agreement

1 A makes an offer to B

Offer

A sends B an offer. An offer (or business proposal) is a legal offer, when three things occur:

1 an object is described

EXAMPLE 2.1

Volkswagen Golf, built in 2000

2 a price is determined

EXAMPLE 2.2

The selling price is €4,000 non negotiable

3 the number of objects is stated

EXAMPLE 2.3

The object of the offer is one single car.

Invitation to enter into negotiations

Consequently, where a specific price is missing there cannot be an offer in the legal sense of the word. When one or two elements are missing, a so-called invitation to enter into negotiations is given to the other party. Looking at the introductory case study, Dumbreck makes Smit an offer to sell, deliver and install a computer network at a price of €40,000.

2 The offer is delivered to B

Valid offer

An offer is a valid offer when it has reached the other party i.e. the offeree, B. This is often referred to as the 'reception theory'. It does not matter when the offeree actually reads the offer.

EXAMPLE 2.4

On 6 May, Dumbreck (Germany) sends Smit (The Netherlands) an offer which had been drawn up on 4 May. Smit receives the offer on 9 May and because of a nasty dose of flu reads the offer on 12 May. The offer becomes valid on 9 May.

Withdraw

Note that up to and including this moment it is possible for offerer A to withdraw the offer made to offeree B. By withdrawing the offer in time the offerer prevents the offer from actually becoming a valid offer. After withdrawing the offer in time, an offer no longer exists.

EXAMPLE 2.5

Peters, from The Netherlands, wants to sell his car to Johnson, from the UK. He puts the offer in a letter and sends it to Johnson on 1 May. Johnson receives the offer on 5 May. If Peters wants to withdraw his offer to Johnson – he can get a better price for his car elsewhere – he can do so up to and including the moment his letter is dropped through Johnson's letter box on 5 May. Peters would be better making use of a faster means of communication (fax, phone, email) than a letter.

3 B considers the offer made by A
The offer made by A is a valid offer: it has reached B and has not been withdrawn by A. How long does B have to think about this offer? If a period of time is mentioned in the offer, then the length of stage 3 in schedule 2.1 is clearly determined. A's offer should preferably be in writing, for obvious reasons. If no period of time is mentioned and the offer is a verbal one then it has to be accepted immediately or else it would no longer exist in a legal sense. If the offer is in writing then it is valid for a reasonable period of time. How long this period will be depends on the object mentioned in the offer (a house will take more time to consider than a book) and also on the persons involved (business experts would be expected to come to a decision more rapidly than those with little experience).

4 B sends his acceptance to A
B now sends his acceptance to A; he is letting the offerer know he has accepted the offer A has made. Up to this point A can still revoke the offer he made to B. *Revoking* an offer in this case would require A to inform B that he is no longer interested in selling goods to B and that he therefore withdraws his valid offer.

Revoke

In certain circumstances it is not possible to revoke an offer, for example:
1 when the offer has already been accepted by the other party. Take a look at the schedule: after point 4, the point at which B sends his acceptance, A can no longer revoke the offer he has made.
2 when it can be deduced from the text of the offer itself that the offer is irrevocable. It is also possible that any given circumstances of a case might make an offer irrevocable.

Irrevocable offer

EXAMPLE 2.6

Andersen from Sweden makes Bernsen from Denmark an offer: 'This offer is valid from 4th December to 11 December.' After the offer reached Bernsen and during this period, should Anderson change his mind, he would be unable to revoke his offer to Bernsen. Andersen's offer is an irrevocable offer.

EXAMPLE 2.7

America Today, a jeans store in The Netherlands, offers Levi 501s at a price of €50 each, with the condition that: 'This offer is valid as long as stocks last.' This is therefore an irrevocable offer: as long as there are Levi 501s in stock, they must be sold at a price of €50. It would not be possible during that period of time for America Today to change the price.

At this point, bear in mind that B can still refuse to accept A's offer. He can do this by rejecting the offer explicitly ('Keep the goods, I do not want them') or by making a new offer to A. B's new offer to A is referred to as a counter offer. Note that by B making this counter offer, A's first offer no longer legally exists!

Let us look at the introductory case study more closely. Smit turns down Dumbreck's offer (point 4) by coming up with further requirements. These in turn force Dumbreck to adjust their original offer and so a new offer (point 1) is made to Smit. Every new offer is received (point 2) and discussed by Smit (point 3), before contacting Dumbreck again.

5 B's acceptance reaches A

Acceptance
Agreement

A now receives the acceptance sent by B and the agreement becomes final: they have reached an agreement at point 5 according to the so-called reception theory. The fact that A might not read B's acceptance until a few days later is irrelevant.

6 Revoking an offer after reaching an agreement

This situation can arise in the period immediately following A's receipt of the acceptance. In circumstances where the offer was made with the reservation 'prices subject to change' or 'prices not binding', it is still possible for A to revoke his offer after it has been accepted but it must be done so immediately.
This is a revocation of the offer after an agreement has become final, which is only possible if one of the reservations mentioned above is added to the offer made by A. And A has to revoke his offer immediately after he has received B's acceptance.

EXAMPLE 2.8

On 2 December Getränkenhandel Mosel from Münster, Germany, sends all its customers a list of wines for sale in their store. At the bottom of the list is the following sentence: 'Prices are subject to change'. Peters, from The Netherlands, reads the list and decides to buy a case of South African red wine at a price of €99. He phones Mosel on 4 December and informs them that he, Peters, would like to buy this particular wine at the price given on the list. From this moment an agreement exists: Peters verbally accepts Mosel's written offer on 4 December, thus reaching an agreement on that date. However, if Mosel wants to sell the case of South African red wine at a price higher than €99, it still has the right on 4 December to revoke the offer of December 2nd. This means that Mosel must immediately inform Peters that the price is no longer €99 a case, but as of this moment has gone up to €119. This is a new offer. Peters has the right to accept this offer and to buy a case of this wine but only at a price of €119.

Note that the preliminary stage mentioned in the first paragraph of this chapter is the period of time from point 1 *up to* point 5.

Let us re-examine the introductory case. An agreement was never finalised because Dumbreck and Smit did not get beyond the stage of talking over the specific details of Smit's proposed computer network. In order to establish both Dumbreck and Smit's legal positions more information is needed about the stances they took during the negotiations. The numerous national laws and international treaties on agreements are unable to help us in this situation.

2.2 Legal aspects of negotiations

What is the legal status of negotiations? A letter of intent is often used to establish the current status of negotiations between the parties involved. It is also intended to be a draft version of the final agreement. Parties have to be accurate about the way the content of the letter of intent is drawn up. Parties state in it the action they will take from that moment on. Is a letter of intent a legally binding document or agreement, or not? Does a letter of intent *per se* place any obligations on the negotiating parties? No statute law provides the answer to these questions and instead case law will have to help us out. This will also help to determine just what Dumbreck's and Smit's legal positions are in the introductory case study.

Letter of intent

Case law – i.e. judgments given in courts of law which establish the law for subsequent cases of a similar nature – has shown that the preliminary stage is governed by the so-called rules of good faith. The following verdict of the Dutch Supreme Court lays down this rule, which is a principle widely accepted by other international courts of law.

Rules of good faith

Case of Baris vs Riezenkamp

Facts

Verdict of the Dutch Supreme Court 15-11-1957, NJ 1958, 67

Baris and Riezenkamp are in negotiations over the sale of an engine. Of crucial concern during the negotiations is the cost of building the engine. After agreement has been reached it turns out these costs are much higher than had been calculated during the negotiations. The Dutch Supreme Court, amongst its other findings concerning this case, gives the following opinion on the legal status of negotiations in general.

View of the Dutch Supreme Court on negotiations

...that parties, by entering into negotiations over a proposed agreement, also enter into a situation which is subject to the rules of good faith. This means that both parties should take the other party's interests into consideration during these negotiations;

...this means in this case that if one party is inclined to enter into an agreement with the other party, there is an obligation on both parties to take reasonable precautions to prevent from entering a contract with the wrong perspective or expectations. This obligation is based on the fact that one may, in general, rely on information given by the other party.

The rules of good faith therefore govern the preliminary stage and thus place an obligation on both negotiating parties to take the other party's interests into consideration. What exactly does 'taking the other party's interests into consideration' mean? It means both parties have to give each other accurate information, and not mislead each other during negotiations. Each party should examine the information given by the other, but has the right to rely – without further investigation – on the information given by that party, especially in a situation with people who are expert in their particular field.

This problem of taking the other party's interests into consideration becomes more relevant when one party pulls out of negotiations. In certain circumstances it could be seen as unfair leaving the other party with (huge) costs spent on negotiations and not paying anything to compensate them for their loss. In a situation where one party has invested more money than usual to obtain a contract, the withdrawal from negotiations by the other party without compensating their costs is not appropriate. One party's profitability might well be compromised by the other having left the negotiating table and not closing the agreement. When one party withdraws from negotiations owing to a lack of money, it can cause considerable problems to the other party, who should have been made aware of this possibility from the outset.

One could argue that as long as no final agreement has been reached, there can be no contract and so claiming compensation for damages suffered as a result of a breach of contract is out of the question. But what about the legal possibility of claiming damages other than for a breach of contract?

One should bear in mind that the use of terms such as 'letter of intent' or 'gentlemen's agreement' cannot prevent an actual legal agreement from arising from negotiations. It is possible – even though parties have used phrases such as 'letter of intent' – that they have in fact agreed on the essentials of a contract. And for that reason an agreement could legally have become final and both parties could be held responsible for the obligations attached to such an agreement. To 'be held responsible' could in fact mean that one party could be liable for the other's costs and loss of profit mentioned earlier on. The name of the document is not the only issue to determine whether or not there is an agreement. One needs to examine the circumstances of the case.

Let us go back to our case study. Smit broke off negotiations with Dumbreck. The question is whether he did so in accordance with the rules of good faith that govern the preliminary stage? Did Smit sufficiently take Dumbreck's interests into consideration when doing so?

2.3 Breaking off negotiations: breach of contract or tort?

In order to determine whether any legal problem could arise from breaking off negotiations one needs to take a close look at the facts and how the negotiations stood at the moment they were broken off. As in the introductory case study, bear in mind that the name of the document, i.e. 'letter of intent', in itself is not important. That which is essential to an agreement are agreements on the elements of price and object.

EXAMPLE 2.9

Price:
- Takeover price, payment of costs related to the takeover, paying off the current management.
- Do both parties agree on these matters?
- Is the buyer indeed willing to pay the price set during the negotiations?
- Have any reservations been made by either of the parties, such as 'for all decisions board approval is necessary'?

EXAMPLE 2.10

Object:
- Takeover of the company, takeover of the employees, takeover of trade names and trade marks.
- Have parties reached an agreement on the same thing; are they still talking about the same object?
- Has a date for transfer of ownership been set?
- The duration of the negotiations is irrelevant to the question of whether or not legal obligations should result from the negotiations.

2.3.1 Breach of contract

If parties have reached an agreement on these two essential issues, object and price, then there is an agreement. In that case, a party breaking off – what he or she refers to as – 'negotiations' is really committing a so-called breach of contract. This party is therefore, according to the rules of civil law, liable to pay damages to the other party. This liability consists of compensation for costs covering the amount that is considered reasonable in that line of business and may also include a loss of profit by the other party. If, such as in the introductory case study, Smit were to have broken off negotiations once all relevant elements of the computer network had been agreed, this would have resulted in a breach of contract on Smit's part.

Breach of contract

2.3.2 Tort

But what if parties did not agree on price and/or object? In that case there is no agreement and no way of getting one's costs compensated by claiming damages as a result of a breach of contract. The only option left to the party that suffered damages, is to claim compensation for these damages based on tort. Using tort makes the above-mentioned legal aspects of negotiations relevant, such as 'good faith' and 'taking the interests of other parties into consideration'.

Tort

What is tort and when does one commit a tort when breaking off negotiations?

1 A tort is a wrongful act/civil wrong between two private individuals.
2 Either party's action is wrongful when it can be regarded as conflicting with the rules of good faith that govern the preliminary stage.
3 Obviously the party breaking off negotiations failed to take the other party's interests into consideration, which is required of both parties when entering into negotiations.
4 Taking the other party's interests into consideration could mean e.g. paying an amount of money to compensate for the other party's costs.

If indeed a tort can be established based on these 4 points, then it may be possible to claim damages.

Stage

The damages one party can claim by means of a tort in cases like this depend on the stage the negotiations were at when the other party broke them off. In its verdict the Dutch Supreme Court (Hoge Raad 12 augustus 2005, NJ 2005, 467, CBB/JPO) departed from its earlier case law on this subject (HR 18 juni 1983, NJ 1983, 723, Plas/Valburg). Now, and in accordance with case law from courts of law in nearly all other European countries, the preliminary stage basically comprises two stages:

1 Stage 1 = first stage, parties start negotiating.
2 Stage 2 = second stage, agreement is within reach, a follow-up to stage 1.

Where negotiations are broken off at the first stage, no damages whatsoever can be claimed from the party that broke them off. Only in a situation where an agreement has almost become final i.e. the second stage, and when one party commits a tort by breaking off negotiations, can the other party be awarded compensation for costs.

1 First stage
At the first stage, both parties are free to break off negotiations, if these negotiations have progressed no further than normal as regards their particular line of business. At this stage the costs of business offers, calculations and travelling expenses are at their own expense.

2 Second stage
At the second stage negotiations have reached a point where an agreement is within reach. Neither party is at liberty to break off negotiations but if one does, that party will have to compensate the other party for the costs incurred. Under certain circumstances compensation for loss of profit is likely.

Depending on the answers to the following questions, claims for compensation for loss of profit may be regarded as reasonable:

1 To what extent did the party that broke off negotiations lay claim to the resources/time/money of the other party?
2 Was the other party in financial need of this assignment?
3 In what way did the party that broke off negotiations let the other party get involved in activities relating to the future contract?

It is also possible – thus being a third option – to ask whichever court of law has jurisdiction (Chapter 3) to force that party to resume negotiations. However, this court will first have to take a close look at the facts, before acceding to that request. If the conflict between the parties is significant and a contract between the two is very unlikely, a court of law may deny such a claim.

The two stages illustrated above represent the Dutch situation. Internationally, two other and different views are relevant:

1 In the USA parties are free to break off negotiations as long as there is no agreement; costs of the negotiations will not be compensated.
2 In the EU good faith governs the negotiations between the parties involved.

As a result, a party that breaks off negotiations and does not act in accordance with the rules of good faith must compensate the costs of the other party.

2.3.3 Breaking off negotiations: what to claim?

When discussing the legal status of negotiations, the documents connected with them (such as a letter of intent or gentlemen's agreement) and the options for claiming damages from the party that pulled out of negotiations are relevant. First go through the facts and try to find reasons that will determine whether or not an agreement on object and price has been reached and thus establish whether or not an agreement between the two parties has become final. In a single overview, schedule 2.2 outlines the steps that need to be taken. **Damages**

SCHEDULE 2.2 Damages

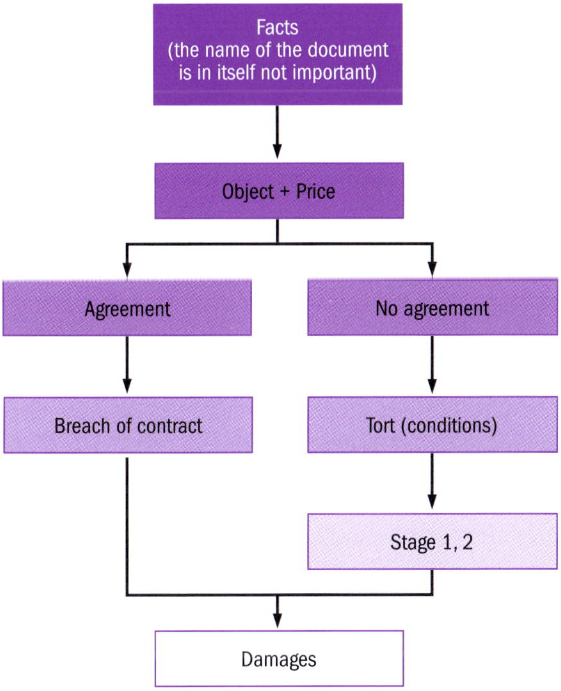

If an agreement has been reached, it is possible to claim compensation for unnecessary costs incurred and/or loss of profit arising from a breach of contract.

If no agreement was reached, damages can be claimed by means of a tort only. One must first establish whether or not a tort was committed. One will therefore have to determine what stage negotiations were at the moment one of the two parties broke them off. If this is clear, it will also be clear what damages will have to be awarded by the appropriate court of law. In some cases a continuation of negotiations might be the solution. Such a

2

solution would only apply if there was only a slight misunderstanding between the parties, which would be easy to solve.

It is also possible (and preferable) for both parties to make an arrangement regarding these matters before starting negotiations. Where negotiating parties agree in their letter of intent that 'no rights or obligations can be derived from the negotiations by either party', no compensation for damages or loss of profit is possible. Another option is that negotiating parties agree in advance that each party will bear its own costs, regardless of the outcome of the negotiations.

2.4 Cases at the preliminary stage

In this section examples will be given about the preliminary stage; how does a court of law determine whether object and price have been agreed upon? The steps indicated in Schedule 2.2 apply in every case and are displayed in the margin on the left side of each example.

In the cases of AGA vs Bouw and VSH vs Shell the circumstances that help us determine object and price are given as well as information concerning the content of letters of intent. The facts and circumstances of both cases can be used to tackle the exercises in this chapter. In both cases there is no agreement and parties have to use tort to claim damages. These cases therefore also provide examples of how to determine the stages the negotiations were at when one party broke them off. Be aware that the Notes accompanying the cases are based on the verdict of the Dutch Supreme Court of 2005.

Case AGA – Bouw

Facts

Court of Appeal Arnhem (The Netherlands) 14-11-1983

AGA B.V., a Dutch producer and distributor of all kinds of gases and fluids, and Mr Bouw, a gas wholesaler and seller and service technician of welding equipment, negotiate over a takeover bid for Bouw by AGA. Bouw breaks off the negotiations and AGA starts litigation against Bouw.

Letter of intent

(...)
2. After negotiating for more than six months over an exclusive sales contract between AGA and Bouw concerning industrial gases and the takeover by AGA of Bouw, the gas wholesaler, parties sign a document on November 26th 1982 with the heading: 'Letter of intent' and with the following contents:
'I. AGA Ltd., in this document hereinafter referred to as AGA, in Amsterdam, and
II. Mr G.A. Bouw, hereinafter referred to as Bouw, in Ede,

considering:

that Bouw is the sole owner of the enterprise Bouw Welding Services and that Bouw and AGA are aiming at close cooperation in the field of selling industrial gases,

hereby declare their intention to reach the following:

1.1 Starting December 1st 1982 Bouw will buy the industrial gases needed for his enterprise exclusively from AGA, under the conditions and prices referred to in the supplement to this letter of intent;

2.1 Starting January 1st 1983 Bouw will lease the wholesale company in industrial gases to AGA for a period of one year. During 1983 AGA will pay costs incurred by Bouw involving the trade in industrial gases, for instance labour costs (except those of Mr Bouw), rent of space, sales and administration. These costs will be fixed by accountants of both parties;
(...)

3.1 On January 1st 1984 AGA will take over Bouw's wholesale company in industrial gases. With this takeover the assets of this company will cost the value in going concern but at the very least the value given to them in the company's books;

3.2 Mr Bouw will remain involved with the enterprise mentioned under 3.1 as a member of the board of directors, and will receive in remuneration 10% of the turnover (free of purchase tax). This arrangement will take effect on January 1st 1983. The enterprise will be continued on the same premises and AGA and Mr Bouw will determine this company's policy together;

3.3 The price of the takeover payable by AGA to Bouw is set at NLG 400,000.-, which will be paid in five annual instalments starting January 1st 1983;

3.4 AGA will co-operate in strengthening Bouw's other activities in the field of gases;
(...)
Agreed to and signed in duplicate on November 26th 1982 in Amsterdam.'

One party breaks off the negotiations: Bouw walks away

On December 1st 1982 Bouw buys industrial gases from AGA for the first time. On December 16th 1982 Bouw breaks off negotiations concerning a draft of the lease contract mentioned in the 'letter of intent' (under 2.1) and informs AGA that he does not want to go through with the deal. After that Bouw never again ordered industrial gases from AGA and went on to supply his enterprise with industrial gases from daily contracts.

Is there an agreement? If so, AGA can claim damages based on a breach of contract

AGA have based their claims on the fact that Bouw had agreed to buy his industrial gases only from AGA starting January 1st 1982, to lease his company to AGA starting January 1st 1983 and to the takeover by AGA to be effected on January 1st 1984.

The name of the document in itself is not important; look at the content of this letter of intent!

The Court of Appeal finds that the stage of negotiations at the time Bouw broke them off had been stated by both parties in the document signed on November 26th 1982, and that both parties started putting into effect paragraph 1.1 of that document on December 1st 1982. This document is referred to by both parties as a 'letter of intent'. This document also states that both parties are 'aiming at co-operation' in the field of selling industrial gases, and 'intend to' undertake several business deals.

No agreement: an exact price has not yet been determined

Paragraphs 1.1, 2 and 3 are closely connected. Also paragraph 1.1 will only last a certain period. The final agreement consists of three elements all of which are closely connected. The 'letter of intent' deals with an essential part of the deal – the takeover price of NLG 400,000.- – but other important aspects have not yet been agreed upon, such as the prices mentioned in 2.1 and 3.1, ...

No agreement: disagreements on the object

... the right to the use of the trade name 'Bouw Welding Services' and the transition of claims on debtors from deliveries of industrial gases as mentioned in the draft of the lease contract.

Final conclusion: no agreement, so no breach of contract by Bouw

The Court of Appeal finds that there are no grounds for accepting the existence of a legally binding agreement between AGA and Bouw, which makes it obligatory for Bouw to buy industrial gases from AGA exclusively, to lease his wholesale business in industrial gases to Bouw and to sell his enterprise to AGA later on. That one of the two parties claims to have said otherwise during these negotiations is therefore not relevant.

Has Bouw committed a tort, thus enabling AGA to claim damages or requiring Bouw to return to the negotiating table?

On the other hand judging by the contents of the 'letter of intent' and the putting into effect of paragraph 1.1, the negotiations were at such an advanced stage that Bouw was not at liberty to break off the negotiations unilaterally, bearing in mind that the legal position of both parties is ruled by good faith, without giving AGA the opportunity to resolve the disagreements with Bouw and to find out if there might be a solution to their problems. This act of Bouw should therefore be considered as conflicting with the rules of good faith.

Only possible in the second stage: can AGA claim that Bouw must resume negotiations?

Furthermore during its enquiry the Court of Appeal did not find any reason to believe that the resumption of negotiations by these two parties should initially be considered pointless. Therefore the demand by AGA that the court should order Bouw to continue negotiations over the lease contract cannot be seen as inappropriate.(Claim awarded: note that neither party is obliged to reach an agreement!)

Case VSH vs Shell

Facts

Verdict of Dutch Supreme Court/ Hoge Raad The Hague (The Netherlands) 23-10-1987

The plaintiff has requested the County Court first to order Shell Chemicals to pay damages of NLG 3,409,876.-, with interest (= 100/60 × NLG 6,600,000.- minus NLG 7,590,124.-). If this request were not granted the plaintiff requested that Shell Petroleum should pay this amount for the damage suffered by VSH.
Both requests are based firstly on non-performance by Shell and secondly on Shell breaking off negotiations contrary to the rules of good faith, this also being wrongful for several other reasons.
In 1975 the plaintiff and Shell started talks, initially about some sort of financial support to be given by Shell to Vaessen-Schoenmaker & Co. Plastics Ltd. (VSP), a daughter company of VSH. Later on – in 1976 and 1977 – parties discussed the possibility of Shell actually acquiring a shareholding in VSP.

Letter of intent drawn up between VS and Shell

At the beginning of July 1977 negotiations between both parties advanced to a point where they legally had to inform the unions, which they did on July 19th 1977 and shortly after that issued a press bulletin with the news that the plaintiff and Shell were '... talking about the possibility of Shell acquiring a major interest in VSP'.

A telex sent by Shell to VSH on July 11th 1977 reads as follows:
'We confirm that we have reached an understanding on the following issues during our meeting of last Friday between yourself and on our part (names negotiators):
1 ... (etc.)

Shell breaks off negotiations

After that VSP is taken over by a third party, Wavin

Is there an agreement between VSH and Shell, is there a breach of contract by Shell?

No agreement: negotiations were conducted by Shell Chemicals, whereas Shell Petroleum would sign the final deal

No agreement: object and price agreed to under the reservation 'subject to Shell Board approval'

No agreement and because of that no breach of contract by Shell; is it possible that Shell has committed a tort?

Establishing a tort: what 'negotiations' over which 'agreement' is VSH referring to?

Preliminary stage is governed by the rules of good faith

10. Takeover of 60% of the shares in VSP by Shell. Both parties have agreed to Shell taking over 60% of the shares in VSP and paying NLG 6,600,000 to the current shareholder VSH (the plaintiff) this being subject to Shell board approval. VSH will keep 40% of the shares. In all probability the takeover will be effected on December 31st 1977
Regards, (etc.).'

The negotiations between the two parties were continued up to August 12th 1977, but on that date Shell informed the plaintiff of the fact that they were no longer interested in acquiring a shareholding in VSP.

6. After that the plaintiff negotiated a merger between VSP and another producer of plastics, Wavin Ltd. Shell is one of two shareholders of Wavin Ltd. As a result of these negotiations VSH sold its 100% interest in VSP to Wavin B.V. for the price of NLG 7,590,124.
(...)

With the Court of Appeal VSH requested to have the agreement of July 8th 1977 reversed and to be compensated for costs and loss of profit. This agreement referred to by VSH was reached by Mr P. Schoenmaker on behalf of VSH and three persons employed by Shell Chemicals, and comprised the takeover by Shell Chemicals or Shell Petroleum of 60% of the shares in VSP and in return the payment of NLG 6,600,000 as confirmed by telex by Shell Chemicals on July 11th 1977.

6.1 Shell pointed out that at first the negotiations were conducted by people employed by Shell Chemicals, but that Shell Petroleum had been the one who intended to sign the final agreement instead of Shell Chemicals and because of that, from the moment the unions were contacted, people employed by Shell Petroleum were also involved in the negotiations. VSH had not been opposed to this.

The telex of July 11th 1977 says, on point number 10: '... parties have agreed to Shell taking over 60% of the shares in VSP and paying NLG 6,600,000 to the current shareholder VSH (the plaintiff) this being subject to Shell Board approval'. VSH has not denied that the people employed by Shell Chemicals made the reservation 'subject to Shell Board approval' during the meeting that was confirmed by the telex of July 11th 1977. VSH claims that the people employed by Shell Chemicals referred to this reservation as 'just a formality' of no significant importance. But Mr Schoenmaker should have known that this reservation is usual in negotiations like these and therefore is valid.

The second basis for compensation for damages is based on the fact, says VSH, that negotiations on July 12th 1977 were at such a stage that Shell was – under the circumstances – not or no longer at liberty to pull out of the negotiations unilaterally. This second basis concerns the circumstances under which a party that breaks off negotiations over an agreement is obliged to compensate for damages suffered by the other party.

2

If VSH had justified expectations that an agreement was within reach, Shell acts contrary to the rules of good faith and commits a tort

The first question to be answered here is what 'agreement' VSH is referring to. VSH claims that when Shell pulled out of detailed negotiations, parties at that stage and at that time had the same opinion on various essential aspects of the final agreement, such as 'the price' and 'the object'.
The Court of Appeal concludes that when VSH refers to an 'agreement', they mean the 'agreement' reached on July 8th 1977, confirmed by Shell by telex on July 11th 1977, that Shell would take over 60% of the shares of VSP in return for a payment of NLG 6,600,000.

At this point parties have to bear in mind that by entering into negotiations their relationship is governed by the rules of good faith, which means that they have to take the other party's interests into consideration. But Shell would still have been at liberty to break off negotiations over this joint venture, unless VSH had justified expectations depending on the circumstances' that a joint venture would have been within reach.

The meeting of July 8th 1977 did not only concern itself with a 60% takeover by Shell of VSP but also with the financial aspects of such a takeover. Parties agreed to increase the capital of VSP by NLG 5,200,000. Mr P Schoenmaker would finance 40% of this increase in capital; Shell would finance 60%. VSH never explained how it would raise the amount of money needed to contribute to the increase in capital. VSH later admitted during court proceedings that it would not have been able to finance this increase in capital.

No justified expectations of VSH regarding a 60% takeover by Shell

On August 8th 1977 VSH and four persons employed by Shell Chemicals held a meeting at a bank. On this occasion Shell pointed out that if the future financial resources of VSH were not secure, Shell would prefer a 100% takeover of VSP. VSH had said in court it had not been opposed to this takeover and parties left that day thinking that from that moment on it would be better to talk about a 100% takeover.

So Shell did not act contrary to the rules of good faith, and therefore no tort was committed when they pulled out of the negotiations in the way they did

So even if Shell had not pulled out of negotiations on August 12th 1977, but had continued negotiating with VSH, there would have been no resulting joint venture in which Shell would have bought only 60% of the shares of VSP. Bearing in mind the necessary investment and the fact that VSH could not finance it, the idea of such a joint venture was therefore not an option from the start and both parties had already dropped this idea by August 8th 1977. So by August 12th 1977 VSH simply could not have had any justified expectations of a joint venture with Shell.

VSH claims that there are also other circumstances that make the actions of Shell wrongful and contrary to the rules of good faith.

Other reasons that indicate a tort committed by Shell in this case?

Firstly VSH claims that Shell's reasons for breaking off negotiations are not valid. In the court's opinion these reasons are irrelevant to the matter of whether damages should be paid to VSH.

Secondly VSH claims that Shell had deliberately refused to resume the negotiations and solve the differences between them. If VSH is referring to the negotiations over a 60% takeover by Shell, then there is nothing to negotiate, in the court's opinion. If VSH is referring to negotiations over a 100% takeover, then this is not in any way connected with the second basis, in the court's opinion.

No tort committed by Shell: no compensation of damage suffered by VSH

This means that the second basis for compensation for damages claimed by VSH cannot be accepted either. All claims for compensation are denied.

Summary

- An agreement becomes final when the offer of one party is accepted by the other party. An agreement thus consists of an offer and an acceptance of that offer.

- An offer:
  - must be distinguished from an invitation to enter into negotiations
  - becomes a valid offer the moment the offer reaches the offeree
  - can be withdrawn up to and including the moment the offer reaches the offeree
  - can be revoked up to the moment the offeree sends his acceptance to the offerer
  - can be revoked by the offerer even after the offer was accepted by the offeree in cases where the offer was made under a reservation such as 'prices not binding'

- An acceptance is valid the moment it reaches the offerer. At this moment the agreement becomes final.

- The period of time up to the moment the agreement becomes final, i.e. the period of negotiations between the parties, is referred to as the preliminary stage.

- The preliminary stage is governed by the rules of good faith. The negotiating parties enter into a situation where one has to take the other party's interests into consideration.

- As a result, breaking off negotiations can conflict with the rules of good faith. Thus breaking off negotiations by one party can lead to a claim for compensation for damages by the other party. This claim must be based on either a breach of contract or on tort. The circumstances of the case determine whether breach of contract or tort applies. And in a case of tort, the stage negotiations were at when they were broken off is relevant in deciding the level of compensation for.

Glossary

Acceptance	Giving word either orally or in writing, that one agrees to the offer that one has received.
Agreement	An agreement becomes final when an offer made by one party is accepted by the other party and the acceptance reaches the offerer.
Breach of contract	One party to a contract does not meet the obligations imposed by the contract, thus resulting in damages to the other party.
Contract	An agreement put in writing.
Damages	Costs and extra expenses one suffers as a result of a breach of contract or a tort committed by another party.
Good faith	Generally accepted and morally justifiable behaviour depending on the situation.
Invitation to enter into negotiations	A proposal to come to an agreement that lacks some of the elements of an offer; an invitation to make an offer
Irrevocable offer	An offer that has become valid cannot be cancelled by the offerer, due to the content of the offer. The offer remains valid and cannot be cancelled e.g. because of the period of time mentioned in the offer.
Letter of intent	A letter of intent is used to state the current status of negotiations between the parties involved and is intended to be a draft version of the final agreement.
Loss of profit	Compensation for loss of profit means making financial restitution to an aggrieved party, putting that party in a position where it would have been had the agreement become final. The compensation for loss of profit is an estimate of the profit the party would have made in a situation had negotiations not been broken off and an agreement become final.
Negotiations	Period of time during which parties, through making offers and counter offers, discuss the content of a possible future agreement and by acceptance of an offer make an agreement.

Offer	A proposal to make an agreement contains a description of the object, the price and the number of objects.
Offeree	He who receives an offer made by another person.
Offerer	He who makes an offer to another person.
Preliminary stage	Stage of negotiations between two or more parties.
Revoking an offer	The offerer cancels his own valid offer orally or in writing; a valid offer no longer exists. Possible up to the moment the offeree sends his acceptance, unless the offer is irrevocable.
Stage	A moment in time, a period of time.
Tort	A wrongful act committed by a private party against another private party, thus acting in conflict with statutory law or in conflict with the rules of good faith that govern the preliminary stage and causing the other party damage.
Valid offer	An offer becomes a valid offer the moment it reaches the offeree
Withdrawing an offer	Preventing an offer from becoming a valid offer by using a faster means of communication than the one used for the offer itself in order to cancel one's own offer. Possible up to and including the moment the offer reaches the offeree.

Exercises

2

The exercises should be answered using schedule 2.2 and the relevant elements of the cases in the previous section.

Exercise 2.1
Bolsch N.V., a Dutch brewer, is determined to acquire a larger market share in the Dutch beer market. For that reason they enter into negotiations with Hopbergen Breweries of Bruges Belgium – famous for its Trappist beers – on 5 January 2016 by sending the brewery a letter inviting them to come to Enschede, The Netherlands.

On this occasion, the Bolsch staff unfold their company's plans:
- a complete takeover of the Hopbergen brewery in the monastery (= convent) near Bruges (Belgium);
- an increase in the production of original Trappist beer;
- the development of two new Trappist beers apart from the famous 'Enkel', 'Dubbel', 'Tripel' and 'Quadrupel';
- a new high-tech brewery, to be built on part of the current location thus modernising the works;
- the exclusion of all monks from the production of Trappist beer;
- the trade name of the Hopbergen beers of course will have to change to 'Bolsch Hopbergen Beers';
- Bolsch offers a minimum takeover price of €4,000,000,–.

The representatives of the Hopbergen brewery tell Bolsch that they in turn will first have to inform the monastery's board, but – provisionally – they also tell Bolsch that though Hopbergen is interested in further negotiations, neither excluding the monks from the production of beer, nor a change in the Hopbergen trade name are negotiable. There is also the possibility that the Hopbergen Brewery might lose its right to use the designation of 'trappist beer' if it were taken over by a large brewery like Bolsch.

At the end of their first meeting, Bolsch and Hopbergen Brewery draw up a letter of intent:

'On January 15th 2016 Bolsch Breweries N.V. and Hopbergen Brewery started negotiations over the possible takeover of Hopbergen by Bolsch. Parties agree that:
- *The current minimum takeover price offered by Bolsch is €4,000,000.*
- *Subjects that have yet to be decided on are the personnel of the future brewery, the new trade name of the beers, and the use of the designation 'trappist beer' after a takeover by Bolsch.*

- *Parties will meet again as soon as the Board of Directors of both companies have had a chance to discuss the proposal, but before April 1st 2016.*
- *Parties have the intention to effect this possible takeover before 1 January 2017 Enschede (signed by both parties) etc.'*

After their second meeting on 8 April 2016, the same points of disagreement still remain. Hopbergen wants further information from Bolsch about the new brewery, the production process in the new brewery and finds that – as the monks are excluded from the production process – that the takeover price should be more than €5,000,000. This extra information costs Bolsch another €30,000 on top of the €50,000 they had already spent on negotiations. Bolsch informs Hopbergen that the requested information will be available on 1 August 2016.

On 1 July 2016 Hopbergen informs Bolsch that the deal is off, as far as they are concerned, because no word has been received from Bolsch since 8 April 2016 and in the meantime they have received a much better offer from another Dutch brewery, Heineken, covering all relevant aspects of the takeover. Bolsch is not amused by this act of Hopbergen, and decides to start litigation against Hopbergen.
Bolsch wants Hopbergen to return to the negotiating table, and if this is no longer possible Bolsch wants compensation for costs and loss of profit (estimated for 2017 alone at up to €500,000,–).

Will the competent court of law have to award the claims submitted by Bolsch?
Motivate the answers carefully, by using all relevant facts of the case.

Exercise 2.2
Since the beginning of the nineteen eighties Frank Brewer has managed to build a successful computer enterprise. In 2014 Brewer employs about 220 people. Unfortunately, the 'golden days' in the computer business are over and Frank thinks it would be a good idea to sell his enterprise to a bigger company. In June 2014 meaningful contact was made with IBM, a company with its roots in the USA.
Frank has engaged an attorney, Mr Anderson, to conduct the negotiations with IBM on his behalf. Frank has given him a number of conditions of sale he wants to have met:
1 The takeover must be finalised before 1 June 2015.
2 There must be a minimum price.
3 The takeover of all personnel must be secured.
4 The council of employees and unions should be kept informed at all times.

Mr Anderson and IBM negotiate over these issues and conditions and reach an understanding that is acceptable to both parties. This understanding is put in writing in a document called 'Letter of intent'. This letter of intent reads as follows:
1 *IBM agrees to the takeover of Brewer shares, that is 100% of the shares in Brewertech Ltd. at a minimum price of €5,000,000.*
2 *IBM guarantees the current position of the employees for a period of two years, as agreed to by the unions.*

3 accountants' reports will determine the exact price of Brewertech Ltd. and whether or not that price should exceed €5,000,000.
4 the takeover will take place on 15 March 2015, at the office of notary Mr Koning.

On 1 February 2015 Brewer receives a message from IBM that 'due to current economic developments, IBM does not want to go through with the takeover and therefore cancels the appointment of 15 March 2015'. Brewer immediately consults Mr Anderson. The attorney is a bit shaken by this news because the only tangible result of the negotiations with IBM is this piece of paper called 'letter of intent'. Anderson tells Brewer that he thinks there is very little he can do. Brewer cannot believe his ears and wants another expert's 'second opinion'.

Is Mr Anderson right, and if so, why? If he is wrong, describe what legal action Brewer should take in this case against IBM's conduct and state the reasons for doing so!

Exercise 2.3
Tango B.V., a Dutch producer and distributor of all kinds of petrol, and Mr Huisman, a small petrol wholesaler, negotiate the takeover of Huisman by Tango. After more than six months of negotiations over an exclusive petrol sales contract between Tango and Huisman and the takeover of Huisman's wholesale petrol company by Tango parties sign a document on 26 November 2012 with the heading: 'Letter of intent' which contains the following:

Letter of intent

Tango B.V., hereinafter referred to as Tango, in Amsterdam, and Mr G.A. Huisman, hereinafter referred to as Huisman, in Ede, considering that Huisman is the sole owner of the enterprise Huisman Petrol Services and that Huisman and Tango are aiming at close cooperation in the field of selling petrol, declare their intention to agree on the following:

1. Starting 1 December 2014 Huisman will buy the petrol needed for his enterprise exclusively from Tango, under the conditions and prices referred to in the supplement to this letter of intent;

2. Starting 1 January 2015 Huisman will lease the wholesale petrol company to Tango for a period of one year. During 2013 Tango will pay Huisman's costs involved with the trade in petrol, for instance labour costs (except for Mr Huisman), rent of space, sales and administration. Accountants for both parties will fix these costs;

3. On 1 January 2016 Tango will take over the Huisman wholesale petrol company. With this takeover the assets of this company will cost the value in going concern but at the very least the value given to them in the company's books;

4. Mr Huisman will remain involved with the enterprise referred to in paragraph 3. He will serve on the board of directors, and will receive 10% of the turnover (exclusive of purchase tax). This arrangement will take effect on 1 January 2016. The enterprise will be continued on the same premises and Tango and Mr Huisman will determine this company's policy together;

5. The price for the takeover to be paid to Huisman by Tango is set at €500,000 to be paid in five annual instalments starting 1 January 2016;

6. Tango will cooperate in strengthening Huisman's other petrol-related activities.

Agreed to and signed in duplicate on 26 November 2014 in Amsterdam.'

On 1 December 2014 Huisman buys petrol from Tango for the first time. On 16 December 2015 Huisman breaks off negotiations over a draft of the lease contract referred to in the 'letter of intent' (paragraph 2) and informs Tango that he does not want to go through with the deal. After that Huisman never again ordered petrol from Tango and went on to supply his enterprise with petrol from daily contracts.

Tango starts litigation against Huisman in order to force him to return to the negotiating table. Huisman in turn states there is no agreement between the two negotiating parties and therefore no claim by Tango should be approved.

Give a well-argued opinion on this matter; will Tango's claim have to be upheld by the Dutch court of law?

3 Courts

One of the three main issues of International Private Law is the question of which court of law has jurisdiction when dispute arises from a contractual or non-contractual relationship. If the opposing parties live in the same country, the jurisdiction of a court of law is not an issue – it does, however, become an issue if the opposing parties are from different countries. A Regulation of the EU (Brussels I Regulation) establishes which court of law has jurisdiction in international legal disputes over real estate, insurance matters, consumer contracts, contracts of employment, tort and breaches of contract in general. This chapter explains the issue of jurisdiction within the EU when legal disputes arise between parties who live in different countries.

Issues of jurisdiction when the litigating parties are from different states

3

Mitchell Ltd., a company established in the UK, closes a contract of sale with Smit B.V., a company established in The Netherlands. Smit is to deliver computer components to Mitchell. The delivery is carried out correctly, but the Dutch seller does not receive payment. Having phoned and faxed several times, Smit wants to starts litigation against Mitchell. However, the question is where to go i.e. what court of law should be asked to settle this legal conflict? It would put Smit at a financial (extra costs for hiring UK lawyers), legal (what is the procedure in the UK?) and practical disadvantage to bring the matter before a UK court of law.

3.1 What court of law has jurisdiction?

In cases of litigation between two parties coming from different states, the question of where to go to resolve the conflict is relevant. When parties, like Mitchell and Smit in the introductory case study, are from countries belonging to the EU, the Brussels I Regulation states the rules on matters of jurisdiction. Chapter 1 describes jurisdiction as being one of the three main issues of international private law ("Question 1"). This "Question 1" and therefore this Brussels I Regulation deal with what court is competent to rule upon a conflict between two parties. When two parties are from different states, the use of the Brussels I Regulation can be helpful in sorting out such matters as these.

Jurisdiction

3.2 Brussels I Regulation: what countries are involved?

Starting 10 January 2015, the Brussels I Regulation applies in all Member States of the EU.

The Brussels I Regulation has undergone an extensive period of review and, from 10 January 2015, the revised Brussels Regulation (that is, the Brussels Regulation (recast)) will be applied by member state courts. Following a detailed consultation, the UK opted into the Brussels Regulation (recast), and it will also be applied by Denmark.

When applying the Brussels I Regulation, the nationality of the parties is of no concern. If one wants to determine what court of law has jurisdiction, the place where the parties live is relevant.

Court of law

3.3 Rules concerning jurisdiction of the Brussels I Regulation

The Brussels I Regulation answers the question of which court of law has jurisdiction when a conflict arises between two contracting parties, whose places of residence or business are in different states. This paragraph gives an overview of the Articles of the Brussels I Regulation that are used most often:

- Art. 25 Brussels I: the parties' choice of a court of law that has jurisdiction (paragraph 3.3.1).
- Art. 24 Brussels I: jurisdiction concerning immovable property (paragraph 3.3.2).
- Art. 20 – 23 Brussels I: jurisdiction concerning individual employment contracts (paragraph 3.3.3).
- Art. 17 – 19 Brussels I: jurisdiction concerning consumer contracts (paragraph 3.3.4).
- Art. 10 – 16 Brussels I: jurisdiction regarding insurance matters (paragraph 3.3.5).
- Art. 4 and 7 Brussels I: general provisions regarding jurisdiction (paragraph 3.3.6).

3.3.1 Choice available to parties (Art. 25 Brussels I)

Choice

Art. 25 Brussels I makes it possible for both parties themselves to choose the court of law that will have jurisdiction should there be a lawsuit between the parties. The agreement on jurisdiction shall be in writing or evidenced in writing. In case parties are doing business for a longer period of time, an agreement on jurisdiction does not necessarily have to be in writing, as long as it meets the practices which these parties have established between themselves. In international trade or commerce, it is also possible to rely on the rules on jurisdiction which are widely known usage in that particular line of international business.

EXAMPLE 3.1

TowWreck Ltd., a company established in the UK, and Nedcar B.V., a company in The Netherlands, close a contract of sale. In this contract parties choose a Dutch court of law to have jurisdiction in case of litigation. A Dutch court of law would therefore have exclusive jurisdiction in such a case according to Art. 25 Brussels I.

Art. 25 Brussels I provides no answers as to which court of law should have jurisdiction when neither party has made a choice, or the choice they made was not in writing. In such a case one has to resort to the other options of Brussels I i.e. answering Question 1 by turning to one of the special provisions of the Brussels I Regulation. Paragraph 3.3 states that the following are the special provisions on jurisdiction of Brussels I: jurisdiction concerning litigation over immovable property, over employment contracts, over consumer contracts and over insurance matters.

3.3.2 Jurisdiction in cases of litigation over immovable property (Art. 24 Brussels I)

Immovable property

Art. 24 Brussels I is a special provision with regard to immovable property. A lawsuit between two parties from different Member States of the EU must be conducted before the court of law of the country where the immovable property is situated. This special provision is an example of exclusive jurisdiction: no other court of law has jurisdiction where this Article applies.

EXAMPLE 3.2

Hendriks, living in Arnhem (The Netherlands), buys a chalet in the French Alps from LeBrun SA, a company established in France. Problems arise over the legal ownership of this house. It turns out that the French seller did not fulfill all the legal formalities required to transfer the ownership of the house to Hendriks. According to Art. 24 Brussels I only a French court of law has jurisdiction in a lawsuit concerning this chalet. This is because the immovable property i.e. the chalet is situated in France. In case the chalet is for temporary private use only, a French court of law also has jurisdiction, because the defendant Lebrun is domiciled in France. Hendriks has to turn to a French court of law to solve his problems.

3.3.3 Jurisdiction in cases of litigation over individual employment contracts (Art. 20 – 23 Brussels I)

Art. 20 – 23 Brussels I are about jurisdiction in cases of litigation over obligations connected with individual employment contracts. These employment contracts are sealed between an employer and an employee coming from different EU Member States.

Individual employment contracts

If the employer has his corporate residence in a non-Member State, but has a subsidiary or establishment in a Member State, then the employer is deemed to have residence in that Member State (Art. 20 Brussels I).

EXAMPLE 3.3

Peters, who is a resident of Cologne (Germany), is an employee of the German branch of Ford Motors in Cologne, though Ford is a company with its corporate residence in the USA. Problems arising out of Peters' employment contract should be brought before a German court of law.

When an employee starts litigation against his employer, the following courts have jurisdiction according to Art. 21 Brussels I:

1 The court of law of the Member State in which the employer has his place of residence, or
2 in another Member State:
  - the court of law of the country where the employee usually carries out his work, or
  - the court of law of the country where the employee usually used to work, or
  - if the employee neither usually works nor has worked in any specific country, before the court of law of the Member State where the business which hired the employee is or was situated.

EXAMPLE 3.4

Sanders, from Enschede (The Netherlands), is employed as a salesperson by Küchen Eck GmbH, a company established in Gronau (Germany). His job there is to sell as many kitchens a day as possible. A conflict arises over salary payments by Küchen Eck which are long overdue. No arrangement as to the jurisdiction of any court of law has been set down in the employment contract. According to Art. 21 Brussels I Sanders has the option of bringing the matter before a German court of law only.

Art. 21 Brussels I makes it possible for another court of law to have jurisdiction, other than the court of law of the country of the employer. The following examples are about Art. 21 Brussels I.

EXAMPLE 3.5

De Waele, a computer engineer living in Liege (Belgium), is employed by SuperBits GmbH, a company from Aachen (Germany). His employer has sent him to work at a daughter company of theirs in Luxemburg for a period of one year. During this period a conflict between De Waele and SuperBits arises over payment of overtime. A court of law in Luxemburg has jurisdiction in this case, should De Waele be prepared to sue his employer, according to Art. 21, 1, (b), i Brussels I.

EXAMPLE 3.6

3

Jansen, a student living in Amsterdam (The Netherlands), applies for a post with Mueller GmbH, a shipping company established in Hamburg (Germany). She is hired by Mueller's Rotterdam (The Netherlands) office. Her job is to assist on the company's cruises along the Rhine. The ship travels from The Netherlands, through Germany to Switzerland, and back. Two months later, Jansen has not been paid anything approaching the salary they had agreed on. If no provisions were made regarding this matter, then a Dutch court of law has jurisdiction under Art. 21, 1, (b), ii Brussels I.

When an employer starts a lawsuit against an employee, only the court of law of the Member State in which the employee has residence shall have jurisdiction (Art. 22 Brussels I).

EXAMPLE 3.7

Sanders, from Enschede (The Netherlands), is employed as a salesperson by Küchen Eck GmbH, a company established in Gronau (Germany). His job there is to sell as many kitchens a day as possible. A conflict arises over the fact that Sanders has not sold a single kitchen for at least a month. Sanders calls his employer all kinds of names in front of all the other employees. Küchen Eck wants to nullify Sanders' employment contract even though no arrangements have been made in the employment contract as to which court of law has jurisdiction. According to Art. 22 Brussels I Küchen Eck can only do this in a Dutch court of law.

3.3.4 Jurisdiction in cases of litigation related to consumer contracts (Art. 17 – 19 Brussels I)

Consumer

A consumer is a person who buys goods or services outside his trade or profession. Whether a contract sealed by this person is actually a consumer contract according to Brussels I, can be deduced from the conditions of Art. 17 Brussels I. In Art. 17 Brussels I three types of contract are mentioned. A contract for a loan repayable by instalments to buy goods is considered a consumer contract under Art. 17 Brussels I. The same goes for a contract of sale of goods to be paid by instalments. The third consumer contract mentioned in Art. 17 Brussels I is a "any kind of contract" with a foreign party as a result of commercial activities in the country of the consumer. If any of the three contracts mentioned applies, and is concluded by a consumer, then the contract is a consumer contract under Art. 17 Brussels I.

In such a case the consumer must use Art. 18 Brussels I in order to determine which court of law has jurisdiction.

Art. 18 Brussels I states that in a case of litigation between a consumer and a seller, the consumer may choose the place where the lawsuit should take place. This can be either in his country or in the country of the seller. If the seller sues the consumer, he may bring proceedings only before the court of law of the country of the consumer.

EXAMPLE 3.8

One fine Saturday morning, De Koning, living in Almelo (The Netherlands), finds a piece of paper on his front doormat. This informs him that this weekend Karmann GmbH, a company established in Münster (Germany), is selling DVD players at a price of €49 each. De Koning immediately jumps into his car, races across the border and buys one of the advertised DVD players in Münster.

According to Art. 17, 1, (c) Brussels I this is a consumer contract: De Koning is a consumer, the German company Karmann is doing business in The Netherlands and the contract sealed by De Koning was one aspect of their commercial activities. In case of non-payment by De Koning, the seller may sue him only before a Dutch court of law, under Art. 18 Brussels I.

Art. 19 Brussels I enables both parties to depart from the provisions of Art. 17 and 18 Brussels I by agreement, but this exception is seldom used.

3.3.5 Jurisdiction in cases of litigation relating to insurance matters (Art. 10 – 16 Brussels I)

Insurance

Art. 10 – 16 Brussels I enable a party to sue an insurer before several courts, though in most cases the court of law of the country where the insurer is established has jurisdiction. The Brussels I Regulation allows many exceptions to these rules and makes it possible to depart by agreement from the provisions of Brussels I Regulation.

EXAMPLE 3.9

Hendriks, living in Arnhem (The Netherlands) has bought a chalet in the French Alps, as mentioned earlier. Due to defective wiring, of which Hendriks had not been aware, the chalet burns to the ground and the entire contents are lost.

Hendriks' insurer, Lachen AG, a company established in Germany, were convinced that Hendriks could not have been unaware of the chalet's bad wiring and refused to pay. It is possible for Hendriks to start litigation against his insurer before a French court of law according to Article 12 Brussels I.

An insurer may only bring a lawsuit before the court of law of the country of the person insured.

3.3.6 General provisions on jurisdiction (Art. 4 and 7 Brussels I)

When none of the special provisions of paragraphs 3.3.2 up to and including paragraph 3.3.5 applies to the case, one will have to resort to the

General provisions

general provisions given by Brussels I. The general provisions of Brussels I are explained in this paragraph and consist of Art. 4 and 7 Brussels I. Under Art. 4 Brussels I the court of law of the country of the defendant has jurisdiction. In any lawsuit there must be one party who puts in a claim against another. This makes the first party the 'plaintiff' and the other party the 'defendant'. The issue is to determine who in fact is the plaintiff and who the defendant. In case this is settled, the defendant always will have residence in a particular country, so one will have no difficulty in determining which court of law has jurisdiction according to Art. 4 Brussels I.

If the defendant, in turn, starts litigation against the plaintiff, the court of law before which the matter was first brought has jurisdiction (Art. 4 Brussels I).

EXAMPLE 3.10

Nijenhuis, a company established in Deventer (The Netherlands), supplies 1,000 kilos of cheese to VandenBroecke, a company from Gent (Belgium). When the Belgian buyer fails to make payment, the Dutch seller decides to enter into a lawsuit against his Belgian client. In this case the seller is the plaintiff and the buyer is the defendant: according to Art. 4 Brussels I, a Belgian court of law has jurisdiction.

Note that this is only one half of the general provision: one has to combine Art. 4 with 7 Brussels I. This is referred to as 'alternative jurisdiction'. This could mean that Art. 4 and 7 Brussels I lead to different conclusions about which court of law has jurisdiction. In that case it is up to the plaintiff to make a choice between the two.

With Art. 7 Brussels I one has to distinguish between paragraph 1 (matters relating to contract) and paragraph 2 (matters relating to tort). Article 7, 1, a Brussels I states that, in matters relating to a contract, the courts for the place of performance of the obligation in question have jurisdiction. Unless otherwise agreed by the parties to a contract, Brussels I provides for a place of performance of the obligation in question. In case of a contract of sale, it is the place for the delivery of the goods in a Member State according to Article 7, 1, b Brussels I. In case the contract is for the provision of services, the place of performance of the obligation in question is the place where the goods were or should have been delivered (Article 7, 1, b Brussels I).

EXAMPLE 3.11

Pompidou SA, a company established in Paris (France), supplies goods to Van Haringen, a company from Scheveningen (The Netherlands). The Dutch buyer does not pay the agreed price into an account the French seller has with Banque Credit Lyonnais in The Hague (The Netherlands). Under Art. 7, 1 Brussels I, concerning a matter relating to a (sales) contract, the place of performance of the obligation in question in this contract of sale is the place where the goods were delivered. The place of delivery is in The Netherlands, so a Dutch court of law has jurisdiction according to Article 7, 1, b Brussels I.

Art. 7, 2 Brussels I states the court of law that has jurisdiction in matters relating to tort. According to this paragraph of the Article jurisdiction lies with the court of law of the country where the harmful event or the offence occurred or could have occurred. If one can determine the place of the tort, one knows what court of law to turn to.

EXAMPLE 3.12

Reynkes, a truck driver from Bonn (Germany), gets into a fight with McDonald, a truck driver from Liverpool (UK), in a bar in Amsterdam (The Netherlands). Reynkes grabs a chair before McDonald does and hits him rather hard with it, causing his new found English 'friend' to lose sight in his left eye and to limp for the rest of his life. McDonald may sue Reynkes before a Dutch court of law under Art. 7, 2 Brussels I.

Note that according to Dutch jurisprudence this criterion on jurisdiction in the case of a tort can also be interpreted as the country where the damages were suffered.

EXAMPLE 3.13

Dutch owners of greenhouses in the western part of the Netherlands suffered severe damage as a result of French mining companies draining salt waste into the Rhine. The Rhine provides the water the greenhouses need to water their crops. A Dutch court of law has jurisdiction according to Article 7, 2 Brussels I, because even though the tort was committed in France, the damage resulting from this tort was suffered in the Netherlands. The effect of such a tort is reason enough for it to be referred to as a "cross-border tort".

In most cases of litigation, Art. 4 and 7, 1, 2 Brussels I assign jurisdiction to courts of law of different countries. This is referred to as 'alternative jurisdiction'. When two courts of law from different countries have jurisdiction, it is up to the plaintiff to choose which one the case will go before.

EXAMPLE 3.14

Dupont from Montpellier (France) delivers goods to Smit B.V., a company from Utrecht (The Netherlands). The Dutch buyer does not pay the agreed price into an account the French seller has with ING Bank in Paris (France). The French seller starts litigation against his Dutch buyer.
Art. 4 Brussels I states that one is required to determine the place of residence of the defendant. The defendant is the Dutch buyer, so under this article a Dutch court of law has jurisdiction. Art. 4 Brussels I has to be combined with Art. 7 Brussels I.
Art. 7, 1 Brussels I is about matters relating to sales contracts. The court of law of the place of performance of the obligation in question had jurisdiction. The contract involved is a contract of sale. In this case the delivery of the goods is not the issue (Article 7, 1, b Brussels I), payment for the goods is (Article 7, 1, c Brussels I). As payment for the goods was to be made in France, a French court of law has jurisdiction (Article 7, 1, a Brussels I).

EXAMPLE 3.15

Dutch owners of greenhouses in the western part of the Netherlands suffered severe damages as a result of French mines draining salt waste into the Rhine. This river provides the water the greenhouses use to water their crops.
Art. 4 Brussels I states that one should determine the place of residence of the defendant. In this case the defendants are the French mining companies, so a French court of law has jurisdiction. But Art. 4 Brussels I also has to be combined with Art. 7 Brussels I.
Art. 7, 2 Brussels I is about matters relating to tort. It states that one should determine the place where the damage was suffered. This is in The Netherlands so a Dutch court of law has jurisdiction. Alternative jurisdiction means that the plaintiff has to make a choice between these two options, and probably will choose to go to a Dutch court of law.

3.4 Execution of the verdict under the Brussels I Regulation

Execution

When a court of law that has jurisdiction according to Brussels I gives a verdict in a case, it is possible to execute this verdict in another Member State of the EU. For this purpose it is necessary to ask the court of law in that State in an additional procedure for a provision to enable the verdict to be carried out in that particular country (Articles 39 – 44 Brussels I).

EXAMPLE 3.16

Mitchell Ltd., a company established in the UK, conclude a contract of sale with Smit B.V., a company established in The Netherlands. Smit is to deliver computer components to Mitchell. The place of delivery is the place of business of the Dutch seller. The delivery is carried out correctly, but the Dutch seller does not receive payment. Payment should have been made into an account Smit has with the ING Bank in Amsterdam (The Netherlands). After having phoned and faxed several times without any luck, Smit decides to start litigation against Mitchell. According to Art. 4 Brussels I, a UK court of law has jurisdiction. Under Art. 7, 1 Brussels I, a Dutch court of law has jurisdiction and the plaintiff therefore has to make a choice. In the event Smit goes to the Dutch court of law whose verdict can nevertheless be executed in the UK. There is no way whatsoever that Mitchell can avoid a verdict by not responding to letters.

3.5 Arbitration

Arbitration

Parties engaged in a lawsuit can agree on letting a third party (i.e. not a 'regular' court of law) resolve their dispute. This is called arbitration and is frequently used to resolve conflicts between parties in the same line of business. In such a case the arbitrator might be a panel of arbitrators, the members being experts in that line of business. It is up to the parties to decide whether they seek a ruling from a regular court of law or opt to go to arbitration. When a legal conflict arises between companies from different states, arbitration is sometimes preferred over litigation before a regular court of law. The Court of Arbitration of the International Chamber of Commerce (ICC) in Paris is a well known arbitration institution. The London Court of Arbitration and the Stockholm Chamber of Commerce also deal with arbitration.

Advantages of arbitration are:
- Arbitration is done by experts in the same line of business as the parties in dispute and can result in a verdict of superior quality. A regular court of law might have problems in acquiring industry-specific information needed to give a verdict in the case.
- The procedure is less formal than a procedure before a regular court of law; arbitration can therefore be faster than a regular court procedure.
- Arbitrators are independent of states and courts of law.
- Arbitration is not open to the public; confidential company information stays behind closed doors.

Disadvantages of arbitration are:
- Arbitration is generally expensive as the arbitrator's salary is paid by the litigating parties.
- When parties choose arbitration, they will no longer have the option of going to a regular court of law.

Parties can agree that any conflict that may arise between them is settled by means of arbitration. They can draw up a clause to that effect in their contract. Parties can also agree, after a conflict has arisen, to settle it by means of arbitration. This requires an additional statement i.e. agreement of both parties.

When parties are domiciled in the same country, the law of that country determines whether arbitration is possible and, if so, how the verdict should be enforced. The same thing happens when a foreign arbitral verdict has to be enforced in e.g. The Netherlands. Under Dutch law permission of the President of the District Court has to be obtained to enforce the verdict in The Netherlands.

EXAMPLE 3.17

In an arbitral verdict given by the Panel of Arbitrators in Germany, the claim made by Boris Back GmbH against Billy's Brötchen GmbH was upheld. Both companies are established in Germany. Because the arbitral verdict might be of use to a subsidiary of Boris Back GmbH established in The Netherlands, Boris Back has to go to the Dutch District Court in order to obtain permission to enforce the arbitral verdict in The Netherlands.

When parties engaged in arbitration are from different states the enforcement of the verdict of the arbitrators is governed by the New York Convention on the Recognition and Enforcement of Foreign Arbitral Awards (1958). At present, 142 of the 192 United Nations Member States and the Holy See have adhered to this Convention. The New York Convention requires courts in these states to recognize written arbitration agreements and to refuse to allow a dispute to be heard before them if it is subject to arbitration. When an arbitral verdict is given in a member state of the New York Convention, the verdict can be enforced in all other member states. The nationality of the parties is not relevant.

EXAMPLE 3.18

Shell, established in The Netherlands, starts arbitral proceedings in the Court of Arbitration of the ICC against Indonesian Petroleum, established in Indonesia, over the sale and delivery of 10.000 barrels of oil. Shell's claim is upheld: the arbitral verdict can be enforced in both The Netherlands and Indonesia immediately, without resorting to a court of law, as both countries signed the New York Convention.

Summary

- The Brussels I Regulation provides rules on jurisdiction and the execution of verdicts when the litigating parties are domiciled in different EU Member States.

- 25 Brussels I: one first has to establish whether the two litigating parties have made their choice about which court of law should have jurisdiction.

- If no such decision can be made one has to resort to the special provisions given in the Brussels I Regulation:
  - 24 Brussels I (immovable property): the court of law of the country where the immovable property is situated, has jurisdiction over the matter.
  - 20–23 Brussels I (employment contracts): when an employer starts litigation against an employee, the court of law of the country of the latter has jurisdiction. In most cases where an employee sues his employer, the court of law where the employer is domiciled has jurisdiction over the matter.
  - 17–19 Brussels I (consumer contracts): the extent of the provisions on consumer contracts is limited to the three types of consumer contract mentioned. In most cases the consumer receives protection of the court of law of the country where he is domiciled.
  - 10–16 Brussels I (insurance): in most cases the court of law of the country where the insurer is established has jurisdiction.

- When no agreement on jurisdiction has been made and none of the special provisions applies, one has to resort to the general provisions of Brussels I. The plaintiff may choose either
  - 4 Brussels I: the court of law of the country where the defendant is domiciled, or
  - another court of law, depending on whether there has been a breach of contract (7, 1 Brussels I) or a tort (7, 2 Brussels I) committed by the defendant.
  - 7, 1 Brussels I: in matters related to contract, the plaintiff has to determine the place of performance of the obligation in question. The court of law of the country where this place is situated, has jurisdiction.
  - 7, 2 Brussels I: the plaintiff should determine the place where the tort was committed or – in case of cross-border torts – the place where the damages where suffered. This decides the court of law that has jurisdiction under 7, 2 Brussels I.

- Execution of the verdict: once the competent court of law has given its verdict, 40 Brussels I rules on its execution.

- When a legal conflict arises between parties in the same line of business, those parties may opt to go to arbitration. The verdict in such cases is given not by a court of law, but by a panel of arbitrators. Their expertise should provide the litigating parties with a better solution to their conflict. Arbitration is not arranged for in Brussels I. The execution of international arbitral verdicts is also governed by other treaties than Brussels I.

Glossary

3

Alternative Jurisdiction	The plaintiff can choose between two courts of law, each with jurisdiction to rule on his lawsuit against a defendant.
Arbitration	Parties engaged in a lawsuit can agree on letting a third party (i.e. not a 'regular' court of law) resolve their conflict.
Brussels I	Brussels I Regulation is on jurisdiction and the recognition and enforcement of judgments in civil and commercial matters
Choice of parties	When parties are from different states they may choose which court of law they would prefer to give a verdict.
Consumer contract	Contract concluded by a person, outside his trade or profession, to buy goods or services for domestic use. Brussels I limits the number of consumer contracts that fall under this Regulation.
Contract	An agreement put in writing.
Court of law	Judicial body, under the control of the public authorities of a country, which has the power by law to give judgment on cases brought before it by parties that are engaged in a lawsuit.
Defendant	The party against whom a lawsuit is brought before a court of law.
Execution of verdicts	Enforcing the judgment of a court of law in the countries where the litigating parties are domiciled and in other countries.
Employment contract	A contract between two parties, an employer and employee, in which the employee conducts certain activities under the employer's direction, for which the employee receives payments as a reward over a certain period of time.
General provisions	The provisions on jurisdiction that apply when there is neither a written agreement on jurisdiction nor any of the special provisions apply.
Immovable property	Property that cannot be moved, such as houses, trees, land and factories.

Insurance	Matters of insurance between an insurance company and the insured.
Jurisdiction	The authority to give a ruling i.e. a verdict in a legal dispute between two parties.
Member States	The Member States of Brussels I are also the Member States of the EU.
Plaintiff	The party instigating a lawsuit and putting in a claim against another party.
Tort	A wrongful act committed by a private party that results in damage to another party.

Exercises

3

Exercise 3.1
Müller, a former German sports hero living in Bentheim (Germany), sells his house there to Jansen, a soccer coach, who lives in Enschede (The Netherlands). The sale is concluded in writing in Enschede and Jansen agrees to pay the price into an account Müller has with the ABN Amro Bank in Enschede. A dispute arises over the legal ownership of the house. It seems that Müller wanted to sell Jansen a house which, according to the German authorities, belongs to a certain Schmitt. Jansen starts a lawsuit against Müller.

What court of law has jurisdiction in this case?

Exercise 3.2
De Boer from Amsterdam (The Netherlands) and Saelens, a Belgian second-hand car dealer from Bruges (Belgium), reach an agreement on the sale of 50 used cars. Talking on their mobile phones they agree that in the event of any legal problems a Dutch court of law should have jurisdiction. A dispute arises over the delivery of the 50 cars to Bruges (Belgium) and De Boer starts litigation against the Belgian buyer before a Belgian court of law.

What court of law has jurisdiction in this case?

Exercise 3.3
De Mol, a pensioner living in Amstelveen (The Netherlands), is interested in buying a second home in the Dordogne (France). In order to fulfil his lifetime dream, he contacts Gounon Immobilier SA, established in Lyon (France). Gounon has the perfect house for De Mol: he invites the Dutch pensioner over to a village in France. De Mol is very enthusiastic about the small French villa. Because there are other potential buyers, he immediately decides to buy. Before signing the contract De Mol states that he wishes to add a rider. De Mol wants Dutch law to apply to the contract as under Dutch law he has the right to change his mind within 2 days of signing the contract. Gounon does not understand a word De Mol is saying. De Mol signs the contract of sale. In the small print at the bottom of the contract it states that in case of litigation a French court of law will have jurisdiction and that French law is applicable to the contract of sale.
The next day and having thought things over De Mol informs Gounon that the deal is off: he is going home. Gounon requests that De Mol should stand by his contractual obligations. De Mol must pay 20% of the selling price on the spot, which De Mol refuses to do. On his way home and a bit shaken by events De Mol causes a collision with a truck owned by DeSnelle, a company from Belgium, and subsequently knocks down

a fence belonging to the Jabouille family, who live in a small town near Strasbourg (France).

1 What court of law has jurisdiction if Gounon starts litigation against De Mol?
2 What court of law has jurisdiction if De Snelle requires compensation for damage to their truck?
3 What court of law has jurisdiction if Arnoux, the insurance company that paid for the Jabouille family's fence, starts litigation against De Mol?

Exercise 3.4
Ancelotti, domiciled in Firenze, Italy, has agreed to act as Weller's financial adviser. A contract to that effect has been drawn up and signed in London UK where Weller lives. Ancelotti has been requested by Weller to advise him on an investment he is planning to make in Ahold N.V., a multinational company, established in Amsterdam, The Netherlands.
Ancelotti, who is not sure whether Ahold will prove to be such a good investment, asks the advice of Westerhagen, a friend of his who is a financial consultant in Cologne, Germany. Westerhagen gives Ancelotti his approval of the proposed investment. Ancelotti advises Weller to proceed with the investment, informing him that this advice was checked twice, by him and by Westerhagen. Due to economic developments in South America and Ahold's accounting problems, the value of Ahold shares drops and Weller loses a great deal of money. Weller is not a happy man and blames both advisers for the bad advice they gave him. Weller decides to sue both Ancelotti and Westerhagen for compensation for his loss. Ancelotti is not a happy man either as Weller refuses to pay the fee agreed on in their contract.

1 In the case of Weller vs Ancelotti: what court of law has jurisdiction?
2 In the case of Weller vs Westerhagen: what court of law has jurisdiction?
3 In the case of Ancelotti vs Weller what court of law has jurisdiction?

4
Law

One of the three main issues of International Private Law is the question of which national legal system should be used to settle a dispute arising from a contractual or non-contractual relationship. If the opposing parties live in the same country, then there is no issue over which law should apply– it does, however, become an issue if the opposing parties are from different countries. A Regulation of the EU (Rome I Regulation) establishes which national legal system applies in cross-border disputes over real estate, insurance matters, consumer contracts, contracts of employment, tort and breaches of contract in general. This chapter explains the issue of what law should be applied when legal disputes arise between parties who live in different countries.

International contracts and conflicts: which law holds the solution?

Mr. Laurent, a schoolteacher living in France, closes a contract of sale with Schmitt GmbH, a company established in Germany. Schmitt is to deliver 10 cases of wine to Laurent. The delivery is carried out correctly. However, because Laurent has not yet paid for several shipments, the German seller has retained the ownership of the goods until payment has been received from the French buyer. Laurent pays the last delivery, but still Schmitt refuses to transfer the ownership of the goods because of several other payments by Laurent that have not been made. Laurent subsequently goes bankrupt.

Obviously, there is a conflict between Schmitt and Laurent, the contracting parties who are from different States. What law has the solution to this conflict? Had French law been applicable to this international contract of sale between Laurent and Schmitt, Laurent would have been the owner of the goods, whereas under German law, Schmitt would still have had the legal right to retain ownership of the total of 1,000 cases of wine for a longer period.

4.1 Introduction to Rome I

In Chapter 1, the three main issues of international private law were discussed, the second of which was the law applicable to contract or the tort involved. This question becomes relevant when the parties involved are from different countries. This is set out by the EU Regulation on the law applicable to Contractual Obligations (hereinafter referred to as Rome I). As natives of any country are inclined to depend on their own national laws to settle legal conflicts, which may arise out of contractual relationships, a choice has to be made. As in the introductory case study, it is necessary to know which national law applies in a certain situation.

European Regulation on Contractual Obligations

The issue (Question 2 of Chapter 1) of which national law applies in a certain situation (i.e. one involving contracts) is dealt with by Rome I. The first issue of international private law, what court of law has jurisdiction in a certain case (Question 1 of Chapter 1), is dealt with by Brussels I (Chapter 3). Looking back at Chapter 3, bear in mind that the answer to Question 1 about which court of law has jurisdiction, has no connection to, or effect on the answer to Question 2. It is, for example, quite possible that a French court of law would have to apply German law, as in the introductory case illustrating the conflict between Laurent and Schmitt.

What is very important to remember at this stage is that Rome I does not provide a competent court of law with an immediate solution to a conflict between two contracting parties. Rome I only gives so-called 'rules of reference'. In other words, the rules of Rome I dictate which law should be applied to a disputed contract. It is this law which will resolve the conflict between the two parties. Rome I does therefore not provide answers to questions such as: 'Can I claim damages?' or 'Is it possible to nullify the contract?', but only answers such as 'German law' or 'English law' and it is these national laws which will provide answers to those questions mentioned above.

Rules of reference

4.2 Conditions on the use of Rome I

Rome I applies to contractual obligations in any situation involving a choice between the laws of different countries. The Member States of Rome I are all EU members except for Denmark.

Member States of Rome I

According to Art. 25 Rome I, Rome I should not be used if there is a Convention or Treaty dealing with the same subject in as much detail as Rome I. As a result, should a problem arise e.g. in an international contract of sale that meets the requirements of Art. 1 of the Convention of the International Sale of Goods (CISG), then Rome I must not be used to solve the legal conflict. In such a case the court of law would immediately turn to the CISG (Chapter 5). However, in cases where the CISG cannot be used or does not indicate where the answer lies, one must return to the applicable law as prescribed by Rome I, and look for an answer there to the legal problems regarding this international sales contract.

EXAMPLE 4.1

In the Introductory case study, Laurent and Schmitt are in conflict over the transfer of the ownership of goods from seller Schmitt to buyer Laurent. Had Laurent been a company, established in France, the parties themselves and their contract would have been subject to Art. 1, 1 CISG (Chapter 5). As the CISG, however, has no provision as to when a party becomes the owner of goods delivered to him, Rome I must be used to determine the law applicable to their contract of sale. The answer to their legal problems lies in whichever national law Rome I indicates.

According to Art. 1, 2 Rome I, Rome I does not apply to e.g. contractual obligations relating to wills and succession, or property rights arising from a matrimonial relationship. Furthermore agreements on arbitration and on which court of law should have jurisdiction (Art. 25 Brussels I) are not governed by Rome I; separate Treaties concern themselves with all these issues.

Universal effect of Rome I

Art. 2 Rome I deals with the so-called 'universal effect' of Rome I. While Rome I only determines the applicable law, Art. 2 Rome I says that that law must be applied. It is irrelevant at this point that this law may not be the law of a Member State.

EXAMPLE 4.2

A company established in Switzerland delivers goods to Moleman, a buyer living in The Netherlands. As agreed on by the parties, the place of delivery of the goods is Amsterdam (The Netherlands). On delivery, the buyer checks the goods and finds them not to be in order. The buyer starts litigation against the seller. A Dutch court of law has jurisdiction (Art. 4 and 7, 1 Brussels I) and has the option of applying Swiss law (Art. 4 Rome I) to the international sales contract, even though Switzerland is not a Member State (Art. 2 Rome I).

4.3 Content of Rome I

This paragraph explains the following Articles of Rome I:
- The choice of law made by contracting parties in Art. 3 and 4 Rome I (paragraph 4.3.1).
- Law applicable to consumer contracts in Art. 6 Rome I (paragraph 4.3.2).
- Law applicable to individual employment contracts in Art. 8 Rome I (paragraph 4.3.3).
- Law applicable under certain circumstances in Art. 9 Rome I (paragraph 4.3.4).
- Formal validity of a contract in Art. 11 Rome I (paragraph 4.3.5).

General provisions of Rome I

Freedom of choice

4.3.1 The choice of law made by contracting parties (Art. 3, 4 Rome I)

The general provisions of Rome I are mentioned in Art. 3 and 4 Rome I. Under Art. 3 Rome I contracting parties have the opportunity to choose the law that will govern their contract: there is 'freedom of choice'. Parties only have this choice of law if they are living or are established in different countries. Nationality is not a relevant factor when applying Rome I.

EXAMPLE 4.3

Becker, from Germany, sells his yacht, which is currently moored in the harbour at Monaco, to Lacoste, who lives in Monaco. The sale of the yacht is concluded in Monaco. Delivery and payment of the yacht are made at Lacoste's apartment. This is an international contract (Art. 1 and 3 Rome I).

EXAMPLE 4.4

Johnson, an Englishman living in Amsterdam (The Netherlands), sells a batch of 1,000 Korean lamps to LeBrun, a Frenchman living in Utrecht (The Netherlands). Delivery and payment are made in The Netherlands. This is not an international contract as both parties are domiciled in The Netherlands. Their nationality is not relevant. Dutch law applies to their contract; they cannot change this by opting for the law of a different country (Art. 1 and 3 Rome I).

A contract shall be governed by the law chosen by the parties. The choice shall be made expressly or clearly demonstrated by the terms of the contract or the circumstances of the case. While it is therefore not mandatory to put this choice of law in writing, it is preferable, when drawing up the contract, that it should be. The choice of law is in most cases put in writing either in the contract itself or in the terms of sale and delivery.
Keep in mind that Rome I at this point provides parties with all kinds of opportunities to choose the governing law. They can make a different choice at different parts of the contract (Art. 3, 1 Rome I). They can also change the choice of law after concluding the agreement (Art. 3, 2 Rome I). Art. 3 Rome I applies to international contracts and, as explained earlier, parties cannot by their choice of law make their contract an international contract.

No choice of law is made by the parties

If no choice of law is made by the parties or the choice made by the parties cannot be demonstrated with reasonable certainty, Art. 4 Rome I takes effect. Art. 4, 1 Rome I says that if no choice of law has been made, the law applicable to the contract can be derived from one of the situations displayed in 4, 1 Rome I (a) tot (h) inclusive. Art. 4, 1 Rome I mentions the law applicable to several contracts e.g.:

- contract for the sale of goods: the applicable law to this contract is the law of the country where the seller has his habitual residence,
- contract for the provision of services: the applicable law to this contract is the law of the country where the service provider has his habitual residence,
- franchise contract: the applicable law to this contract is the law of the country where the franchisee has his habitual residence,
- contract of distribution: the applicable law to this contract is the law of the country where the distributor has his habitual residence.

Where the contract is not covered by Art. 4, 1 Rome I, the contract shall be governed by the law of the country where the party who is to effect the

Characteristic performance

characteristic performance of the contract has his habitual residence (Art. 4, 2 Rome I). The characteristic performance is the same as the significant action of this particular contract. A significant action can never be paying an amount of money as this happens with nearly all contracts.

Examples of characteristic performances under Art. 4, 2 Rome I:
- contract for rent: the characteristic performance is effected by the landlord,
- employment contract: the characteristic performance is effected by the employee,
- contract for an agent: the characteristic performance is effected by the agent.

Note that the payment of money between contracting parties occurs in all the contracts mentioned above. For that reason payment can never be seen as a characteristic performance of any contract.

4

EXAMPLE 4.5

Murphy Ltd., a seller established in the UK, delivers goods to Jansen, a buyer living in The Netherlands. At the moment of delivery in Amsterdam, the buyer checks the goods and finds them not to be in order. The buyer starts litigation against the seller. What law should be applied to this contract? Parties have not already made a choice of law (Art. 3 Rome I) and therefore we need to establish the law applicable to the contract by means of Art. 4 Rome I. Art. 4, 1, (a) Rome I says that a contract for the sale of goods shall be governed by the law of the country where the seller has his habitual residence. As the seller is from the UK, British law must be applied to this sales contract.

Immovable property

Art. 4, 1, (c) Rome I states that a contract relating to a right in rem in immovable property or to a tenancy of immovable property shall be governed by the law of the country where the property is situated. Notwithstanding Art. 4, 1, (c) Rome I, Art. 4, 1, (d) Rome I states that a tenancy of immovable property concluded for temporary private use for a period of no more than 6 consecutive months shall be governed by the law of the country where the landlord has his habitual residence. That is, if the tenant is a natural person and has his habitual residence in the same country as the landlord. If that is not the case, one must opt for Art. 4, 2 Rome I.

EXAMPLE 4.6

Jansen, living in Amsterdam (The Netherlands), and De Bruijn, living in Rotterdam (The Netherlands), close a contract of sale concerning a villa. This villa is situated near Montpellier (France). Jansen and De Bruijn draw up a preliminary contract, in which buyer De Bruijn retains the right to declare the contract avoided if financing the purchase should prove to be impossible. Jansen and De Bruijn make an appointment with a notary, established in France, to sign the 'compromis de vente', a legal document required by French law for the sale of immovable property. However, De Bruijn refuses to sign this document, relying on the provision mentioned in the preliminary contract. Seller Jansen nullifies the preliminary contract. According to Art. 4 Rome I French law governs this contract, as the villa is situated in France.

Art. 5 Rome I determines the law applicable to a contract for the carriage of goods. This contract shall be governed by the law of country in which, at the moment the contract is concluded, the carrier has its principle place of business. But this is only the case when:

- the place of loading of the goods, or
- the delivery address for the goods, or
- the place where the consigner is situated,

is the same country as the one where the carrier is established.
The correct interpretation of Art. 5 Rome I has given rise to controversy e.g. in situations where all the places mentioned in Art. 5 Rome I are in different countries.

EXAMPLE 4.7

Huisman Fruit & Vegetables B.V., a company in The Netherlands, come to an agreement with Giscard Import & Export Trading S.a.r.l., a company established in France. The agreement is about a weekly delivery of fresh fruit and vegetables from Huisman to Giscard for a period of 6 months. Giscard has arranged for Klein Transporte GmbH, a company established in The Netherlands, to take care of the transport of the goods. Klein will collect the goods from a warehouse belonging to Huisman. As Giscard and Klein made no decision about applicable law, Dutch law will govern the contract for the carriage of goods under Art. 5 Rome I. Both the place where the carrier is situated, as well as the place of loading of the goods, is situated in The Netherlands.

Also note that with some contracts it is almost impossible to determine the characteristic performance: in case of contracts of joint venture, in contracts dealing with the cooperation between two parties, contracts for the exchange of goods a characteristic performance is not easily determined (Art. 4, 4 Rome I). In such cases (international) courts of law have tended to decide for themselves the characteristic performance.

4.3.2 Law applicable to consumer contracts in Art. 6 Rome I

Consumer contracts

In Art. 6 Rome I special provisions are given concerning certain consumer contracts. Art. 6 Rome I takes effect only when no choice of law has been made by the parties to the consumer contract.

Under Art. 6, 1 Rome I, a *consumer* is someone acting outside his trade or profession. If the consumer closes a contract with a person acting in the exercise of his trade or profession, the *professional*, this contract shall be governed by the law of the country of the consumer, provided that the professional:

- pursues his commercial or professional activities in the country where the consumer has his habitual residence, or
- by any means, directs such activities to that country or to several countries including the country where the consumer has his habitual residence.

The law of the country of the consumer must be applied to the consumer contract, if no choice of law (Art. 3 Rome I) was made by the consumer and the professional (Art. 6, 2 Rome I).

EXAMPLE 4.8

In the market square at Enschede (The Netherlands), Rekers, from Almelo (The Netherlands), buys a tree for his garden from Bäumer GmbH, a company established in Germany. The German seller had put an advertisement in the local newspaper for the Enschede region, inviting all citizens to come to the Enschede market square on that particular Saturday to buy a tree from Bäumer. According to Art. 6, 1 Rome I, Rekers is a consumer and the sales contract is also a consumer contract. So Dutch law is applicable to this contract, because the contract was concluded in the State where the consumer lives, i.e. The Netherlands, and was preceded by an advertisement.

According to Art. 6, 2 Rome I any choice of law made by the parties under Art. 3 Rome I cannot ultimately deprive the consumer of the protection of the law of his own country, which would be the applicable law under Art. 6 Rome I. So under this provision a consumer, engaged in a lawsuit against a contracting party, may use whichever law is more favourable to him, even if the consumer and his counterpart have already chosen to apply a different law to their contract.

Schedule 4.1 illustrates the relationship between Art. 3 Rome I (choice of law made by the parties), Art. 4 Rome I (applicable law when no choice was made) and Art. 6 Rome I (special provisions for law applying to certain consumer contracts).

SCHEDULE 4.1 Relationship Art. 3, 4 and 6 Rome I

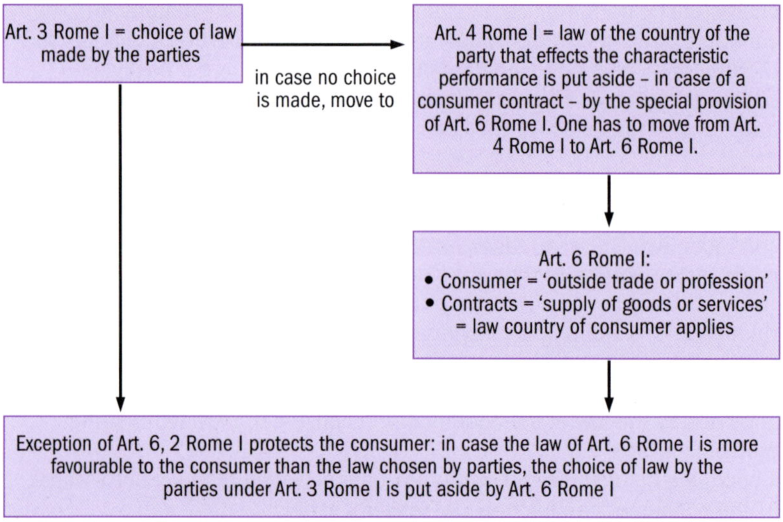

4.3.3 Law applicable to individual employment contracts (Art. 8 Rome I)

Employment contracts

Art. 8 Rome I is another special provision, which applies to individual employment contracts. These employment contracts should also be international contracts (Art. 1 and 3 Rome I), in order for Rome I to apply.

There are two options concerning the law applicable to an individual employment contract:

- parties – employer and employee – choose the applicable law themselves according to Art. 3 Rome I, or
- if they have not chosen the applicable law, they must turn to the law given under Art. 8 Rome I.

Art. 8, 2 Rome I says that if an employer and employee have not chosen the law which will apply to the employment contract, then the law of the country where the employee usually works is the law which will apply.

EXAMPLE 4.9

Vink, living in Deventer (The Netherlands), is employed by Hausmacher Immobilien GmbH, a company established in Bielefeld (Germany). As no choice of law was made by employer and employee in the individual employment contract (Art. 3 Rome I does not apply), Art. 8, 2 Rome I determines that German law will govern this contract. Germany is the country where Vink usually works. This would also seem fair enough to the German colleagues of this Dutch employee.

If the employee is working in several different countries at the same time, the law of the country of the employer should be used instead, according to Art. 8, 3 Rome I.

EXAMPLE 4.10

Jansen, a student living in Amsterdam (The Netherlands), applies for a post with Mueller GmbH, a shipping company established in Hamburg (Germany). She is hired by Mueller's Rotterdam (The Netherlands) office to assist on Rhine cruises organised by the company. The ship travels from The Netherlands, through Germany to Switzerland, and back. Two months later, Jansen has not been paid anything approaching the salary they had agreed on. If no provisions were made regarding this matter, then Dutch law is applicable under Art. 8, 3 Rome I. Jansen was hired by the Rotterdam (The Netherlands) Mueller branch office, therefore Dutch law applies to this employment contract.

According to Art. 8, paragraph 1 Rome I, any choice of law made by the parties (employer and employee) under Art. 3 Rome I cannot ultimately deprive the employee of the protection of the law of the country where he usually works, which would be the applicable law under Art. 8, 2 Rome I. Art. 8, 1 Rome I states that an employee, engaged in a lawsuit against his employer, may use whichever law is more favourable to him, even though employer and employee have already chosen to apply a different law to the employment contract.

Schedule 4.2 illustrates the relationship between Art. 3 Rome I (choice of law made by the parties), Art. 4 Rome I (applicable law when no choice was made) and Art. 8 Rome I (special provisions for law applying to individual employment contracts).

SCHEDULE 4.2 Relationship Art. 3, 4 and 8 Rome I

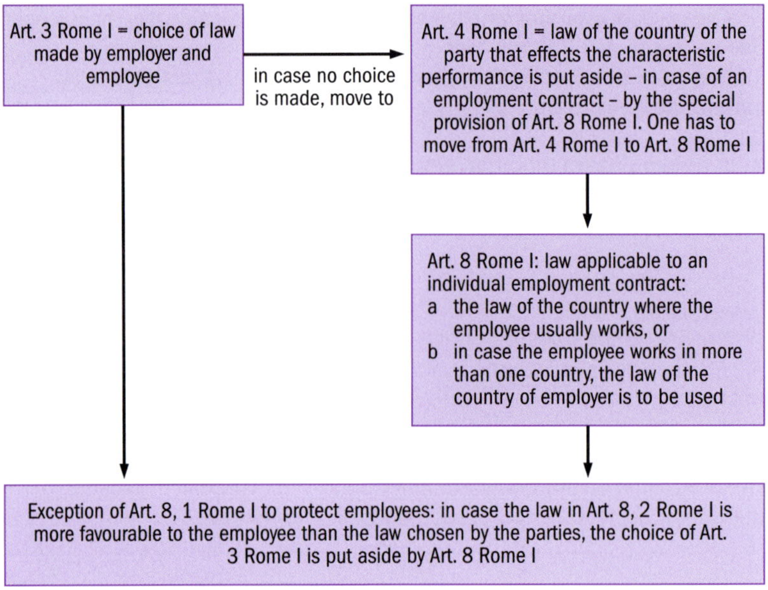

The following case from the Dutch Supreme Court demonstrates how Dutch courts apply Art. 8, 1 Rome I.

Case of Sanchez

Facts

Dutch Supreme Court (Hoge Raad) 8-1-1991, NJ 1991, 296

Juan Sanchez Martinez, of Spanish nationality, had been an employee of the Spanish airline Iberia since 1951. He worked for Iberia in Spain until 1961, in Switzerland until 1972, in Germany until 1975, and finally in The Netherlands.

There he had the position of general manager ('Director de la Compania en Holanda') with the Dutch branch of Iberia. Sanchez lived in Amsterdam in an apartment paid for by Iberia. He received his salary plus expenses in NLG; he also received an amount of money in Spanish pesetas from Iberia, which he used to pay for his pension plan in Spain, among other things. Sanchez reported to his Spanish superiors, who gave him their instructions directly from Spain.

Art. 3 Rome I applies: valid choice made in writing for Spanish law

Art. 25 Brussels I: the choice as regards the court with jurisdiction was made in writing

The contract by which Sanchez was appointed general manager in The Netherlands was finalised in Madrid. The contract had the following paragraph, which was signed by both parties: 'Taking into account that my working contract has been finalised in Spain, any question related to the practice or suspension of the position as manager shall be subject to Spanish law and Spanish courts.'

On April 13th 1983 Sanchez was fired for taking bribes.

Sanchez sued his employer before a Spanish court of law and demanded that his discharge be reversed. All Spanish courts of law denied his claim. Then he turned to the Dutch Magistrate's Court in Amsterdam and requested the reversal of his discharge (...).

Verdict: effect of Art. 8, 1 Rome I for Sanchez

Iberia claims that Spanish law should be applied here, because both parties agreed to this in writing. Sanchez claims that Dutch law, which would be more favourable to him, should be applied instead.

The Dutch Supreme Court decides that Dutch law should be applied here according to art. 8, 1 Rome I. Even though both parties made a choice of law under art. 3 Rome I, this choice cannot deprive Sanchez of whatever protection is available to him under Dutch law, (according to art. 8, 2 Rome I), The Netherlands being the country where Sanchez usually works.

4.3.4 Law applicable under certain circumstances (Art. 9 Rome I)

An exception to the rules mentioned in Art. 3 – 6 Rome I inclusive, is given in Art. 9 Rome I. This article was put into Rome I as a result of a verdict given by the Dutch Supreme Court. The fundamental point of this exception is that a court of law can decide to ignore the rules of Art. 3 – 8 Rome I inclusive and instead apply the mandatory rules of another law to the contract in question if there are special circumstances which would allow this. The verdict of the Dutch Supreme Court does not indicate what circumstances are 'special' enough in order to do this. Furthermore, in the case itself the exception was mentioned but not used.

Mandatory rules

4

The content of Art. 9 Rome I is derived from the Alnati case.

Case of Alnati

Facts

Dutch Supreme Court (Hoge Raad) 13-5-1966, NJ 1967, 3

A Dutch potato trader buys a quantity of potatoes in France and then sells them to a client in Brazil. Van Nievelt, a ship owner established in The Netherlands, transports the potatoes from Antwerp (Belgium) to Rio de Janeiro. A Dutch insurance company insures the consignment on board the ship 'Alnati'. When the potatoes are delivered in Brazil, there is some damage to the cargo, caused by seawater.
In the documents concerning this freight, the applicable law chosen is Dutch. As Dutch law has fewer options to claim damages from the Dutch insurance company than Belgian law, parties quarrel over what law should be applicable in this case. Dutch law, according to the choice made by both parties, or Belgian law, because it contains several mandatory rules about transport and the liability of the transport company.

Verdict

Because both parties chose to apply Dutch law, the fact that mandatory Belgian (international private) laws exist presents no obstacle to any Dutch court of law wishing to apply Dutch law, even though Dutch law differs from mandatory Belgian law.
However, when conflicts like this arise, it is possible for a Dutch court of law to take into consideration the interests of a foreign state in the execution of some of its laws outside its territory and therefore a Dutch court of law has the authority to give preference to this law over the law of another country chosen by the contracting parties. But in this case there are no circumstances that oblige the Dutch court of law to use Belgian law instead of the Dutch law chosen by the parties.

4.3.5 Material and formal validity of a contract (Art. 10, 11 Rome I)

Material validity

Art. 10 Rome I concerns the material validity of a contract. This Article provides rules to establish whether the content of a contract is valid or not. The decision is based on the law which is applicable to the contract under Rome I.

EXAMPLE 4.11

Blits Images B.V., a photo agency established in Amsterdam (The Netherlands), makes an agreement with Bild Zeitung (Germany) about the sale and supply of 5 photos of a former German tennis celebrity and his new girlfriend in Amsterdam. The contract states that Dutch law is applicable (Art. 3 Rome I). Whether or not it is legal to distribute these photos i.e. the material validity of this contract depends on Dutch law.

4

Formal validity

Art. 11 Rome I is about formal validity. Formal validity means whether or not a contract can be deemed valid after having examined the legal formalities involved in that contract. Formalities are whether a contract must be put in writing, or whether a notary's document is required. Art. 11, 1 Rome I: as long as the contract meets the formal requirements of the law chosen by the parties (Art. 3 Rome I, choice of law) or the law of the country where the contract was concluded (that is, in the event this is different from the law chosen by the parties) the contract is formally valid. Thus, according to Art. 11, 1 Rome I there are two circumstances in which a contract can be deemed to be formally valid. It is enough for a contract to be formally valid if only one applies.

EXAMPLE 4.12

Rubens, from Brussels (Belgium), concludes a verbal contract with Schneider, from Emden (Germany), at an auction in Frankfurt (Germany). The contract concerns the sale and delivery of a painting by Rubens to Schneider. Both parties decide that Belgian law should be applicable to their contract. According to German law, the contract is valid only if it is in writing. Under Belgian law, it can be made verbally. According to Art. 11, 1 Rome I the contract is formally valid, because Belgian law is applicable to this contract under Rome I.

4.4 Combination of Brussels I and Rome I

Rome I

Chapter 3 of the Brussels I Regulation deals with which court on law has jurisdiction. This chapter explains the Rome I Regulation on the law applicable to international contracts. As will be seen, the combination of Brussels I and Rome I in the following case gives rise to confusion in the Dutch Supreme Court. In cases such as this, one has to make a clear distinction between Brussels I and Rome I, and between *court of law* and *law*.

Case of BOA

Facts

Dutch Supreme Court (Hoge Raad) 25-09-1994, NJ 1994, 750

What court of law has jurisdiction: a French court of law or a Dutch court of law?

In 1986 the French enterprise SNPAA reaches an agreement with BOA Ltd. in Enschede over the delivery and installation of a so-called paper presser (in Dutch: 'baalpers'). BOA has delivered the presser to France, assembled it on behalf of SNPAA, and put the presser into operation. But payment by the French contracting party fails to arrive.

Link between Dutch law as the applicable law and a Dutch court of law having jurisdiction?

At the Rechtbank (the County Court) in Almelo BOA demands payment of NLG 75,000.-, the price the parties had agreed upon. The defendant, SNPAA, resists this and claims that in this case a French court of law instead of a Dutch court of law should have jurisdiction, either on the basis of art. 4 Brussels I, or on the basis of art. 7 Brussels I. According to BOA the Dutch court of law has jurisdiction, based on the fact that payment should have been made in the Netherlands (art. 7 Brussels I).

The Rechtbank finds that the contract is governed by French law and declares itself not competent. During the appeal, the Gerechtshof (the Court of Appeal) states that Dutch law is applicable, based on art. 4, 1 Rome I, and that therefore a Dutch court of law has jurisdiction in this case. Eventually the case is brought before the Hoge Raad (the Dutch Supreme Court).

Verdict

Art. 4 and 7 Brussels I: alternative jurisdiction for courts of law, plaintiff BOA chooses Art. 7 Brussels I

The first issue to be resolved here is whether art. 7 Brussels I gives jurisdiction to the Rechtbank. Because BOA claims payment, it is therefore necessary to determine first what law governs the agreement that contains this obligation and, according to this law, where the place of payment should be. In this case, payment should have been made at the BOA company in Enschede, and the Rechtbank of Almelo therefore had jurisdiction in this case, based on art. 7 Brussels I.

Art. 4 Rome I: applicable law if no choice was made by BOA and SNPAA

The first question is answered by using art. 4 of the European Communities Convention on Contractual Obligations (Rome I); it is irrelevant that this convention has not yet come into effect in The Netherlands.
The 'characteristic performance' according to art. 4, 2 Rome I is carried out by BOA in this specific contract, so that it is likely that the contract is most closely connected with the Netherlands and that Dutch law governs the contract. There are no grounds to believe that the fifth paragraph of art. 4 should not be put into operation nor that the agreement is more closely connected with France.

Art. 3 Rome I: applicable law chosen by BOA and SNPAA

After reaching the conclusion that Dutch law governs the contract, because no choice of law was made, the Gerechtshof (...) subsequently examined whether the parties concerning their contract made a choice of law. The Gerechtshof answered this question in the affirmative, finding that the Smecoma terms of sale are to be applied to this contract and that these terms say that Dutch law governs a contract that is closed according to these terms.

(Note that the Art. 3 and 4 Rome I exclude each other, so both articles *cannot* be used *together* in the way the Hoge Raad does!)

4.5 Law applicable to international torts Rome II

Rome I deals with the law applicable to international contracts, and becomes relevant when such contracts are breached by one of the contracting parties. As a result, Rome I does not apply to torts, which are civil wrongs between parties that do not have a contract. The so called 'Rome II' Regulation, the Regulation (864/2007) on the law applicable to non-contractual obligations (hereafter referred to as Rome II) applies in situations where, with regard to non-contractual obligations in civil and commercial matters, there is a conflict of laws.

EXAMPLE 4.13

4

Mannesmann, living in Münster (Germany), buys a Deck & Blacker hand drill at MegaDrill, a hardware store in Enschede (The Netherlands). Due to faulty wiring in the drill, Mannesmann suffers burns on both hands. Note that Mannesmann and MegaDrill are from different countries and Megadrill is not the manufacturer of the hand drill. This example is about product liability, a non-contractual responsibility of the manufacturer Deck & Blacker, established in the UK. What law governs Mannesmann's claim for compensation?

Article 3 Rome II states that any law specified by this Regulation shall be applied whether or not it is the law of a Member state. As in Rome I, Article 14 Rome II gives parties the option of agreeing to submit their non-contractual obligations to the law of their choice. This can be only done by agreement, before or after the event that caused the damage, occurs. If no such agreement is made by the parties, the general rule of Article 4 Rome II applies. Article 4 Rome II states that the law applicable to a non-contractual obligation is the law of the country in which the damage occurs. This law then applies, regardless of the country in which the event giving rise to the damage took place. In Articles 5 up to and including Article 12 Rome II special provisions are given, that derogate from the general provision of Article 4 Rome II.

EXAMPLE 4.14

The answer to the question in Example 4.13 is provided by Article 5 (Product Liability). Though Mannesmann has his habitual residence in Germany, German law does not apply to his claim for damages. Article 5, 1, (a) Rome II does not apply as the hand drill was not marketed in Germany. Under Article 5, 1, (b) Rome II Dutch law applies to Mannesmann's claim, as the hand drill was bought by Mannesmann and marketed by MegaDrill in The Netherlands.

EXAMPLE 4.15

Under Article 10 TFEU, the EU has fined several Belgian building companies for price agreements and other acts of unfair competition. A claim by Dutch building companies, who felt that their commercial interests were affected by these acts of unfair compettion, was governed by Dutch law according to the provisions of Article 6 Rome II (Unfair competition and acts restricting free competition).

EXAMPLE 4.16

Dutch owners of greenhouses in the western part of the Netherlands suffered severe damages as a result of French mines draining salt waste into the Rhine. This river provides the water the greenhouses use to water their crops. Under Article 7 Rome II (Environmental damage), Dutch law governs this claim for compensation by the Dutch owners of greenhouses, as The Netherlands is the country where the damage was suffered.

EXAMPLE 4.17

Coca Cola is a registered trademark all over the world, including The Netherlands. Jansen, living in Enschede (The Netherlands), alters this trademark and prints Cocaine (in the same typeface and colours as the protected Coca Cola trademark) on t-shirts. He sells these t-shirts in a store in Bruges (Belgium). Because the trademark is protected under Dutch law, Dutch law will govern this tort, as is explained in Article 8 Rome II (Infringement of intellectual property rights).

EXAMPLE 4.18

Workers at Nederlandse Spoorwegen, a Dutch provider of railway transport, engage in a week's strike, supported by their Union. Deutsche Bahn, a German provider of railway transport, suffers damage, as several international trains have to be cancelled as a result of this strike. Dutch law governs a claim by Deutsche Bahn for compensation under Article 9 Rome II (Industrial action).

EXAMPLE 4.19

Verrecke, a Belgian national, has an account with Van Lanschot Bankiers, established in The Netherlands. Due to a mistake by ABN Amro Bank, also established in the Netherlands, the sum of €1,000,000.- is added to Verrecke's account at Van Lanschot. Verrecke is pleasantly surprised. Article 10 Rome II (Unjust enrichment) applies to this case. Article 10, 1 Rome II is not applicable as there is no relationship between Verrecke and ABN Amro. Article 10, 2 Rome II is not applicable, as Verrecke does not have his habitual residence in The Netherlands. Under Article 10, 3 Rome II Dutch law governs a claim by ABN Amro against Verrecke, as The Netherlands is the country where the unjust enrichment took place.

Summary

- When a contract involves two parties living in different countries, it is clear that a choice has to be made as to which law governs the contract. The Rome I Regulation provides rules on these matters (Art. 1, 2 Rome I).

- If the contracting parties choose the applicable law themselves in accordance with Art. 3 Rome I, this choice should be made in writing.

- If no choice of law is made by the contracting parties, the contract is governed by the law indicated by Art. 4 Rome I. This states that the law applicable to the contract is the law of the country to which the contract is most closely connected. This in most cases is the country of the party who is to effect the characteristic performance under the contract. However, if the contract concerns either the carriage of goods or immovable property, then different criteria apply.

- A choice of law made by contracting parties under Art. 3 Rome I is sometimes set aside by special provisions for consumer contracts (Art. 6 Rome II).

- A choice of law made by contracting parties under Art. 3 Rome I is also sometimes set aside by special provisions for individual employment contracts (Art. 8 Rome II).

- A choice of law by contracting parties under Art. 3 Rome I can even be set aside – on very rare occasions – by the mandatory rules of another country 's law (Art. 9 Rome I).

- Art. 10 Rome I provides rules on the material validity of the contract. Art. 11 Rome I provides rules on the formal validity of a contract.

- As Rome I applies to contractual obligations only, it does not apply to (international) torts. The Rome II Regulation on the law applicable to non-contractual obligations applies to international torts. In general, this Regulation applies the law of the country where the damage arising from the tort is suffered. Special provisions apply in certain kinds of tort e.g. product liability, unfair competition, infringement of intellectual property rights and industrial action.

Glossary

Characteristic performance	If no choice of law has been made by the parties to a contract, or their choice is not clear, then according to Art. 4 Rome I one has to determine what the characteristic performance of the contract is. Paying money to another party is a common feature of many contracts and for that reason is not in any way 'characteristic'. So, the party receiving payment is therefore the one effecting a characteristic performance of the contract. If the country of the party carrying out the characteristic performance is known, one has to apply the law of that country to the contract.
Consumer contract	Contract made by a person acting outside a trade or profession at the time of concluding the contract. Art. 6 Rome I describes the necessary conditions for a contract to be a consumer contract under the Rome I. Both parties to this contract must be from different states.
Formal validity	The validity of a contract depends on whether the required legal formalities for that type of contract are fulfilled.
Freedom of choice	Contracting parties are free to choose the law which will apply to their contract. The decision should preferably be in writing, but under Art. 3 Rome I this is not mandatory.
Immovable property	Property, houses and land and their accompanying legal rights and obligations.
Individual Employment Contract	A contract of employment, where employer and employee are from different states. The employee works under the direction of the employer for a period of time and in return for which he receives payment.
Mandatory rules	Rules which, either by the authority of their content or of the organisation that issued them, must be followed.
Material validity	The validity of a contract is based on its content e.g. are the rights and obligations described in the contract legal?

Rome I	European Regulation on the law applicable to Contractual Obligations. The convention provides rules as to which law determines the obligations of contracting parties who are situated in different states.
Rules of reference	Rome I does not provide immediate solutions to legal problems, but rather indicates which laws should be applied to the problems.
Tort	An act or omission committed by a person or legal entity resulting in damage to another person or legal entity, without any justification for this act or omission.
Universal effect	Whichever law is specified by Rome I will apply, regardless of the fact that this might mean applying the law of a state that has not signed Rome I.

Exercises

Exercise 4.1
Ancelotti, domiciled in Firenze, Italy, has agreed to act as Weller's financial adviser. A contract to that effect has been drawn up and signed in London UK where Weller lives. Ancelotti has been requested by Weller to advise him on an investment he is planning to make in Ahold N.V., a multinational company, established in Amsterdam, The Netherlands.
Ancelotti, who is not sure whether Ahold will prove to be such a good investment, asks the advice of Westerhagen, a friend of his who is a financial consultant in Cologne, Germany. Westerhagen gives Ancelotti his approval to the proposed investment. Ancelotti advises Weller to proceed with the investment, informing him that this advice was checked twice, by him and by Westerhagen. Due to economic developments in South America and Ahold's accounting problems, the value of Ahold shares drops and Weller loses a great deal of money. Weller is not a happy man and blames both advisers for the bad advice they gave him. Weller decides to sue both Ancelotti and Westerhagen for compensation for his loss. Ancelotti is not a happy man either as Weller refuses to pay the fee agreed on in their contract.

1 What law governs the financial consultancy agreement between Weller and Ancelotti?
2 Suppose that Italian law governs the contract between Ancelotti and Weller and they have both agreed to this. According to Italian law, their contract should have been made in writing, which it was not. However, with regard to Rome I, is it nevertheless possible that the contract might indeed be formally valid?

Exercise 4.2
Van Bemmel B.V. is a company established in The Netherlands that both manufactures shoes and acts as a wholesaler for several brands of shoes. Van Bemmel buys a batch of men's shoes from Hereford Ltd., a company established in the UK, at a price of €20,000. Both parties agree in a telephone conversation, that in the event of any legal problems arising a UK court of law would have jurisdiction and also that the shoes would be collected by Van Bemmel at a Hereford-owned warehouse in Bruges (Belgium). Van Bemmel hires Danzas, a transport company established in France, to collect the goods in Belgium and deliver them to The Netherlands. Payment by Van Bemmel will be made in cash as soon as the goods are collected in Belgium.

4

1 What law applies to the contract of sale between Hereford and Van Bemmel?
2 What law applies to the transport contract between Van Bemmel and Danzas?
3 Van Bemmel has a contract with a German agent, Mr. Müller. No choice of law has been made by Van Bemmel and Müller. What law will apply to their contract?
4 Van Bemmel has made a distribution contract with Christlkindl Schuhe GmbH, a company established in Zug (Switzerland). This Swiss company will handle both the Swiss and the Austrian markets. It is agreed verbally between the two parties that Swiss law will apply to the contract. What law actually does apply to the distribution contract between Van Bemmel and Christlkindl Schuhe GmbH?
5 For many years Van Bemmel has been hiring three Italian craftsmen who manufacture all shoes by hand in their workshop in Rome (Italy) and deliver to Van Bemmel impeccable work of the highest quality. If *Dutch* law were chosen as the law applicable to their contracts of employment, would it nevertheless still be possible for the craftsmen to apply *Italian* law to their employment contracts, should the employees wish to do so?
6 Due to a strike by Italian customs authorities, which is supported by their Unions, a large shipment of shoes for Van Bemmel is held up at the Italian border. As a result, Van Bemmel is not able to present his new collection of shoes to his Dutch customers at the appropriate time. Van Bemmel suffers damage as a result of this strike. What law governs a claim by Van Bemmel against the Italian customs authorities?

5
CISG

The contract of sale is perhaps the most common form of contract. This chapter is about the formation of an international contract of sale, about the rights and obligations of both the seller and buyer and about dealing with breaches of contract by either of the two. The chapter also explains the Convention on the International Sale of Goods (CISG), which lays down rules on these matters and provides remedies for breaches of international contracts of sale.

International contract of sale: what are the options when a conflict arises?

On 1 April 2009 Trapper Jeans B.V. from Enschede (The Netherlands) close a contract with Sigmund GmbH from Emden (Germany). The contract concerns the sale and delivery of 1,500 pairs of outdoor trousers in various sizes. According to the contract the goods are to be delivered to the place of business of Sigmund GmbH on 5 May 2009. Sigmund pays €25,000 in advance. On delivery it turns out that the quality of the zip is below standard. A mistake has also been made about the sizes: nearly all the trousers are either size 'S' (too small) or size 'XXL' (very large indeed) and this is not what the parties agreed. Replacing the zip with a better one and sorting out the problem of sizes will take four weeks. A new delivery will therefore be made on 5 June 2009. This new date creates a problem for Sigmund GmbH, which, on 11 April 2009, made contracts with five stores in Germany to deliver the trousers on 10 May 2009. Sigmund is now liable for penalties of up to €5,000. There is, however, the possibility of buying the trousers from StarGap B.V. (The Netherlands), though this will cost Sigmund an extra €10,000. Without any doubt this case gives rise to numerous questions. Apart from the questions about which court of law has jurisdiction and which law is applicable to the contract, questions arise as to the options of both parties to this contract to settle their conflict.

5.1 Introduction to the CISG

In Chapter 1 the third main issue (Question 3) was whether a specific treaty can provide an immediate solution to a conflict between contracting parties. In a case concerning a contract of sale, the United Nations Convention on the International Sale of Goods (CISG) is the specific treaty to be used to solve problems relating to this type of contract. If the contract of sale in question meets the requirements of Articles 1 to 6 CISG inclusive, the CISG is applicable. This means that, Rome I (Chapter 4) cannot be used by whichever court of law has jurisdiction. However, should the CISG (Question 3) fail to resolve a conflict between contracting parties, then the solution must lie in whichever law is applicable to the contract according to Rome I (Question 2).

United Nations Convention on the International Sale of Goods (CISG)

While Rome I refers to an applicable law, where the answer to a legal problem might be found, the CISG provides immediate answers to legal problems relating to contracts of sale. These include answers to questions like: can I declare this contract null and void, can I claim compensation for damage suffered because delivery was not made in time, is it still possible to revoke my offer, is the seller allowed to repair a defect in the machine he supplied?

5

Note that Brussels I (Chapter 3) applies to nearly all legal obligations. Rome I (Chapter 4) refers to contractual obligations only. The CISG applies to only one type of contract, the (professional) contract of sale. As this type of contract is the one most often used in the world, it comes within the scope of this book.

As of 26 September 2014, 83 Member States of the United Nations have adopted the CISG Treaty. For this reason, the CISG has become more and more important over the years.

83 Member States

5.2 Application of the CISG

In order to be able to apply the CISG to a contract of sale, any court of law that has jurisdiction has to check whether the requirements of Art. 1, 1 CISG have been met.

Apply the CISG to a contract of sale

According to Art. 1, 1 CISG this treaty is about contracts concerning the sale of *goods* (so not 'services'), which are international contracts closed between undertakings ('places of business are in different States') and the CISG can be used only:

a when the States (of the contracting parties) are Contracting States; *or*
b when the rules of international private law lead to the application of the law of a Contracting State.

If both contracting parties are from Member States of the CISG, direct application of the CISG is possible (Art. 1, 1, a CISG).
If one of the parties is not from a Member State of the CISG (e.g. the United Kingdom is not a Member State), one cannot, according to Art 1,1, a CISG, apply the CISG. But there is a second option: perhaps an indirect application of the CISG under Art. 1, 1, b CISG is possible. According to Art. 1, 1, b CISG, the rules of private international law, i.e. Rome I, should lead us to the law of a Member State of the CISG, in order for the CISG to be applicable.

EXAMPLE 5.1

Art. 1, 1, a CISG (immediate application of the CISG). Starweiner AG, from Bitburg (Germany), supplies 1,000 bottles of beer to Groenen B.V., a Dutch company established in Groningen. However, the Dutch buyer does not pay in time. The German seller wants to nullify the contract. Should a lawsuit between the German seller and the Dutch buyer arise, would the competent court of law use the CISG to answer this question? According to Art. 1, 1, a CISG the answer is 'yes', as both Germany and The Netherlands are Contracting States of the CISG.

In the opening case study, the court of law that has jurisdiction over the conflict between Trapper and Sigmund will have to determine whether the requirements of Art. 1 CISG are met. There are two companies, Trapper and Sigmund, that close an international and professional contract of sale concerning goods. And as both parties are from countries that have signed the CISG, the CISG has to be applied to determine what legal options Trapper has.

5

EXAMPLE 5.2

Art. 1, 1, b CISG (indirect application of the CISG). Nieuwenhuis V.o.f, a Dutch company from Alkmaar, supplies 1,500 kilos of Leerdammer cheese to Brown Ltd., a company established in the UK. The English buyer pays only half the price, claiming that he only received half the amount he ordered. As this is absolute nonsense, the Dutch seller wants to claim the other half of the price from the English buyer.
Can the court of law that has jurisdiction use the CISG in this case? Art. 1, 1, a CISG does not apply as the United Kingdom is not a Contracting State. Turn to Art. 1, 1, b CISG: 'rules of private international law' in this context means turning to Rome I to determine the law applicable to this case. Under Art. 3 Rome I, the parties made no choice of law in this case. So one has to turn to Art. 4, 1, a Rome I which states that a contract for the sale is governed by the law of the country, where the seller has his habitual residence. When the case concerns a contract of sale the seller effects the characteristic performance. In this example there is a Dutch seller and because The Netherlands is a Contracting State of the CISG, the court of law must apply the CISG in this case.

Note that in Example 5.2, if the seller had not been from a Member State of the CISG, the CISG would not have been applicable. In such a case one would have to return to the law applicable to this contract of sale according to Rome I (Chapter 4).

Art. 2 CISG makes clear that contracts for the sale of goods to consumers are not governed by the CISG. Therefore, problems arising out of contracts for the sale of goods for personal, family or household use can be solved either by the applicable law according to Rome I or by other, more specific, rules of law.

Art. 6 CISG makes it possible for the contracting parties to exclude the application of the CISG to their contract. It is possible for the parties to agree to use only a part of this Treaty or to change the effect of certain

provisions of the Treaty. If parties do decide to opt out of the CISG, this should be made quite clear. In general, the choosing of an applicable law does not automatically mean the CISG no longer applies.
Once parties have opted out of the CISG , the second main issue i.e. Question 2 returns. What law applies if a problem should arise out of the sales contract? In most cases, the seller will try in his terms of sale and delivery to force the buyer to agree to use the law of the country of the seller as the law applicable to the contract of sale. The seller would thus be more sure of his legal position.

5.3 Content of the CISG

The object of the CISG is a contract of sale. The first thing to be dealt with (in paragraph 5.3.1) is the formation of the contract. The content of the Articles of the CISG are identical to the process used to determine the legal position of the parties during the 'preliminary stage' described in Chapter 2. In paragraph 5.3.2 a breach of contract is defined and the subsequent options are laid out for both seller and buyer should the other party commit a breach of contract.

5.3.1 Formation of the contract of sale according to the CISG

Formation of the contract

As explained in Chapter 2, an agreement consists of an offer and its acceptance (Art. 18, 21, 23 CISG). The offer is valid the moment it reaches the other party. The offerer has the opportunity to withdraw the offer up to and including the moment the offer reaches the offeree (Art. 15 CISG). If the offer becomes valid, the offeree has time to think it over. The time allowed for consideration depends on the content of the offer and whether or not the offer was in writing (Art. 18 CISG). Up to the moment the offeree sends his acceptance, the offerer has the option of revoking his offer – unless the offer is irrevocable (Art. 16 CISG). The offeree can decide to accept the offer, refuse it or make a counter offer to the offerer. If he decides on a counter offer, there will then be a new offer on the table (Art. 17, 19, 22 CISG). The moment the acceptance reaches the offerer there is an agreement (Art. 18 CISG).

The CISG will be dealt with by studying small cases, all of them dealing with either one or some Articles of the CISG. First the relevant Articles of the CISG are mentioned, and these are followed by the accompanying exercises. The answers to all exercises can be found in the Articles of the CISG mentioned above each exercise and in paragraph 5.4. Studying the exercises gives a good overview of legal problems which can arise from international sales contracts and how the CISG can provide solutions.

Exercises 5.1, 5.2 and 5.3 should be tackled with reference to Art. 14 – 23 CISG. The answers can be found in paragraph 5.4.

EXERCISE 5.1

Anderson, a company established in Sweden, wants to make an agreement with Bonhoff, a company established in The Netherlands. He tells Bonhoff that he is willing to sell a machine at a price of €500,000. Just before Bonhoff sends his acceptance to Anderson, he receives a message from

Anderson informing him that Anderson is revoking his offer. Bonhoff, who was inclined to accept the offer made by Anderson, is of the opinion that revoking the offer in this case is not possible. So Bonhoff sends his acceptance to Anderson.

Question: Has an agreement been reached in this case?

EXERCISE 5.2
Anders, a company established in Germany, offers Egberts, a company established in The Netherlands, a consignment of coffee. Anders informs Egberts in writing that the time limit for acceptance is three months. One month after his offer to Egberts, Anders sees an opportunity to sell the coffee to Christensen, a company in Denmark, at a much higher price. Anders revokes the offer made to Egberts. Nevertheless Egberts accepts the offer after Anders has revoked it.

Question: Has an agreement been reached in this case or not?

EXERCISE 5.3
Food Company B.V., a company established in The Netherlands, makes an offer to Ulbricht GmbH, a company established in Germany. The contract concerns the sale and delivery of a high tech machine for the production of food. In the offer, Food Company includes a copy of their terms of sale and delivery. Ulbricht GmbH sends its acceptance of the offer containing their own terms of sale and delivery, which differ on various points from those of Food Company. Problems arise when, after delivery, the machine does not function properly and several leaks in the hydraulic system result in the severe pollution of the products. In turn, the products cause health problems in consumers. Food Company states that they have excluded every liability for this kind of damage in their terms of sale and delivery and are of the opinion that they are not liable in any way. According to the terms of sale of Ulbricht GmbH, Food Company is indeed responsible for this kind of damage.

Question: Which terms of sale and delivery apply to this contract?

Exercise 5.4 is to be made by using Art. 31 – 34 CISG. The answer is located in paragraph 5.4.

EXERCISE 5.4
Andreotti, a company established in Italy, sells to Breitmann, a company established in Switzerland, a number of watches at a price of €10,000.

Question 1: If no place of delivery is agreed upon, where should delivery of the watches take place?
Question 2: If the seller has to arrange transport of the watches, is he free to choose the means of transport?

5.3.2 Committing a breach of contract under the CISG

Breach of contract

In a contract of sale there are two parties: a seller and a buyer and the CISG is therefore set up accordingly. Both seller and buyer can commit a breach of contract i.e. not abiding by the obligations under their contract of

sale or the CISG. A breach of contract enables the other party to resort to certain options available under the CISG.
Schedule 5.1 shows what the obligations of both seller and buyer are, and what the options for both seller and buyer are should there be a breach of contract. The Articles of the CISG containing this information are mentioned in Schedule 5.1. This schedule is of help in nearly all the exercises on the CISG that follow.

SCHEDULE 5.1 Breach of contract: options for seller and buyer

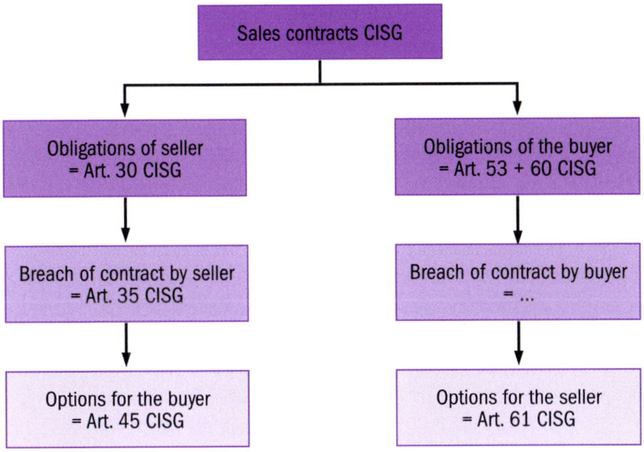

- Art. 46 + 47 CISG = require performance within an additional period = Art. 62 + 63 CISG

or
- Art. 49 CISG = declare the contract avoided (effects = Art. 81 - 84 CISG) = Art. 64 CISG

or
- Art. 50 CISG = reduction of the price = ...

and
- Art. 74 CISG = claim damages = Art. 74 CISG

Bear in mind that following a breach of contract, the seller and the buyer cannot both resort to all the options mentioned above at the same time. The buyer e.g. cannot require performance within an additional period and declare the contract avoided at the same time (Art. 46, 47, 49 CISG). This is because the delivery to be made by the seller is based on the same contract. Declaring the contract avoided by the buyer cannot be combined with a reduction of the selling price (Art. 50 CISG), as payment by the buyer is based on that same contract. Claiming damages – if the buyer or the seller has suffered damage – is an option always available to both parties, regardless of other options being used (Art. 74 CISG).

Require performance

Nullify the contract

Damage

Exercises 5.5 and 5.6 should be tackled with reference to Art. 35 – 44 CISG. The answers are located in paragraph 5.4.

EXERCISE 5.5

Abels, a company established in The Netherlands, sells to Bartels, a company established in Germany, a quantity of radios at a price of €150,000. The moment they are delivered to Bartels it becomes clear that these radios have an electronic defect.

Question: Has the seller fulfilled his legal obligations?

EXERCISE 5.6

Biondi, a company established in Italy, manufactures shirts. Biondi buys from Ten Bate, a company established in The Netherlands, a large quantity of textiles. The fabric should consist of 80% cotton and 20% polyester. The textiles are supplied to Biondi. When Biondi supplies the shirts to Christoffel, a company established in Belgium, Christoffel refuses to accept them, because the fabric consists of only 25% cotton. Biondi claims compensation from Ten Bate because they delivered the wrong fabric.

Question: Does Biondi have a right to compensation for damage suffered?

Exercises 5.7, 5.8 and 5.9 should be tackled with reference to Art. 45 – 52 CISG. The answers are located in paragraph 5.4.

EXERCISE 5.7

Schubert, a company established in Germany, sells a quantity of shirts to Hermsen, a company established in The Netherlands. The shirts are to be delivered before 1 May and arrive on 29 April. Unfortunately, the size labels of the shirts are wrong. Hermsen gets a little nervous because he is to supply these shirts to Berin SA, a company established in France, on May 2nd. If the shirts are not delivered to Berin on that date, Hermsen is liable to a penalty of €25,000. Another Dutch company is willing to change all the labels within one day at a price of €15,000.

Question: What options does Hermsen have, if Schubert cannot deliver the shirts with the right labels in them before 1 May?

EXERCISE 5.8

A sales contract is concluded between Bertelsmeier, a company established in Germany, and Michielsen, a company established in The Netherlands. Bertelsmeier sells Michielsen a machine. It is agreed that should any problem arise, a claim should be made in writing to the German seller. It appears that the machine does not function properly, so the Dutch buyer puts in his claim in writing within the three-week period they had agreed on. The German seller informs the Dutch buyer that he will repair the machine within one month. A more speedy repair of the machine is impossible, due to the lack of necessary parts. The buyer does not react to this immediately, but three weeks after he put in his claim he informs the seller that the contract is going to be nullified. The Dutch buyer wants to be reimbursed the price he paid for the machine which he will return.

Question: Is this possible?

EXERCISE 5.9

Angelo, a company established in Italy, sells a machine to Bouvais, a company established in France. The machine is to be delivered before 1 March. When Angelo fails to deliver the machine on time, Bouvais submits a written demand that Angelo make his delivery within 14 days. Angelo does not respond and Bouvais, after informing Angelo in writing that he considers their contract cancelled, orders a new machine on 15 March from another seller. On 20 April Angelo still wants to deliver the machine to Bouvais.

Question: Does Bouvais have to accept this delivery from Angelo?

Exercises 5.10 and 5.11 should be tackled with reference to Art. 53 – 60 CISG. The answers are located in paragraph 5.4.

EXERCISE 5.10
Amelie, a company established in France, buys a machine from Gomez, a company established in Spain. No arrangement is made in the contract concerning where payment for the machine should be made.

Question: Where does payment for the machine have to be made?

EXERCISE 5.11
Arragon, a company established in Spain, sells a machine to Hendriksen, a company established in The Netherlands. The machine is sold at a price of €300,000. Payment for the machine has to be made into Arragon's account on the day of delivery. The machine is to be delivered to Hendriksen's factory on 1 March. But the factory is closed on this date and Arragon cannot deliver the machine to Hendriksen that day.

Question: Does Hendriksen nevertheless have to pay?

Exercise 5.12 should be tackled with reference to Art. 61 – 65 CISG. The answer is located in paragraph 5.4.

EXERCISE 5.12
Allez Medical, a company established in France, sells to Becker, a company established in Germany, a number of medical instruments, custom made for Becker, at a price of €50,000. Becker pays €20,000 in advance. When Allez wants to deliver the instruments on the day both parties had agreed on, Becker refuses to accept and pay for the instruments. An amount of €30,000 should have been paid on delivery. Allez offers Becker a period of three weeks in order to fulfil his legal obligations. Becker does not respond.

Question: What options does Allez Medical have? Also look at Art. 81 – 84 CISG.

Exercises 5.13 and 5.14 should be tackled with reference to Art. 61 – 69 CISG. The answers are located in paragraph 5.4.

EXERCISE 5.13
Arranguez, a company established in Spain, has to deliver a machine to Bleckmann, a company established in Germany. It is agreed that buyer Bleckmann will take care of the transport. Bleckmann hires Derksen, a company established in The Netherlands, to deliver the machine. Derksen's truck is subsequently struck by lightning and both the truck and the machine are destroyed.

Question: Does Bleckmann have to pay Arranguez for the machine?

EXERCISE 5.14

Look at the facts in exercise 5.12. Suppose these medical instruments are lost in circumstances beyond the control of Becker (an 'Act of God') in the three weeks Allez Medical has given him.

Question: Does Becker nevertheless have to pay?

Exercise 5.15 should be tackled with reference to Art. 71 – 73 CISG. The answer is located in paragraph 5.4.

EXERCISE 5.15

Magiot, a company established in France, has a contract with Boon, a company established in The Netherlands, in which Magiot is to deliver cattle feed to Boon once a month for one year. By the time Magiot has made 5 of the scheduled deliveries to Boon, the Dutch buyer has still not paid for 3 of them owing to financial difficulties, he claims to have suffered. Magiot refuses to continue the deliveries. Boon is in urgent need of this cattle feed, and demands that Magiot continue the deliveries.

Question: Does Magiot have the legal right to stop all future deliveries? What are the options for Magiot regarding the 3 deliveries that have not been paid for?

Exercise 5.16 should be tackled with reference to Art. 74 – 77 CISG. The answer is located in paragraph 5.4.

EXERCISE 5.16

Alberts, a company established in The Netherlands, is to deliver a large quantity of grain to Birndorff, a company established in Germany. The grain is to be delivered by Birndorff to Christensen, a company established in Denmark.
It is agreed that Alberts will deliver to Birndorff on 1 June. Birndorff has agreed to deliver the grain on 5 June to Christensen. Alberts does not fulfil his obligations. If Birndorff wants to fulfil his, he has to buy the grain elsewhere, but, due to an increase in grain prices, he would have to pay an extra €10,000.

Question: What are the options for Birndorff in this case?

Exercises 5.17 and 5.18 should be tackled with reference to Art. 85 – 88 CISG. The answers are located in paragraph 5.4.

EXERCISE 5.17

Amelink, a company established in The Netherlands, sells a machine to Miromar, a company established in Spain. Miromar has to delay the receipt of the machine. Amelink incurs costs through having to store the machine.

Question: Does Miromar have to pay the expenses incurred by Amelink?

EXERCISE 5.18

Following up on exercise 5.17, suppose Miromar receives the machine, but it does not function properly. Miromar declares the contract null and void.

Miromar stores the machine, waiting for Amelink to collect it, in an unlocked and unguarded shed. The machine is stolen. Miromar has already paid for the machine.

Question: Is it possible for Miromar to demand a refund from Amelink of the money it has paid?

5.4 Answers to CISG Exercises

Exercise 5.1
Art. 16, 1 CISG: it is still possible for Anderson to revoke the offer, as Bonhoff had not sent an acceptance. No agreement reached.

Exercise 5.2
Art. 16, 2, a CISG: Anders' offer is an irrevocable offer, because there is a fixed time for acceptance of the offer. There is an agreement between Anders and Egberts.

Exercise 5.3
According to Art. 19, 2 CISG Ulbricht GmbH's acceptance makes an agreement final only if the difference in the terms of sale do not materially change the terms of the offer made by Food Company. However, under Art. 19, 3 CISG, different arrangements on liability do materially change the offer. So, Ulbricht's GmbH 'acceptance' basically is a counter offer i.e. a new offer to Food Company according to Art. 19, 1 CISG. Because Food Company delivered the goods without complaint, it can be assumed that the company accepted Ulbricht GmbH's new offer and therefore also accepted its terms of sale and delivery. So Ulbricht GmbH's terms of sale and delivery apply. As a result of this, Food Company is liable for the damage.

Exercise 5.4
Art. 31 (c) CISG: if no place of delivery has been determined by the parties, then the place of delivery of the goods is the seller Andreotti's place of business at the time the contract was concluded.
Art. 32, 2 CISG: the seller is free to choose the means of transport, but only those means that are appropriate under the circumstances and are normally used for transport of that kind.

Exercise 5.5
Art. 35, 1 and 2, (a) CISG: this is a breach of contract by the Dutch seller Abels because the radios are not fit for normal use. Exception in Art. 35, 3 CISG: if Bartels, the German buyer, knew he was buying radios with these defects, then of course there is no breach of contract.

Exercise 5.6
No, because according to Art. 38 CISG Biondi should have checked the goods on delivery, which it did not (Christoffel finally checked the goods). For this reason, even though, under Art.39 CISG, there was a breach of contract committed by Ten Bate, Bondi loses the right to make a claim.

Exercise 5.7
Art. 35 CISG: The seller Schubert commits a breach of contract as the goods do not match the description in the contract. So resort to Art. 45 CISG: after examination of the goods (Art. 38 CISG) and informing the seller in time (Art. 39 CISG), the options available to the buyer Hermsen are:
1 to reduce the price according to the value of the goods (Art. 50 CISG), or
2 to claim damages (Art. 74 CISG)
3 no other options available to the buyer are relevant to this exercise.

Exercise 5.8
According to Art. 48, 1 CISG, the German seller Bertelsmeier has the right to repair the machine. There is no unreasonable delay, as Bertelsmeier needs a month to order the new parts. The request indicated in Art. 48, 2 CISG is included in the question of the German seller, as explained in Art. 48, 3 CISG. If the Dutch buyer Michielsen did not want the German seller to repair the machine, he should have told him so right away. Note that the German seller has the *right* to repair the machine if he so wishes; the Dutch buyer has no right to insist that it be repaired.

Exercise 5.9
Following the period of two weeks given to the Italian seller Angelo by the French buyer Bouvais (Art. 46 and 47 CISG), the contract has been correctly nullified using Art. 49 CISG. The contract therefore no longer exists and there are no further obligations.

Exercise 5.10
Art. 57, 1, (a) CISG: if no place for payment has been agreed, the seller's place of business is therefore the place for payment. So, the place for payment in this case is where Gomez, the Spanish seller, has his place of business.

Exercise 5.11
Art. 53 and 60 CISG: Hendriksen is obliged to receive the goods and to pay the price. It is Hendriksen 's own fault that the factory was closed on the day of delivery.

Exercise 5.12
There is a breach of contract by the German buyer Becker (Art. 53 and 60 CISG). So, Allez Medical, the French seller, has the right to declare the contract avoided under Art. 64 CISG. The results of declaring the contract avoided are described in Art. 81,1 CISG (no contract means no contractual obligations), Art. 81,2 CISG (restitution of the down payment to Becker) and Art. 84 CISG (compensation for Becker for interest lost).

Exercise 5.13
As explained in Art. 67 CISG, the risk passed from Arranguez to Bleckmann the moment the goods were handed over to the first carrier, Derksen. According to Art. 66 CISG Bleckmann therefore is obliged to pay, even though the goods have been destroyed.

Exercise 5.14

Check Exercise 5.12. The risk passed from Allez Medical to Becker the moment Allez Medical wanted to deliver the goods to Becker. So, Becker has to pay (Art. 69 and 66 CISG).

Exercise 5.15

According to Art. 73, 2 CISG, the French seller Magiot has the right to cancel all 7 future deliveries. It seems obvious that Boon is not going to pay for these deliveries. Art. 73,1 CISG states that Magiot also has the right to cancel the contract because of the 3 deliveries that were not paid for. Art. 81, 2 CISG requires the restitution of the cattle feed that is still on the Boon premises.

Exercise 5.16

Art. 35 CISG: breach of contract by Alberts, the Dutch seller. Art. 45 CISG provides certain options for the German buyer Birndorff. These allow Birndorff to declare the contract with Alberts avoided according to Art. 49 CISG and, having done so, buy other grain elsewhere. He can also:

1 Art. 75 CISG = claim the difference in price from Alberts (this is only possible if the contract of sale between Alberts and Birndorff has been nullified beforehand).
2 Art. 74 CISG = claim other damages.

Exercise 5.17

Art. 85 CISG: as long as the costs incurred by seller Amelink are reasonable, Miromar has to pay them. Until the moment Miromar actually pays for the goods and the additional costs, Amelink has the right to retain the goods.

Exercise 5.18

The Spanish buyer Miromar in this case has neglected his obligations mentioned under Art. 86, 1 CISG. According to Art. 86, 2, last sentence CISG, the rights and obligations of Miromar are governed by Articles 81 – 84 CISG. This means that, under Art. 82, 1 CISG, nullifying the contract is out of the question, as it would be impossible for Miromar to make restitution of the machine.

5.5 Art. 7 Brussels I, determining place of performance of obligation in question

The problem discussed in this paragraph concerns one of the general provisions of Brussels I. Why discuss a problem with Brussels I in this chapter? Because, once the problem is clear, its first solution lies in the CISG, which is the topic of this chapter. Note that in this paragraph both the CISG and Rome I are used in a different way from before.

The general provisions of Brussels I are to be found in the Articles 4 and 7 Brussels I. Art. 4 Brussels I states that the court of law of the country of the defendant has jurisdiction. According to the principle of alternative jurisdiction, Art. 4 Brussels I had to be combined with Art. 7 Brussels I.

According to Art. 7 Brussels I, in matters relating to contract, the criterion for establishing which court of law should have jurisdiction is the place of performance of the obligation in question. Problems arise in a situation where no place of delivery can be determined i.e. this place is not clearly agreed on by both parties. The result would be that there is no alternative jurisdiction and that the plaintiff would have no choice. In that situation, according to Art. 4 Brussels I, the plaintiff would have to settle for the court of law of the defendant. However, there are two solutions to this problem with Art. 7 Brussels I, which provide an alternative jurisdiction in favour of the plaintiff. If the first offers no solution, try the second.

Solution 1

If both parties are from countries that are Contracting States of the CISG (Art. 1, 1, (a) CISG) then the provisions of the CISG will determine which country's law will ultimately determine which court of law should have jurisdiction.

5

EXAMPLE 5.3

A company established in France supplies goods to a company established in The Netherlands, but the Dutch buyer does not pay the price they agreed on. Should there be litigation by the French seller against the Dutch buyer, what court of law has jurisdiction?
Art. 4 Brussels I: determine the place of residence of the defendant. The defendant is the Dutch buyer, so a Dutch court of law has jurisdiction. However, because the matter concerns a sales contract, combine Art. 4 with 7 Brussels I. In case there is a contract of sale, but the provision of Article 7, 1, a Brussels I does not give a solution as to which court of law has jurisdiction, try solution 1. Both France and The Netherlands are Contracting States of the CISG (Art. 1, 1, (a) CISG), so use CISG to find the place of payment. According to Art. 57, 1, (a) CISG the seller's place of business is the place of payment. The seller is from France, so the conclusion to solution 1 is that French law will decide what court of law has jurisdiction. So the French plaintiff can choose between a Dutch court of law (Art. 4 Brussels I) and whichever court of law under French law would have jurisdiction (Art. 7 Brussels I with solution 1).

Note that the example would employ the same argument if the place of *delivery* (Art. 31 CISG) had been the problem.

Solution 2

If one of the parties (or both) is not from a Contracting State of the CISG, then Solution 1 is of no use. In that case one should try and solve this problem by means of Rome I. The rules of Rome I will provide a law that will determine what court of law has jurisdiction.

EXAMPLE 5.4

A company established in The Netherlands supplies 1,500 kilos of Leerdammer cheese to a company established in England. The English buyer pays only half the price, claiming that he only received half the quantity he ordered. As this is absolute nonsense, the Dutch seller wants to claim the other half of the purchase price from the English buyer in a court of law. What court of law has jurisdiction in this case?
Art. 4 Brussels I: determine the place of residence of the defendant. As the defendant is the English buyer, an English court of law therefore has jurisdiction.
Combine Art. 4 with 7 Brussels I. Art. 7 Brussels I refers to the place of performance of the obligation in question, meaning in this case the place of payment, which is not mentioned in the contract.
Try solution 1: Art. 1, 1, (a) CISG does not apply: UK is not a Contracting State of the CISG.
Resort to solution 2, using Rome I. Look at Art. 3 Rome I: the parties did not make a choice of law, so resort to Art. 4 Rome I. We are dealing with a Dutch seller, so solution 2 leads to the conclusion that Dutch law will determine what court of law has jurisdiction The Dutch plaintiff can therefore choose between an English court of law (Art. 4 Brussels I) and the court of law that will have jurisdiction according to Dutch law (Art. 7 Brussels I with solution 2).

Summary

- The United Nations Convention on the International Sale of Goods (CISG) concerns itself with contracts for the sale of goods when the places of business of the contracting parties are in different Member States, and if certain conditions are fulfilled (Art. 1, 2 and 6 CISG).

- The formation of the contract concerns: offer, acceptance, withdrawing an offer, revoking an offer, irrevocable offers, terms of sale and delivery and reaching an agreement (Art. 14 – 24 CISG).

- In a contract of sale the seller has an obligation to deliver the goods to the buyer (Art. 30 – 35 CISG). If the seller commits a breach of contract (Art. 35 – 44 CISG) the buyer may resort to certain options given to him by Art. 45 CISG. The buyer may insist on delivery (Art. 46 CISG) or delivery within an additional period (Art. 47 CISG). The seller may try to resolve delivery problems (Art. 48 CISG). The buyer is entitled to declare the contract avoided (Art. 49 CISG) and to claim damages (Art. 74, 75 CISG). The buyer may also reduce the price to be paid for the goods that were delivered (Art. 50 CISG). Additional provisions concerning claims for compensation for damage can be found in Art. 75 – 80 CISG.

- If the buyer commits a breach of contract i.e. does not pay the price and accept the goods (Art. 53 – 60 CISG), the seller has options too (Art. 61 CISG). The seller may require payment (Art. 62 CISG), or payment within an additional period (Art. 63 CISG), or he may declare the contract with the buyer avoided (Art. 64 CISG). The seller has the right to claim damages (Art. 74 CISG). Additional provisions concerning claims for compensation for damage can be found in Art. 75 – 80 CISG.

- The risks concerning the goods pass from seller to buyer at the moment defined in Art. 66 – 70 CISG.

- In general, the effects of nullifying a contract are described in Articles 81 – 84 CISG. Art. 85 – 88 CISG are about the goods to be returned in case the contract is nullified.

Glossary

Application of CISG	The CISG applies when both parties are from countries that are Contracting States of the CISG, or if the rules of international private law lead to the application of the law of a Contracting State.
Breach of contract	One of the two parties to a contract of sale does not abide by the obligations imposed on it by the contract or the CISG.
Contracting States	The Contracting States of the CISG are 83 of the member states of the United Nations.
Damages	Claim for compensation for damages suffered
Declaring the contract avoided	A declaration by one of the two parties to a contract that it considers their contract to be null and void, i.e. to be cancelled as a result of a fundamental breach of contract by the other party.
Formation of the Contract of sale	An offer becomes an agreement as soon as the acceptance of the offeree reaches the offeror.
Performance within additional period	Same as Require performance, but within an extra period of time added to performance within allow one party to fulfil an obligation an additional period
Require performance	A demand from one party to the contract that the other party should abide by its contractual obligations. Thus the contract requires the seller to deliver the goods ordered, and the buyer should accept them and make payment.
UN Convention on the International Sale of Goods	The CISG is a Convention drawn up by the United Nations and affects only those countries who have become Members of the United Nations and have signed the Convention.
Reduction of price	Option available to the buyer to reduce the price to be paid for goods if the goods were of lesser quality than agreed on.

5

Exercises

As seen in the introductory case, a legal conflict over an international contract for the sale of goods has links with Brussels I (Chapter 3), Rome I (Chapter 4) and the CISG (Chapter 5). In this paragraph the questions to the exercises can only be answered by using all three chapters.

5

Exercise 5.19
Jansen, a company established in The Netherlands, buys a large number of leather handbags from Gomez, a company established in Portugal. The handbags are to be delivered to The Netherlands by the Portuguese enterprise. On arrival in The Netherlands the handbags prove to be of inferior quality than the parties had agreed upon. Jansen asks himself the following questions.

1 In this case what court of law has jurisdiction?
2 What law is to be applied to the contract?
3 What options do I have? Can I claim compensation? Give Jansen a complete overview of his legal possibilities!

Exercise 5.20
Picchi, an Italian manufacturer of fashionable shoes, established in Rome, supplies a number of shoes to Van Bemmel, a company established in The Netherlands. It is agreed orally between the two parties that Dutch law will be the law applicable to this contract and that the court of law in Amsterdam will have jurisdiction should litigation arise between the two parties. As it turns out the Dutch buyer does not pay. The Italian seller starts a lawsuit in Rome against the Dutch company and demands payment of the price with interest.

1 Is it possible for the Italian seller to start litigation against the Dutch buyer in an Italian court of law?
2 Has a breach of contract been committed by the Dutch buyer? Is it possible to claim interest from the Dutch buyer?

Exercise 5.21
Bourdon SA, a company established in France, and McCormick Ltd., a company established in the UK, conclude an agreement in Spain. The UK company is to sell to the French company a number of goods with a total value of €50,000. It is agreed orally that the court of law in France will have jurisdiction and that French law will be the law applicable to this contract. When the French buyer wants to collect the goods in England, as agreed by both parties, it turns out they are not available. The English seller informs his French buyer that he will not be able to supply them, due to the great demand for his products. The French buyer, who is in great

need of these goods, is informed there is no chance he will receive them in the near future.
Bourdon is not keen to start litigation against McCormick in France, because according to French law their contract of sale should have been in writing. The Spanish attorney, who was present at the conclusion of the agreement, then told him that this was not necessary in Spain.

1 In this case: looking at the formalities, is this contract valid or not?
2 What court of law has jurisdiction?
3 What can Bourdon, who has already paid for these goods, claim from the English seller and what action must he take?

Exercise 5.22
On 1 April Trapper Jeans B.V. from Enschede (The Netherlands) conclude a contract with Sigmund GmbH from Emden (Germany). The contract concerns the sale and delivery of 1,500 pairs of outdoor trousers in various sizes. According to the contract the goods are to be delivered to the place of business of Sigmund GmbH on 5 May. Sigmund pays €25,000 in advance. On delivery it turns out that the quality of the zip is below standard. A mistake has also been made about the sizes: nearly all the trousers are either size 'S' (too small) or 'XXL' (very large indeed) and this is not what the parties agreed on. Replacing the zip with a better one and sorting out the problem of sizes will take four weeks. A new delivery will therefore be made on 5 June. This new date creates a problem for Sigmund GmbH which, on 11 April, made contracts with five stores in Germany to deliver the trousers on 10 May. Sigmund is now liable for penalties of up to €15,000. There is, however, the possibility of buying the trousers from StarGap B.V. (The Netherlands) though this will cost Sigmund an extra €10,000.

1 What court of law has jurisdiction in this case?
2 If the CISG is not applicable, what law should be applied to the sales contract between Trapper Jeans B.V. and Sigmund GmbH?
3 What legal options does Sigmund have according to the CISG in the event:
- it decides to wait for Trapper Jeans to deliver the trousers on 5 June and in doing so incurs a penalty of €15,000?
- it decides to buy the trousers from StarGap B.V. (instead of Trapper Jeans B.V.) in order to deliver to his German customers in time?

6
The free movement of goods, persons, services and capital

Essential to the European Union are the freedom of movement of goods, of people in general and workers in particular, of capital, of services and the freedom of establishment (the freedom to settle in another EU country and start a business there). The protection of these freedoms is an essential function of EU law. This chapter explains these freedoms and the rights and obligations of both the Member States of the EU and their nationals. Do Member States have the right to ban products from their home market? Do German nationals have the right to enter The Netherlands to look for work? Under what circumstances can Belgian nationals deduct gifts to Dutch charitable organisations from their home income tax? Can Dutch law limit gambling only to Dutch businesses holding a license from the Dutch authorities – thus excluding foreign businesses? This chapter provides the answers to questions such as these.

The free movement of bread

Nannini Sarl, a company established in Italy, is the sole representative in Italy for frozen bread which is prepared in France. This bread is sold in France by BCS, a company established in France. *The Laboratoire Interrégional* in Marseilles (France) issued a certificate for this bread which states that it is 'a product of good quality, healthy and fit for human consumption'. Nannini buys this French bread from BCS and imports it into Italy. However, Nannini very rapidly encounters problems with the Italian authorities who believe that Nannini has violated Italian law no 580/67 of 4 July 1967, regarding the use and trading of grains, farina, bread and pasta. They therefore impose an administrative fine on Nannini. This Italian law states that in Italy it is forbidden to sell bread with a moisture content higher than 34%, with a grain percentage lower than 1.40%, or which contains bran. The French bread imported by Nannini does not meet these requirements and therefore Nannini is fined and not allowed to sell this bread in Italy. Nannini appeals against the judgement to the Italian judicial authority *Pretore di Pordenone*, which subsequently asks the European Court of Justice for a preliminary ruling. The Italian legislation involved is considered a restriction of the free movement of goods and therefore ruled unlawful.

6.1 Introduction to the free movement of goods

Free movement of goods

The free movement of goods is one of the most important principles of the EU. To enable the free movement of goods within the Member States of the EU, tariff barriers were removed, but many other obstacles created by Member States still remain, such as the one mentioned in the opening case study.
The principle of the free movement of goods is upheld by Art. 34, 35 and 36 TFEU. Obstacles put up by Member States that endanger the free movement of goods within the territory of the EU, are prohibited. The objective of Art. 34, 35 and 36 TFEU is to remove these obstacles, known as quantitative restrictions, together with measures having an equivalent effect (as a quantitative restriction). However, these Articles give Member States the right in some cases to uphold barriers among themselves whenever this is justified. Art. 34 and 35 TFEU have direct effect (Chapter 1) which means that any national of a Member State engaged in a lawsuit can depend on these Articles in a national court of law. Art. 34, 35, and 36 TFEU do not apply to trade barriers between a Member State and a non Member State.

6.2 Quantitative restrictions

Quantitative restriction

A *quantitative restriction* is an act of a Member State which restricts the import or export of a product by amount or by value or for a certain period of time.

EXAMPLE 6.1

British meat is *banned* from the Dutch market. A ban is a quantitative restriction and in conflict with Art. 34 TFEU.

EXAMPLE 6.2

It is allowed to import Italian Chianti wine into the Netherlands, *but* due to a *Regulation* by the Dutch government *only to a maximum of 5,000 crates a month*. A quota is a quantitative restriction and in conflict with Art. 34 TFEU.

6.3 Measures having an effect equivalent to quantitative restrictions

Measures having equivalent effect

Measures having equivalent effect under Art. 34 and 35 TFEU are usually administrative measures taken by a Member State which, like quotas, are capable of restricting the free movement of goods. So, standards on size, quality or weight, inspection requirements or certification requirements are considered measures having an equivalent effect.

In the Dassonville case, the European Court of Justice produced its own definition of '*measures having equivalent effect*': all trading rules enacted by Member States which are capable of hindering, directly or indirectly, actually or potentially, intra-community trade are to be considered as measures having an effect equivalent to quantitative restrictions.

Since then, this criterion has been used in other cases in the European Court of Justice to establish whether or not a measure having equivalent effect is present. The definition of 'measure having equivalent effect' includes nearly every measure taken by a Member State that in some way affects or may affect the free movement of goods. A measure having equivalent effect is prohibited under Art. 34 and 35 TFEU and therefore has to be cancelled by the Member State responsible for it. EU law is of a higher level than the laws of individual Member states (Chapter 1, case Costa v. ENEL).
In the opening case study the Italian law about the moisture content of bread meets the definition of the Dassonville case, and therefore can be seen as a measure having equivalent effect.

EXAMPLE 6.3

6

To import whiskey from Ireland into the Netherlands, the Dutch government requires a certificate stating the origin of the product. This certificate is to be issued by the producer of the whiskey. A measure having equivalent effect does not forbid the import of goods, but imposes conditions that more or less obstruct the free movement of these goods within the EU. According to the Dassonville case, this requirement of the Dutch government is considered a measure having equivalent effect.

EXAMPLE 6.4

Chicken meat imported from Belgium is inspected at the Dutch border under a regulation issued by the Dutch government. This regulation is a measure having equivalent effect. It does not forbid the import of goods, but imposes extra measures that more or less obstruct the free movement of goods within the EU. According to the Dassonville case, this requirement of the Dutch government is a measure having equivalent effect.

There is a breach of Art. 35 TFEU, when national law gives an advantage to domestic production over exported products. In cases before the European Court of Justice Art. 35 TFEU is rarely the issue.

EXAMPLE 6.5

In order to export watches out of France one has to obtain an export license from the French authorities. This license can only be obtained after the watches have been inspected. As an inspection is not mandatory for watches for the home market, this measure taken by the French government is a measure having equivalent effect and an infringement of Art. 35 TFEU.

6.3.1 Distinctly and indistinctly applicable measures having equivalent effect

Within the measures having equivalent effect, one has to distinguish two categories. There are distinctly and indistinctly applicable measures having equivalent effect. This distinction is relevant when it comes to deciding if a restriction of the free movement of goods is justifiable. These justifications will be dealt with in paragraph 6.4.

Distinctly applicable measures

Distinctly applicable measures are measures taken by a Member State which do not apply equally to both domestic and imported products. In general these are measures that apply to imported goods only and either make it impossible for certain goods to be imported (which otherwise could have been brought in) or make it more difficult to obtain imported products than domestic products.

EXAMPLE 6.6

At the border, as a result of Dutch legislation, Dutch customs authorities inspect only Belgian chicken meat. Dutch, German or British chicken meat is not inspected in any way. This legislation on the inspection of Belgian meat is a distinctly applicable measure.

Indistinctly applicable measures

Indistinctly applicable measures are measures taken by a Member State that apply to both domestic and imported products in the same way, but still pose an obstacle to the free movement of goods. The Italian law in the opening case study applies to all bread sold in Italy, so it applies to both foreign and domestic bread. The measure having equivalent effect is an indistinctly applicable measure.

EXAMPLE 6.7

According to French government legislation, all wine should have a certificate stating the origin of the product. While there is no actual ban on imports, this measure could be in conflict with the free movement of goods.

Table 6.1 illustrates the theory on the free movement of goods up to this point, combined with the options for justification.

TABLE 6.1 Impediments to the free movement of goods

Under Art. 34 and 35 TFEU concerning the free movement of goods, the following are prohibited: 1 Quantitative restrictions (ban, quota), and 2 Measures having equivalent effect (m.h.e.e.) to a quantitative restriction Dassonville case = definition of a m.h.e.e.
With regard to m.h.e.e. one must distinguish between: 1 Distinctly applicable m.h.e.e. 2 Indistinctly applicable m.h.e.e.

If an act by a Member State conflicts with the free movement of goods, then it is prohibited, unless there is a justification for the restriction.

Justifications for quantitative restrictions and distinctly applicable m.h.e.e. could lie in Art. 36 TFEU (paragraph 6.4). To justify indistinctly applicable m.h.e.e. the European Court of Justice has developed case law (paragraph 6.5).

If no justification can be found, the act of the Member State remains in conflict with the principle of the free movement of goods and has to be revoked. If the act of a Member State is justified, the restriction of the free movement of goods is allowed and the national law remains in force.

6

6.4 Art. 36 TFEU: derogation from Art. 34 and 35 TFEU

Art. 36 TFEU which allows Member States to derogate from Art. 34 and 35 TFEU has been interpreted narrowly by the ECJ. As explained above, *quantitative restrictions and measures having equivalent effect (= distinctly applicable measures)* of Art. 34 and 35 TFEU are tolerated in the situations described in Art. 36 TFEU. According to Art. 36 TFEU restrictions on the free movement of goods are justified on grounds of:

1 Public morality

EXAMPLE 6.8

Goods of an indecent and obscene nature may be banned under national laws. The ban on pornographic material under UK law is a quantitative restriction on imports according to Art. 34 TFEU. It therefore conflicts with the free movement of goods, but on grounds of public morality, this UK law is justifiable under Art. 36 TFEU, when the production and sale of domestic pornographic material is also prohibited in the UK. Otherwise UK law would be discriminatory towards foreign products and therefore a non justifiable breach of the free movement of goods.

2 Public policy or public security

3 Protection of health and life of humans, animals or plants

EXAMPLE 6.9

The German Reinheitsgebot is an ancient set of rules governing German breweries, according to which beer may only contain natural ingredients. The Reinheitsgebot was used to ban foreign beers from the German market. This ban is not justifiable under Art. 36 TFEU, as foreign beers are not a danger to public health in Germany.

EXAMPLE 6.10

English law forbids pharmacists replacing prescribed drugs by equivalent ones. As this discriminates against imports, this law is a measure having equivalent effect and therefore forbidden under Art. 34 TFEU. However, the measure is upheld by the English government as a means of avoiding anxiety and maintaining public confidence in prescribed drugs, and for these reasons is justifiable according to the European Court of Justice under Art. 36 TFEU.

EXAMPLE 6.11

An inspection of plants by British authorities to control a plant pest applies only to imported apples. According to the European Court of Justice, this inspection is justifiable under Art. 36 TFEU, as only imported apples pose a threat to the health of English plants.

4 *Protection of national treasures possessing artistic, historic or archaeological value*

EXAMPLE 6.12

At the request of the Greek government, this justification was added to the list of Art. 36 TFEU. The intention of the Greek government was to uphold national legislation to protect the ancient Greek cultural heritage. There was a national ban on exporting pillars from the Acropolis. It is a quantitative restriction and therefore in conflict with the free movement of goods, but justifiable under Art. 36 TFEU.

5 *Protection of industrial and commercial property*

EXAMPLE 6.13

The holder of the rights to intellectual property (patents, trademarks, copyright) can uphold his right even if this would mean an obstruction to the free movement of goods. National legislation to protect designations of origin, like 'Rioja wine' and 'Parma ham', which designations are part of the industrial property of a country.

6.5 Case law to justify restrictions on the free movement of goods

As explained above, Art. 36 TFEU allows national measures that obstruct the free movement of goods to be upheld in certain situations. With regard to indistinctly applicable measures having equivalent effect, two cases of the European Court of Justice are relevant. In general, in the case Cassis de Dijon (paragraph 6.6 contains the full text of this case) the European Court of Justice provides the so-called 'rule of reason' to justify indistinctly applicable measures having equivalent effect in general. When indistinctly applicable measures having equivalent effect, concerning the pricing of goods, apply to national legislation of a Member State, the criterion of the KECK case becomes relevant. As a result a Member State can uphold national measures that restrict the free movement of goods.

Rule of reason

The rule of reason from the Cassis de Dijon case is that 'obstacles to movement within the Community resulting from disparities between national laws relating to the marketing of products must be accepted insofar as those provisions may be recognised as being necessary in order to satisfy mandatory requirements relating in particular to the effectiveness of fiscal supervision, the protection of public health, the fairness of commercial transactions and the defence of the consumer.'

The following definition of the rule of reason contains the conditions that must be fulfilled in order to apply this principle:

1 EU law regarding this subject is not available
The rule of reason mentions 'disparities between national laws' that 'must be accepted', so it becomes obvious that there is no relevant EU law available. In other words: in this area the Member State is free to issue its own legislation as there is no EU legislation on the subject.

2 The measure in question is an indistinctly applicable measure
The rule of reason refers to measures having equivalent effect that do not discriminate between domestic and imported products.

3 The national measure must be in proportion to the protection of national interests. Proportionality of a measure means that the measure should be reasonable when looking at the circumstances of the case.

4 The national interests protected must be of sufficient weight to justify their restriction on the free movement of goods. These grounds are: the effectiveness of fiscal supervision, the protection of public health, the fairness of commercial transactions and the defence of the consumer. However, this list is not exhaustive, as is shown by other rulings given by the European Court of Justice. According to the European Court of Justice, these grounds are to include the promotion of national culture and the protection of the environment. These grounds are not identical with the grounds mentioned in Art. 36 TFEU.

Note that if all four conditions apply to the measure taken by the Member State, this measure is allowed according to the rule of reason and is permitted to obstruct the free movement of goods. In the opening case study, the Italian law referred to is not justifiable under the Cassis de Dijon case. There is no EU law on the subject mentioned in the case, the measure applies to all bread to be sold in Italy, so it seems reasonable that there should be legislation on the content of bread. However, none of the circumstances mentioned under 4 applies. This Italian law therefore conflicts with the free movement of goods and has to be annulled by the Italian government.

However, when it comes to indistinctly applicable measures having equivalent effect concerning the pricing of goods, the European Court of Justice developed another criterion in the KECK case. According to the European Court of Justice, national legislation on the pricing of goods (e.g. national legislation on maximum and minimum prices) is not prohibited under Art. 34 TFEU, as long as this legislation applies equally to both foreign and domestic products. National legislation on the pricing of goods can nevertheless become an indistinctly applicable measure having equivalent effect, if such legislation effectively discriminates between foreign and domestic goods. If equal treatment of foreign and domestic goods basically means discrimination between these goods, then this national legislation conflicts with the free movement of goods and has to be cancelled.

EXAMPLE 6.14

Due to the minimum price of 'jenever' (Dutch gin) in The Netherlands, the advantage in price of a Belgian importer of jenever is lost, because the minimum price of jenever in The Netherlands is set at a higher level than the cost price (selling price to which transportation costs are added) of jenever produced in Belgium. While Dutch legislation applies equally to both Dutch and Belgian jenever, it effectively means that the importation of Belgian jenever into The Netherlands is no longer cost effective. Dutch legislation on the pricing of jenever is not a quantitative restriction, but an indistinctly applicable measure having equivalent effect. This measure cannot be justified as its effect is to discriminate between foreign and domestic goods and it therefore poses an obstacle to the free movement of goods. The Dutch government should annul this legislation.

6.6 The free movement of workers

The free movement of workers is an essential element of the internal market. The principle is enshrined in Articles 45–48 TFEU which apply to nationals of the EU only (Article 20, 21 TFEU).
Article 45 TFEU prohibits any discrimination based on nationality between workers of the Member States in the areas of employment, remuneration and conditions of work. These Articles, as well as Regulations 1612/68 and 2004/38, require equal treatment in all matters relating to the work practices of those in employment and the elimination of obstacles to the mobility of workers, particularly the right to be joined in a host country by family members and the right of the family to integrate into the host country.

EXAMPLE 6.15

Deutsche Post had two systems of remunerating its employees who worked abroad temporarily. One for employees who lived in Germany the moment they became employees and one for employees who lived outside Germany, but in the EU, the moment they became employees of Deutsche Post. The compensation paid to 'German employees' for their work abroad turned out to be much higher than that paid to the others. The ECJ ruled that this arrangement was in conflict with Article 45 TFEU.

EXAMPLE 6.16

The requirement that teachers in vocational schools in Ireland should be proficient in the Irish language is not contrary to Article 45 TFEU, as the promotion of the Irish language is a national policy of the Irish government.

EXAMPLE 6.17

Mrs. Simonetti, an Italian widow living in Marseille (France) claims a travel card allowing reduced fares, which is issued by the French authorities to parents of large families. During his lifetime, the late Mr. Simonetti was employed in Marseille and had always claimed the card. Regulation 2004/38 covers all social and tax advantages, whether or not deriving from contracts of employment. Since the Simonetti family had the right to remain in France under Regulation 1251/70, Mrs. Simonetti has the right to the same 'social advantages' as the French, and so the card has to be issued to Mrs. Simonetti.

6.6.1 Definition of 'worker'

Article 45 TFEU does not define the word 'worker', and as a result the ECJ has interpreted the principle of 'worker'. The criteria for a person to be considered a 'worker', according to the ECJ are the following:

- Someone may only be called a worker when the activities he performs serve some economic purpose.
- If a person performs services for, and under the direction of, another person, in return for remuneration during a certain period of time, that person may be considered a worker.
- A person is considered to be a worker when he is insured against one of several risks in relation to salaried workers.

Note that these criteria are similar to the requirements under the national laws of several Member States for a contract to be an individual employment contract. The interpretation of the term 'worker' by the ECJ has been widened to include the following examples.

EXAMPLE 6.18

According to the case law of the ECJ, a worker under Article 45 TFEU would include:

- Anyone who has lost his job, but is capable of finding a new job;
- A part-time music teacher from Germany receiving supplementary benefit in the Netherlands to bring his income up to subsistence level;

- A member of a religious community, who pays for his 'keep' and receives pocket money but not a formal salary, where commercial activity is a genuine and inherent part of membership of the community;
- A member of the Baghwan religious community who earns his keep in exchange for work;
- A professional sportsman or woman.

However: a person in the process of detoxification obliged to work in a community centre, was not seen as a worker. A student while studying is also not considered to be a worker.

The rights that under Article 45 TFEU apply to a worker, also apply to his or her spouse, the partner with whom the worker has contracted a registered partnership, his or her children under 21 years of age and dependant relatives in the ascendant line (i.e. parents or grandparents) of the worker and his spouse or partner. Member States should allow family members to enter and arrange for the worker to have accommodation available for his family in the area where he works when he arrives for the first time. The worker's children must have the same access to education as other children in that EU Member State.

EXAMPLE 6.19

Mrs. Schmidt, of German nationality, marries Mr. Nwankwo, of Nigerian nationality. Mrs. Schmidt accepts a job with the UK branch of Bayer AG in London, and both go to live in the United Kingdom. Her husband has the right of residence and the right to work in the UK. After one year the marriage breaks down and Mrs. Schmidt returns to Germany. Mr. Nwankwo, her ex-husband, no longer has the right of residence in the UK as he is not a national of an EU Member State and the marriage did not last for at least three years.

6.6.2 The migration rights of a worker

A worker has three "migration rights" i.e. the right to entry, the right of residence and the right to remain.

The right to entry as a job seeker is directly effective. It gives the worker and his family the right to leave their home state and enables the worker to pursue activities as an employed person in another Member State. A job seeker must be able to prove that he is genuinely looking for work and is capable of finding it. The right to entry also applies to the family of the job seeker, on condition each family member has a valid identity card or passport. Member States may only demand entry visas for family members who are not EU nationals.

The Benelux states (Belgium, the Netherlands and Luxemburg) signed an agreement with France and Germany in 1985 at Schengen in Luxemburg. The Schengen agreement concerns the entry of people into a foreign country. As a result, border formalities became less strict for EU nationals moving between the participating 'Schengen countries' which now also include Austria, Belgium, Czech Republic, Denmark, Estonia, Finland, France, Germany, Greece, Hungary, Iceland (not a European Union Member State),

Italy, Latvia, Liechtenstein (not a European Union Member State), Lithuania, Luxembourg, Malta, Netherlands, Norway (not a European Union Member State), Poland, Portugal, Slovakia, Slovenia, Spain, Sweden and Switzerland (not a European Union Member State). Not all EU Members have signed the Schengen agreement and those countries that did, did not implement the Schengen agreement in full as e.g. co-operation in police matters between the 'Schengen countries' leaves room for improvement.

The second migration right of a worker is the right to reside in the Member State they entered. For this he has to have a residence permit, which will be valid for at least 5 years. To obtain this he has to show the document of entry and a confirmation of engagement from an employer or a certificate of employment. Workers and their families are entitled to automatically renewable residence permits valid in this Member State. A residence permit may not be withdrawn because a worker is temporarily unable to work through illness or accident, or through involuntary unemployment of less than 12 months.

Unemployed workers also have a right to enter another Member State looking for work. They have a three-month period to find new employment in that Member State. The Member State is not allowed to oblige these persons to register in that Member State. If a person receives unemployment benefit in his home state, he also has the right to receive it in that Member State where he seeks (new) employment.

Temporary workers who work less than 3 months in a Member State may reside in the Member State during that period of employment, but are not entitled to a residence permit. Temporary workers working from 3 to 12 months in another Member State are entitled to a temporary residence permit for the duration of the work.

EXAMPLE 6.20

Handke, a welder of German nationality who was working and living in Antwerp (Belgium) gave up his job, and thus became voluntarily unemployed. This means that he no longer has the right to an automatic renewal of his residence permit.

EXAMPLE 6.21

Boerrigter, a student of French and of Dutch nationality, is going to work in Paris (France) for five months for his internship. This means that he becomes a temporary worker for longer then three months and as a consequence needs a residence permit for the duration of his internship.

The third migration right is the right to remain i.e. the right of permanent residence. A worker and his family members have the right of permanent residence in a Member State after having resided legally there for a period of five years. The right of permanent residence is the logical consequence of the right of residence of workers. Members of the worker's family may also exercise it, even after the death of the worker.

The right to remain also exists in the following cases where the worker did not complete a period of residency of 5 years:

- *Retired workers*: A worker, who reaches the statutory age for entitlement to an old-age pension, provided he has been employed in that state for at least the previous twelve months and has been continuously resident there for more than two years.
- *Incapacitated workers*: A worker, who ceases to work as an employed person in a Member State as a result of permanent incapacity for work, provided he has been permanently resident in that state for more than two years.
- *Frontier workers*: a worker who is employed in another Member State while retaining his residence in the home state, provided that he has been continuously employed for three years and returns to his state of residence daily or at least once a week.

Time spent working in another Member State counts as working in the state of residence for retirement and incapacity purposes. Retiring or incapacitated workers are not obliged to fulfil residence and employment requirements if married to a national of the Member State in question. Members of a worker's family are entitled to permanent residence if the worker himself is entitled to remain. If a retired or incapacitated worker with entitlement to residency dies, his family may remain permanently after his death. Irrespective of nationality, the family members of a worker who have the right of residence or the right of permanent residence in a Member State shall be entitled to take up employment or self-employment in that Member State.

6

6.6.3 Restrictions of the freedom of movement of workers

The free movement of persons may be restricted on grounds of public policy, public health and public security (Article 45, 3 TFEU).

Public policy covers a wide spectrum of activities, from measures taken to forbid a public meeting (to prevent a disturbance) to a decree concerning the preservation of public decency on a beach. It is difficult to determine how an individual's behaviour may constitute a threat to public policy.

EXAMPLE 6.22

Van Zanten, a member of the Dutch Parliament, is not allowed to accept an offer of employment from a Belgian local authority, in order to safeguard the general interests of the Member State Belgium.

EXAMPLE 6.23

Mrs. Adoui and Mrs. Cornuaille, two women of French nationality and working in Belgium, were on the verge of extradition from Belgium to France. The extradition was ordered because they were employed as prostitutes in Brussels and for that reason, according to the Belgian authorities, posed a threat to public policy. The ECJ disagreed, because the Belgian authorities did not act in the same way with regard to Belgian nationals with the same profession.

Public security has not been defined by the ECJ, but is often invoked as an alternative justification to that of public policy by Member States seeking to exclude an individual. Clearly, terrorist activities may pose a threat to both public policy and public security.

Public health may only be invoked as a justification for refusal of entry or residence (for the first time) where the individual suffers from a disease which may be a threat to public health, such as syphilis or tuberculosis. Diseases or disabilities which may threaten public policy or public security, such as drug addiction and profound mental disturbance, can also be justifiable reasons. The development of a disease or disability after obtaining the first residence permit does not justify a refusal to renew it. Note that these restrictions of the free movement of workers apply to both distinctly and indistinctly applicable measures.

6.7 The freedom of establishment

As the freedom of movement of persons mainly concerns workers, self-employed persons do not fall under Articles 45–48 TFEU. Articles 49–55 TFEU apply instead and prohibit restrictions on the right of establishment.

This freedom of establishment under Article 49 TFEU includes the right to take up and pursue activities as a self-employed person in another Member State and to set up and manage undertakings under the same conditions laid down for the nationals of that Member State. Undertakings in this Article means companies or firms constituted under civil or commercial law, including co-operative societies, a sole trader or a partnership under public or private law, except for those who are non-profit making (Article 54 TFEU).

EXAMPLE 6.24

Schmitt, Jansen and Müller, all of German nationality, are physiotherapists and have completed their education in Enschede (The Netherlands). They now have plans to set up a practice of their own in Enschede which would be permissible under the terms of Article 49 TFEU.

In order to make it easier for workers and self-employed persons to take up and pursue activities in other Member States the EU issues Directives on the mutual recognition of diplomas and certificates and other evidence of formal qualifications. As a result of these Directives, Member States have made homologation or franchise agreements that include a general system for the recognition of higher education diplomas of each Member State. Following these agreements, a Member State may rely on the professional qualifications awarded to the worker and the self-employed person in another Member State. Thus these professional qualifications are sufficient not only to purse a profession in the Member State that awarded them, but also in another Member State (Article 53 TFEU). Member States are allowed in certain cases to ask a self-employed person from another Member State, who intends to run a business in that Member State, to undergo an adaptation period or an aptitude test.

EXAMPLE 6.25

Greece, a Member State of the EU, found that the principle of mutual recognition of diplomas also had a down side. Greek nationals had to accept that the professional qualifications of those nationals from other Member States who were pursuing a profession in Greece, while different from Greek qualifications, nevertheless fell within the framework of the franchise agreements. As a result, the Greek authorities imposed an extra check on the professional qualifications of workers from other Member States. The ECJ found this check to be contrary to Articles 49, 53 TFEU, as Greece has no right to query the basis on which professional qualifications have been awarded by another Member State.

The freedom of establishment may in some cases be restricted on grounds of public policy, public security or public health. Note that these restrictions of the freedom of establishment apply to both distinctly and indistinctly applicable measures.

6.8 The freedom to provide services

Articles 56–62 TFEU safeguard the freedom of EU nationals to provide services to other EU nationals, who do not live in the same EU Member State. Article 57 TFEU gives a description of these services: services rendered against remuneration are included as well as services of a commercial or industrial nature and the services of craftsmen. Services relating to the freedom of movement of goods and persons, as well as to the transport of these goods, are excluded from Article 56 TFEU, as they are governed by their own rules.
Where restrictions on the freedom to provide services remain, Member States must apply them equally to all EU nationals, regardless of nationality (Article 61 TFEU). Note that these restrictions of the freedom to provide services apply to both distinctly and indistinctly applicable measures.

EXAMPLE 6.26

German law restricts the ownership and operation of pharmacies to persons with a professional pharmaceutical qualification. Should one not have this professional qualification, one cannot own or operate a pharmacy. The ECJ found that this law accords with Article 56 TFEU, as the objective of this law is to ensure that the provision of medicinal products to the public is reliable and of good quality.

EXAMPLE 6.27

Dutch legislation on games of chance is based on a system of exclusive licenses. The organisation or promotion of games of chance in the Netherlands is prohibited, unless a license for that purpose has been issued. The relevant Dutch authorities can only issue licenses. In the Netherlands, furthermore, games of chance cannot be played interactively via the Internet. The Lotto, a non-profit-making foundation governed by private law, holds the exclusive license to run sports-related prize competitions, the lottery, and numbers games. Its objectives, according to its constitution, are the raising of funds through the organisation of games of chance and the distribution of those funds among institutions working in the public

interest, particularly in the fields of sport, physical education, general welfare, public health and culture.
The Ladbrokes group, established in the UK, is engaged in the organisation of sports-related prize competitions, and are well known for their betting business. It offers a number of mainly sports-related games of chance on their Internet site. They do not physically carry on any activity in the Netherlands. The Ladbrokes group stated that they hold a license issued by the UK authorities. This license allows them to offer sports-related prize competitions and other games of chance via the Internet and by telephone. Ladbrokes are subject in the UK to very strict legislation for the prevention of fraud and of addiction to games of chance.
The Lotto alleged that the Ladbrokes group were, without a license from the Dutch authorities, offering games of chance on the Internet to persons residing in the Netherlands.
The ECJ finds that legislation such as the Dutch legislation referred to here, constitutes a restriction on the freedom to provide services. However, this restriction is justified by the objectives of consumer protection and the prevention of both fraud and incitement to spend money on gambling, as well as the need to preserve public order. As there is no EU law on this subject, Member States are entitled to legislate on this matter. The fact that Ladbrokes has a license from the UK authorities does not automatically mean that Dutch interests have been fully safeguarded.

6.9 The freedom of capital

Article 63 TFEU prohibits all restrictions on the free movement of capital and payments between Member States and between Member States and other non EU Member States.

However, some restrictions on the free movement of capital are allowed, as is shown by Article 65 TFEU. Member States are allowed to uphold tax laws, if the place of residence of a national and the places where he invests his capital are different. They are also allowed to restrict the free movement of capital in order to prevent infringements of taxation laws or to ensure the necessary supervision of financial institutions. Restrictions on the free movement of capital on grounds of public policy or public security are also allowed.

EXAMPLE 6.28

German law allows gifts to charitable organisations in Germany to be tax deductible. These charitable organisations must first satisfy certain requirements before this can happen. This tax advantage, however, does not apply to organisations established in and recognised as charitable in other Member States.
Persche, a German national, made a gift to the Centro Popular de Lagoa (Portugal), a retirement home to which a children 's home is attached. Persche claimed a tax deduction in respect of this gift, but the German District Tax Office denied his claim. This was because the beneficiary of the gift was not established in Germany and Persche had not filled in the correct form for the tax deduction. The ECJ found this German tax law to be contrary to the free movement of capital (Article 63 TFEU). The ECJ felt that the ability to deduct a gift from one 's income tax was important for anyone thinking of making a donation. This German law could thus have prevented German taxpayers from making donations to charitable bodies outside Germany and was therefore contrary to the principle of the free movement of capital.

6.10 Cases of the European Court of Justice on the free movement of goods, workers and capital, the freedom to provide services and the freedom of establishment

Notes:

Case Dassonville

Court of Justice, Case 8/74, 11 July 1974

Facts

A Belgian law prohibits dealing in spirits with a name of origin recognised by the Belgian government, without a document attesting to that supplied by the government of the country of origin. The wholesaler, Dassonville, established in France, offered 'Scotch Whisky' for sale without being in the possession of the above document in a branch established at Ukkel. The Belgian public prosecutor prosecuted Dassonville because he had been selling 'Scotch Whisky' without having the required (British) certificate of origin. It so happened that he had imported the whisky via France, where such a certificate is not required. The products had freedom of movement because of the clearance through customs in France (Art. 10 EEC Treaty). The United Kingdom became an EU member on 1 January 1975. The Belgian judge asked the Court a preliminary question, which in short asked whether the Belgian Regulations were in violation of Art. 28 TFEU (now Article 34 TFEU).

Grounds

Certificate of origin

2. The first question asks whether a national provision prohibiting the import of goods bearing a designation of origin (where such goods are not accompanied by an official document issued by the government of the exporting country certifying their right to such designation) constitutes a measure having an effect equivalent to a quantitative restriction within the meaning of Art. 28 of the Treaty (now Article 34 TFEU).

4. It emerges from the file and from the oral proceedings that a trader, wishing to import into Belgium Scotch whisky, which is already in free circulation in France, can obtain such a certificate only with great difficulty, unlike the importer who imports directly from the producer country.

'The Dassonville formula'

5. All trading rules enacted by Member States which are capable of hindering, directly or indirectly, actually or potentially, intra-community trade are to be considered as measures having an effect equivalent to quantitative restrictions.

If there is no EU law on this subject, national laws are allowed as long as they do not obstruct the free movement of goods

6. In the absence of a community system guaranteeing the authenticity for consumers of a product's designation of origin, if a Member State takes measures to prevent unfair practices in this connection, it is nonetheless subject to the condition that these measures should be reasonable and that the means of proof required should not act as a hindrance to trade between Member States and should, in consequence, be accessible to all community nationals.

No justification under Art. 30 TFEU ... (now Article 36 TFEU).

7. Even without having to examine whether or not such measures are covered by Art. 30 (now Article 36 TFEU), they must not, in any case, by virtue of the principle expressed in the second sentence of that article, constitute a means of arbitrary discrimination or a disguised restriction on trade between Member States.

... for measures such as a certificate of origin ...

8. That may be the case with formalities, required by a Member State for the purpose of proving the origin of a product, which only direct importers are really in a position to satisfy without facing serious difficulties.

... which for that reason is a 'm.h.e.e.' prohibited under Art. 28 (now Article 34 TFEU).

9. Consequently, the requirement by a Member State of a certificate of authenticity which is less easily obtainable by importers of an authentic product that has been put into free circulation in a regular manner in another Member State other than by importers of the same product coming directly from the country of origin, constitutes a measure having an effect equivalent to a quantitative restriction as prohibited by the Treaty.

Notes:

Case Cassis de Dijon

Court of Justice, Case 120/78, 20 February 1979

Facts

In September 1976 the German enterprise Rewe applied to the *Branntweinmonopol* for a license to import a shipment of liqueur of the famous brand 'Cassis de Dijon' from France. The *Monopolverwaltung* let Rewe know that the sale of 'Cassis de Dijon' – with 15 to 20% volume of alcohol – was prohibited on account of a Regulation of the *Branntweinmonopolgesetz*, according to which the selling of spirits for human consumption was legitimate only if it contained at least 32% volume of alcohol. For some liqueurs an exception had been made in a special Regulation, but because 'Cassis de Dijon' did not belong to these liqueurs, the *Monopolverwaltung* explained it was not able to allow the sale of this product on German territory. Rewe lodged an appeal. The *Hessische Finanzgericht* suspended the case and requested the Court of Justice of the European Community, through a preliminary ruling according to Art. 234 EEC Treaty, to pass judgement i.e. on the next question:
Should the notion 'measures with a similar effect as quantitative import restrictions' in Art. 28 EEC Treaty (now Article 34 TFEU) be interpreted as including the settlement arranged in the German *Branntweinmonopolgesetz* of a minimum percentage of ethyl alcohol in spirits, as a result of which traditional products of other member states, which contained less than the decreed percentage of ethyl alcohol, could not be allowed into trade and commerce in the German Federal Republic?

'The Cassis de Dijon principle' = the rule of reason = justifications for restricting the free movement of goods

Restrictions are justified according to German government

Grounds

4. The plaintiff takes the view that the fixing by the German rules of a minimum alcohol content leads to the result that well-known spirits products from other member states of the community cannot be sold in the Federal Republic of Germany and that the said provision therefore constitutes a restriction on the free movement of goods between Member States which exceeds the bounds of the trade rules reserved to the latter. In its view it is a measure having an effect equivalent to a quantitative restriction on imports contrary to Art. 28 of the EEC Treaty (now Article 34 TFEU). Since, furthermore, it is a measure adopted within the context of the management of spirits monopoly, the plaintiff considers that there is also an infringement of Art. 37, according to which the Member States shall progressively adjust any state monopolies of a commercial character so as to ensure that when the transitional period has ended no discrimination regarding the conditions under which goods are procured or marketed exists between nationals of Member States.

8. Obstacles to movement within the Community resulting from disparities between the national laws relating to the marketing of the products in question must be accepted insofar as those provisions may be recognised as being necessary in order to satisfy mandatory requirements relating in particular to the effectiveness of fiscal supervision, the protection of public health, the fairness of commercial transactions and the defence of the consumer.

9. The government of the Federal Republic of Germany, intervening in the proceedings, put forward various arguments which, in its view, justify the application of provisions relating to the minimum alcohol content of alcoholic beverages, adducing considerations relating on the one hand to the protection of public health and on the other to the protection of the consumer against unfair commercial practices.

The lower the % of alcohol, the more one drinks of it and that is a threat to public health

10. As regards the protection of public health the German government states that the purpose of the fixing of minimum alcohol contents by national legislation is to avoid the proliferation of alcoholic beverages on the national market, in particular alcoholic beverages with a low alcohol content, since, in its view, such products may more easily induce a tolerance towards alcohol than more highly alcoholic beverages.

'Nonsense'

11. Such considerations are not decisive since the consumer can obtain on the market an extremely wide range of weakly or moderately alcoholic products and furthermore a large proportion of alcoholic beverages with a high alcohol content freely sold on the German market is generally consumed in a diluted form.

6

Consumer need not be protected by the mandatory fixing of minimum alcohol contents, as he can see for himself on the label the exact % of alcohol the beverage contains

13. As the Commission rightly observed, the fixing of limits in relation to the alcohol content of beverages may lead to the standardisation of products placed on the market and of their designations, in the interests of a greater transparency of commercial transactions and offers for sale to the public. However, this line of argument cannot be taken so far as to regard the mandatory fixing of minimum alcohol contents as being an essential guarantee of the fairness of commercial transactions, since it is a simple matter to ensure that suitable information is conveyed to the purchaser by requiring the display of an indication of origin and of the alcohol content on the packaging.

Notes:

Case Rüffler

Decision of the Court of Justice of 23 April 2009, Case C 544/07

Facts

After living in Germany, where he was employed, Mr Rüffler took up residence in Poland and has, since 2005, been permanently resident there as a retired person. At the time when the dispute arose, Mr Rüffler's only income came from two pensions paid in Germany: an invalidity pension, taxed in Germany, and an occupational pension paid by the Volkswagen company, which was taxed in Poland.

In 2006, Mr Rüffler applied to the Polish tax authorities for the income tax to which he is liable in Poland on his occupational pension received in Germany to be reduced. Rüffler requested that his income tax be reduced by the amount of the health insurance contributions which he has paid in Germany. However, under Polish legislation, only health insurance contributions paid to a Polish insurance institution can be deducted from income tax.

Preliminary ruling

When his application was rejected, Mr Rüffler brought an action before the Regional Administrative Court in Wrocław (Poland), which then asked the ECJ whether the restrictions imposed on the right to a reduction of tax is compatible with Community law.

Freedom of movement for workers after retirement

The Court notes first of all that persons who, after retirement, leave the Member State of which they are nationals and in which they have carried out all their occupational activity in order to take up residence in another Member State are exercising the right which the TFEU gives to every citizen of the EU to move and reside freely within the territory of the Member States.

Polish legislation discriminates between tax payers

The Court finds that rules such as those provided for under Polish law introduce a difference in the treatment of resident taxpayers, this being a difference between Rüffler and other Polish taxpayers. Polish legislation discriminates between tax payers on grounds of whether health insurance contributions capable of being deducted from the amount of income tax due in Poland have or have not been paid under a national compulsory health insurance scheme. Under those rules, only taxpayers whose health insurance contributions are paid in the Member State of taxation benefit from the right to a reduction of income tax.

The Court points out that resident taxpayers paying contributions to the Polish health insurance scheme and those coming under a compulsory health insurance scheme of another Member State are in objectively comparable situations as regards taxation principles since, in Poland, both are subject to an unlimited liability to tax.

6

In conflict with Article 45 TFEU

Thus, the taxation of the income of Rüffler in that Member State i.e. Poland, his state of residence, should be carried out in accordance with the same principles and, consequently, on the basis of the same tax advantages, including the right to a reduction of income tax equal to other Polish residents.

Notes:

Case Engelmann

Decision of the Court of Justice

State monopoly over games of chance in Austria

Austrian legislation gives Austria a state monopoly over games of chance. As a result the right to organise and operate games of chance is reserved to the State. The objective of this legislation is that the State has the authority to regulate and supervise games of chance. This legislation also enables the State to derive the maximum amount of revenue from them. The Austrian Minister for Finance is permitted to grant a total of 12 concessions for operating games of chance. A concession gives its holder the right to organise and operate gaming establishments. The concessionaire must be a public limited company having its head office in Austria and must be subject to supervision by the ministry. The organisation of games of chance without authorisation may lead to criminal proceedings. A single company, Casinos Austria AG, currently holds the 12 concessions. They were granted and renewed without a public tendering procedure.

Engelmann acts in conflict with Austrian law

Engelmann, a German national, operated two gaming establishments in Austria without previously having applied for a concession from the Austrian authorities. By a judgement at a court of first instance, he was found guilty of unlawfully organising games of chance and ordered to pay a fine of €2.000,-.

Preliminary ruling

The Regional Court in Linz (Austria), to which Engelmann appealed, referred questions to the ECJ for a preliminary ruling. These questions were on the compatibility of Austrian legislation on games of chance with freedom of establishment and freedom to provide services.

Freedom of establishment

Freedom to provide services

First of all, the Court of Justice finds that Austrian law at this point conflicts with the TFEU. The obligation in Austria that persons holding concessions to operate gaming establishments should have their head office in Austria constitutes a restriction on freedom of establishment. That obligation discriminates against companies, which have their head office in another Member State, and prevents those companies from operating gaming establishments in Austria through an agency, branch or subsidiary.

Protection of consumers

The Court investigated whether it would be possible to justify that restriction of the freedom of establishment on grounds of preventing gaming establishments from being run for criminal or fraudulent purposes. However, the Court holds that the categorical exclusion of operators whose place of business is in another Member State is disproportionate, as it has no bearing on either the prevention of criminal or fraudulent activities or the protection of its customers from such activities.

Limit opportunities for gambling

Recover investments

The Court finds that limiting the number of concessions may be justified by the need to limit opportunities for gambling. Also the Court finds that the grant of concessions by the ministry for a period of 15 years may also be justified by the need of the holder of the concession to have sufficient time to recoup his investments.

Transparency in granting concessions

Discrimination on grounds of nationality

However, the Court finds the absence of a competitive and transparent procedure when the concessions were granted to Casinos Austria AG to be contrary to the freedom of establishment and the freedom to provide services. Thus, the grant of a concession only to an operator located in the same Member State without such a competitive and transparent procedure taking place is a difference in treatment to the detriment of operators located in other Member States. Such a difference in treatment is contrary to the principle of equal treatment and the prohibition of discrimination on grounds of nationality, and constitutes indirect discrimination on grounds of nationality which is prohibited by EU law.

Summary

6

- Articles 34, 35 and 36 TFEU uphold the principle of the free movement of goods.
- Under this principle, the following is prohibited:
  1 Quantitative restrictions (ban, quota), and
  2 Measures having equivalent effect (m.h.e.e.) to quantitative restriction The Dassonville case provides a definition of m.h.e.e.
- With m.h.e.e., distinguish between:
  1 Distinctly applicable m.h.e.e.
  2 Indistinctly applicable m.h.e.e.
- When an act of a Member State is a either a quantitative restriction or a m.h.e.e., either way, this act conflicts with the free movement of goods. This act is therefore a restriction on the free movement of goods and prohibited, unless there is a justification for the restriction.
- For quantitative restrictions and *distinctly* applicable m.h.e.e., a justification could lie in Art. 36 TFEU. To justify *indistinctly* applicable m.h.e.e. the European Court of Justice developed case law: the 'rule of reason' from the Cassis de Dijon case.
- If no justification can be found, the act of the Member State remains in conflict with the principle of the free movement of goods and has to be revoked. If the act of a Member State is justified, the restriction of the free movement of goods is allowed and the national law remains in force.
- The free movement of persons comprises the free movement of workers and the freedom of establishment for self-employed persons. Free movement for workers means that a worker from a Member State has the right to enter another Member State, take residency there and, having been a worker there, remain in that Member State. In general, a worker and his family must be treated in the same way as nationals of that Member State in which he finds employment.
- Freedom of establishment is the right to take up and pursue activities as a self-employed person in another Member State and to set up and manage undertakings under the same conditions as those laid down for nationals of that Member State.
- The TFEU safeguards the freedom of EU nationals to provide services to other EU nationals in different EU Member States.
- The TFEU prohibits all restrictions on the free movement of capital and payments between Member States and between Member States and other non EU Member States.

Glossary

Distinctly applicable measures	Measures taken by a Member State, which do not equally apply to both domestic and imported products.
Free movement of goods	In order to stimulate economic activity among EU businesses i.e. undertakings, goods must be able to circulate unrestricted within the EU.
Indistinctly applicable measures	Measures taken by a Member State that apply equally to both domestic and imported products.
Justification	If a quantitative restriction or a measure having equivalent effect is established, it is possible to avoid its prohibition under either Art. 34 or 35 TFEU. If the restriction is justified, the Member State may uphold its own legislation. If the restriction is not justified, the Member State has to annul this part of its legislation as it conflicts with the free movement of goods.
Measure having equivalent effect	All trading rules enacted by Member States which are capable of hindering, directly or indirectly, actually or potentially, intra-community trade are to be considered as measures having an effect equivalent to quantitative restrictions. These measures are acts of Member States that do not forbid imports (or exports) but basically make it economically less viable to import (or export) goods within the EU.
Quantitative Restriction	A quantitative restriction is an act of a Member State which restricts – by amount or by value or for a certain period of time – the import or export from another Member State of a product.
Rules of reason	Rule of law that enables a Member State to justify acts which are considered indistinctly applicable measures of that state.

Exercises

Exercise 6.1
Bertolucci SpA is a leading Italian producer of modernistic etchings on a stone background. It contracts with the Hard Rock Café in London (UK) to supply 10 etchings per month for a trial period of a year. The etchings will be sold in the cafe to customers and passers-by.
The first shipment arrives in London in May 2012; customs authorities have several doubts about these etchings:
1 the customs authorities consider some of the etchings to be pornographic and not allowable under UK legislation to be imported in the UK;
2 the etchings are produced using a chemical which is not permitted for use in any products marketed in the UK; and
3 to import goods like these one has to have a license issued by the UK authorities declaring the origin of the products. Bertolucci had not asked for the license.

1 Does the first reason for rejecting the goods (= '1)') conflict with Art. 34 TFEU? If so, is there any justification for this restriction under EU law? Mention relevant case law in the answer.
2 The second reason for rejecting the goods (= '2)') conflicts with Art. 34 TFEU. Is there any justification for this restriction under EU law? Mention relevant case law in the answer.
3 Does the third reason for rejecting the goods (= '3)') conflict with Art. 34 TFEU? If so, is there any justification for this restriction under EU law? Mention relevant case law in the answer.

Exercise 6.2
BestBreakfast Ltd, a company established in the UK, is a manufacturer of fruit flavoured yoghurt and breakfast muesli. It has recently decided to try to export to the rest of the European market. In order to ensure the products are in good condition when they reach the shops in the Member States, certain measures are taken by BestBreakfast Ltd in developing three special European product lines:
1 the first is frozen yoghurt containing only natural ingredients,
2 the second is unfrozen yoghurt, to which preservatives have been added,
3 the third is muesli in sealed cellophane bags.

All the ingredients of the products are listed on the packaging. BestBreakfast Ltd found that the products were particularly popular in Germany and for four months sales boomed until Germany imposed a ban, justified on 'public health grounds', on the importation of any dairy product containing preservatives. So the unfrozen yoghurt was banned from the German market by German authorities.

A new German consumer protection law also forbade the application of the description *yoghurt* to frozen yoghurts. Following this, consignments of frozen yoghurt were turned back at the German frontier.
Meanwhile, consignments of muesli were subject to long delays at the German frontier whilst checks for health reasons were carried out. These involved opening half the packets in every fifth case of muesli. Payment was required for the inspections and parking fees were imposed on the trucks. When BestBreakfast Ltd challenged the parking fees and charges for the health checks, they were told that the fees and charges were the equivalent of an internal tax imposed on domestic food products to finance a system of factory inspection in the German food industry.

1 A ban is in itself prohibited under Art. 34 TFEU. But is the ban on the yoghurt with preservatives justified under EU law or not? Mention relevant case law in the answer.
2 The second problem concerns the German law that prohibits BestBreakfast from selling frozen yoghurt as yoghurt on the grounds that the term 'yoghurt' cannot be used to describe frozen yoghurt. Is this Regulation justified under EU law or not? Mention relevant case law in the answer.
3 Are these 'checks' on the muesli for health reasons and charging BestBreakfast for inspections and parking of trucks prohibited under Art. 34 TFEU? If so, is there any justification for this (these) restriction(s) on the free movement of goods?

Exercise 6.3
A directive of the European Parliament and the Council of the EU states that any lawyer should be entitled to pursue his activities on a permanent basis in another Member State, using the professional title he would have in his home country. He may give advice on the law of his home Member State, on Community law, on international law and on the law of the host Member State.

The exercise of that right is subject to neither an adaptation period nor an aptitude test. Joint practice of the profession of lawyer in the host Member State is also authorised under certain conditions.

Member State Luxemburg has requested the ECJ to annul that directive. In the view of Luxemburg, this measure introduces a difference in the treatment of national and migrant lawyers and does not guarantee adequate consumer protection or the proper administration of justice.

1 What conditions must be met in this case for the ECJ in order to award the action to annul the Directive? Mention the relevant Article of the TFEU in your answer. Argue your response well, using relevant case law of the ECJ.
2 Is Article 45 TFEU applicable in this case? Is a migrant lawyer considered a worker? Argue your response well, based on case law of the ECJ.
3 What does the "principle of equal treatment" mean?
4 What is your opinion on the claim of Luxemburg? Argue your case well.

Exercise 6.4
Answer the following multiple-choice questions:

6

1 The Treaty on the Functioning of the European Union (TFEU):
- **a** Legislates for the completely free movement of people.
- **b** Deals with the free movement of persons, but contains just concrete measures regarding free movements of economic activities.
- **c** Concerns only the free movement of workers.
- **d** Contains no legislation regarding the movement of people.

2 According to the TFEU what rights does the principle of the free movement of workers bestow?
- **a** The right to enter another Member State.
- **b** The right to enter another Member State and the right of residence.
- **c** The right to enter, the right of residence and the right to remain in another Member State.
- **d** The right to work in another Member State.

3 What does the rule of equality of treatment for workers mean?
- **a** A worker moving to another country is entitled to the same treatment as those in the country that he/she has left.
- **b** A worker moving to another country is entitled to the same treatment as those in the country where the worker is going.
- **c** A worker moving to another country is entitled to more favourable treatment than the workers of the country that he/she has left.
- **d** A worker moving to another country is entitled to more favourable treatment than those in the country where he/she is going.

4 A worker who is going from his home state to work in another Member State:
- **a** Has the right to receive a pension only in the Member State where he works.
- **b** Has the right to receive a pension in that Member State, only if he works there his whole life.
- **c** Can only receive a pension in his home state and has no right to a pension in another Member State.
- **d** Has the right to receive a pension in another Member State under the same conditions that apply to native workers in that country.

5 Who can be considered a worker under Article 45 TFEU?
- **a** A student.
- **b** A student, who works after class.
- **c** A self-employed person.
- **d** A tourist.

6 Who of the following would be entitled to the right of free movement of workers?
- **a** A Russian worker who found employment in the Netherlands.
- **b** The children of an American worker who seeks employment in Italy.
- **c** The children of a German worker, who found employment in France.
- **d** The husband of a Dutch worker who found employment in Turkey

7 The right to employ only a native worker would be permitted in the case of:
- **a** The position of porter at the city hall in The Hague.
- **b** The position of doctor with the medical service of a social security organisation.

c The position of mayor of Amsterdam.
d The position of professor at a university

Exercise 6.5
The Commission brought actions for a breach of EU law against six Member States (Belgium, Germany, Greece, France, Luxembourg and Austria) because they reserved access to the profession of notary to their own nationals. In the Commission's opinion this was discrimination on grounds of nationality, which is prohibited by the TFEU. The Commission also complained that Portugal, together with the Member States mentioned above other than France, did not apply the EU directive on recognition of professional qualifications to notaries. The Member States concerned in these cases, while acknowledging that notaries generally provide their services in those States as members of a independent profession, argue that a notary is a public office-holder who exercises official authority and whose activities are thus excluded from the rules on freedom of establishment.
In order to assess whether notaries exercise official authority within the meaning of the TFEU, the Court then analysed the powers of notaries in the Member States concerned. Only those activities that are directly and specifically connected with the exercise of official authority can be exempted from the application of the principle of freedom of establishment. The Court found that the activities of notaries as currently defined in the Member States in question are not connected with the exercise of official authority within the meaning of the TFEU. Consequently, the nationality condition required by the legislation of those States for access to the profession of notary constituted discrimination on grounds of nationality which is prohibited by the TFEU.

1 What Article of the TFEU prohibits discrimination on grounds of nationality within the EU?
2 What could be the consequences for a Member State, if they do not implement a Directive?
3 The principal issue here is whether the profession of notary requires the exercise of official authority within the meaning of the TFEU. Where in the TFEU does it state that activities which are connected, even if only occasionally, with the exercise of official authority are exempt from the rules on freedom of establishment?
4 The ECJ found in this case that a notary does not exercise any official authority and is not employed by the state. Can you think of the reasons why the ECJ made this decision?

7 Competition law

One of the basic principles of the European Union is the protection of fair trade and competition between Member States of the EU and businesses established in the Member States. Agreements between businesses, which could potentially undermine trade between Member States, are prohibited under EU law. Also, where a business's dominant position in the market leads to anti-competitive behaviour i.e. the abuse of that dominant position, such a dominant position becomes illegal under EU law. Anti-competitive behaviour by businesses within the EU can be heavily punished. This chapter deals with the EU rules on competition.

Agreements between undertakings may affect the trade within the EU

The Bayer Group is one of the main European chemical and pharmaceutical groups. It is represented in all Member States by national subsidiaries. It produces and markets a range of medicinal products for treating cardio-vascular disease under the trade name 'Adalat' or 'Adalate'.
In most Member States, the Bayer Group fixes the price of this range of medicinal products, directly or indirectly. Between 1989 and 1993, the price of Adalat in France and Spain was much lower than in the United Kingdom. The price difference of about 40% caused Spanish wholesalers (from 1989) and then French wholesalers (from 1991) to export that medicinal product in large quantities to the United Kingdom. This practice is referred to as parallel imports: the import of goods into the UK, which have already been sold by the Bayer Group in other countries, as opposed to goods imported directly into the UK from the Bayer Group in Germany. That practice of parallel imports caused a loss of turnover of DEM 230 million for Bayer's British subsidiary.
The Bayer Group then unilaterally changed its supply policy. Its objective was to fulfil orders from Spanish and French wholesalers only at the level of their habitual needs. So the Bayer Group delivered just enough to supply the Spanish and French market, but no more. For that reason, parallel exports to the United Kingdom were made almost impossible.
The Spanish and French wholesalers did not agree to this change of policy and asked for the deliveries to be continued at the same level as before. The Commission investigated the Bayer Group and found its conduct to be in conflict with EU competition law.

7.1 Introduction to competition and cartel law

As shown in the opening case study, agreements between undertakings or decisions taken by associations of undertakings may have a negative effect on trade between the Member States. Thus, these agreements and decisions may affect trade within the EU in the same way as quantitative restrictions or measures having equivalent effect as quantitative restrictions, taken by Member States.

Cartel law

In the EU, the cartel law of the TFEU states that the principle of one common market must be protected and cannot be affected by the acts of one or more undertakings. Art. 101 TFEU prohibits agreements between undertakings, decisions by associations of undertakings and concerted practices, which may affect trade between Member States. Art. 102 TFEU prohibits the abuse of a dominant position by an undertaking.

Art. 101 TFEU prohibits: *all agreements between undertakings, decisions by associations of undertakings and concerted practices which may effect trade between Member States and which have as their object or effect the prevention, restriction or distortion of competition within the common market.* In Art. 101, 1, several examples are mentioned of anti-competitive behaviour, such as the fixing of purchase and selling prices, the limitation or control of production or markets, the division of markets or the control of sources of supply, etcetera. This Article always concerns itself with the behaviour of at least two undertakings.

Art. 102 TFEU prohibits *the abuse of a dominant position by one or more undertakings within the common market or a substantial part of it,* as this is also incompatible with the principle of a common market i.e. the EU market where goods, persons, services and capital can circulate freely. In most of the following cases we see that the dominant position of one undertaking is under discussion. There is nothing wrong with attaining a dominant position, but the abuse of such a position is prohibited under EU law.

These Articles are referred to as *cartel law*.

What is the difference between the free movement of goods of Art. 34, 35 and 36 TFEU (dealt with in Chapter 6) and the cartel law of Art. 101 and 102 TFEU? Art. 34, 35 and 36 TFEU are concerned with quantitative restrictions and measures having equivalent effect to these restrictions. Such acts are carried out by Member States and are contrary to the principle of the free movement of goods. Art. 101 and 102 TFEU are about agreements, decisions or other acts of private undertakings that are contrary to the idea of a common market. Of course any act contrary to the free movement of goods could very well be incompatible with the common market. The key issue is to know *who* took the measure or made the agreement: was it a Member State or a private undertaking?

7.2 The cartel law of Art. 101 TFEU

To decide whether the act of an undertaking should be prohibited under Art. 101, all elements of the first paragraph of this Article should be present. In the event a question is raised e.g. on whether the agreement between two undertakings conflicts with Art. 101, 1, the agreement should be tested against all the relevant elements. Art. 101, 1 prohibits three types of behaviour (listed as 1, 2 and 3). Note that prohibition under Art. 101, 1 takes effect even if only one of these three types is present and as long as all other conditions of Art. 101, 1 (listed as 4, 5, 6 and 7) are met.

1 'All agreements between undertakings'
These 'agreements' may be oral or in writing. So, the form in which the agreement is made is not decisive at this point. An agreement may be derived from letters, shipping documents, faxes, internal memos sent by undertakings, etcetera.

Undertaking

The meaning of 'undertaking' should also be interpreted liberally. Any person engaged in economic or commercial activity involving the provision of goods or services is considered to be an undertaking. Complications may arise when a subsidiary company is involved though, in principle, a parent company is responsible for the conduct of its subsidiary. The fact that the subsidiary company may indeed have a separate legal identity is irrelevant if it cannot independently determine how it acts in the market place and instead has to follow instructions given by the parent company.

2 'Decisions by associations of undertakings'

Association of undertakings

An association of undertakings is e.g. a trade association such as the *Vereeniging van Cementhandelaren* (Association of Cement Dealers). It consists of several undertakings who are in the same line of business. Where 'decisions' are mentioned, no formal agreement is necessary for a decision to have an anti-competitive effect. The meaning of 'decisions by associations of undertakings' is also widely interpreted by the European Court of Justice.

3 'Concerted practices'

Concerted practices

The European Court of Justice gave a definition of 'concerted practices' in the case of ICI. Parallel behaviour of undertakings may be interpreted as a concerted practice *if it leads to conditions of competition which do not correspond to the normal conditions of the market.* A concerted practice is present when parties *knowingly substitute practical co-operation between them for the risks of competition.*

4 'May affect trade between Member States'
An agreement affecting trade within one Member State or exports outside the EU, basically is not covered by Art. 101 TFEU. Instead, the Article tries to define the difference between EU competition law and the competition law of each Member State. However, in the case of Vereeniging van Cementhandelaren, the European Court of Justice decided that although the agreement was effective only in the Netherlands and only among members of that association, it nevertheless posed a barrier to other undertakings wishing to enter the Dutch market. The agreement was therefore considered to be in conflict with Art. 101, 1 TFEU. In the case of Grundig vs. Consten, the European Court of Justice gave its definition of 'may affect trade between Member States' as follows: it is important *whether the agreement is capable of constituting a threat, either direct or indirect, actual or potential, to freedom of trade between Member States in a manner which might harm the attainment of the objectives of a single market between states.*

May affect trade between Member States

5 'Object or effect'
This element concerns itself with the object or the effect of such agreements or concerted practices or decisions. With regard to the element of 'object', where the object of an agreement, practice or decision is clearly to restrict competition, a market analysis by the Commission to determine the effects of the agreement, practice or decision is not required by the European Court of Justice. Concerning the element of 'effect' such a market analysis by the Commission to determine the effects of the agreement, decision or practice, is required by the European Court of Justice. The result of such an investigation may enable the European Court of Justice to find out exactly which agreement, decision or practice conflicts with Art. 101 TFEU.

6 'Prevention, restriction or distortion of competition'
As seen under element 4 in the case of Grundig vs. Consten, the European Court of Justice explained what is meant by agreements *that may effect the trade between Member States*. If an agreement, decision or practice affects trade between Member States, it must also, for that reason, have an appreciable effect on competition and therefore have as its result the *prevention, restriction or distortion of competition*.

Other principles to be derived from the case of Grundig vs. Consten are:
- the list comprising Art. 101, 1 (a) up to and including (e) TFEU is illustrative and not exhaustive;
- prohibition under Art. 101, 1 TFEU, applies to *vertical agreements* (= agreements between producers and distributors, or between distributors and retailers, although potentially beneficial to consumers, are capable of partitioning the market) as well as to *horizontal agreements* (= agreements between undertakings that operate on the same level);
- only those parts of the agreement that affect trade between Member States should be prohibited, not the agreement as a whole;
- trademark rights should not be enforced if this would lead to a division of the market.

Schedule 7.1. illustrates the difference between vertical and horizontal agreements.

SCHEDULE 7.1 Horizontal and vertical agreements

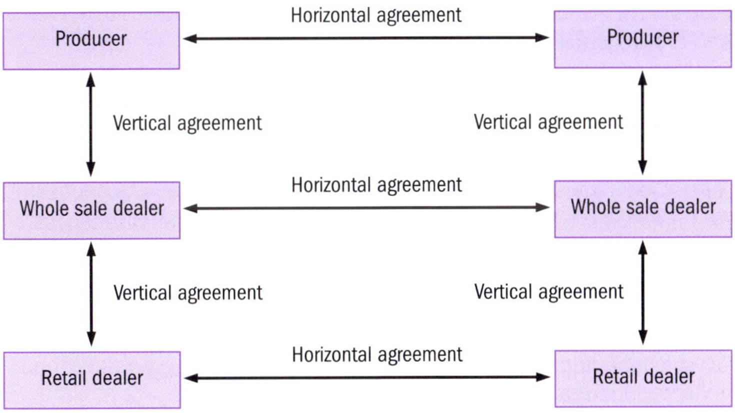

7 'Within the EU'
Art. 101, 1 TFEU bans all agreements between undertakings located within the EU. This Article also bans agreements, practices or decisions between undertakings outside the EU, if the effects of those are felt within the EU or the agreement is implemented within the EU. Art. 101 TFEU applies whenever trade between Member States may be affected.

Art. 101 TFEU also applies where undertakings are (partly) established outside the EU. Suppose an agreement or act restricting competition within the EU is effected by a subsidiary company, established in the EU, of an undertaking, established outside the EU. If the subsidiary company has no freedom to determine its own course of action, the parent company established outside the EU will be held accountable for the agreement reached or act committed by the subsidiary company. Basically, the result is that Art. 101 TFEU takes effect outside the EU.

This is also the case when an act resulting from an agreement, reached by two undertakings outside the EU, takes effect in the EU. In that situation, Art. 101 TFEU applies to these undertakings, even though they are established in non-EU Member States.

EXAMPLE 7.1

7

In the opening case study, there is a *decision by an association of undertakings*. The Bayer Group decides to supply their daughter companies only at the level of their habitual needs. This decision *may affect trade between Member States* (export from France or Spain to the UK is impossible) and has as its *effect* (the consequences are clear, an investigation as to the object of the decision is not necessary) the *prevention, distortion and restriction of competition* (look e.g. at Art. 101, 1, b) *within the EU* (Germany, France, Spain, UK).

7.2.1 Effects of the prohibition under Art. 101, 1 TFEU

Art. 101, 2 TFEU states that, without any further act needed from any of the undertakings, or a Member State or institution of the EU, the agreements and decisions that conflict with Art. 101, 1 TFEU will be cancelled automatically.

7.2.2 Exemptions under Art. 101, 3 TFEU

Art. 101 TFEU in its entirety, is rendered directly applicable by National Competition Authorities (NCAs) and national courts of law, together with the Commission. So, if an undertaking claims exemption under Art. 101, 3 TFEU and shows that its conditions are met, the relevant NCA or national court of law is now entitled to consider the agreement or decision as lawful, and the Commission does not have to give its opinion on the matter first. The Regulation provides that all national competition authorities are empowered to apply EU competition law. Previously only the Commission could declare that an agreement satisfied the requirements of Art. 101, 3 TFEU. By this Regulation a new regime has been established which enables the Commission and national competition authorities to cooperate with one another in conducting investigations.

In other words, the grounds for an exemption are listed in Art. 101, 3 TFEU: the provisions of paragraph 1 may be declared inapplicable in situations where there has been:

- any agreement or set of agreements between undertakings,
- any decision or set of decisions by associations of undertakings,
- any concerted practice or set of concerted practices,

which contributes to the improvement in production or distribution of goods or the promotion of technical or economic progress, while allowing consumers a fair share of the resulting benefit, and which does not:

a impose on the undertakings concerned restrictions which are not essential to the attainment of these objectives;
b afford such undertakings the opportunity to eliminate competition in respect of a substantial part of the products in question.

Companies can no longer apply to the Commission to determine whether an agreement or practice infringes Art. 101, 1 TFEU or for an exemption under Art. 101, 3 TFEU. The Commission and the NCAs have formed the European Competition Network (ECN).

Over the years, the Commission has issued so-called block exemptions. Several Regulations state types of agreements between undertakings, decisions by associations of undertakings and concerted practices which do not fall under the prohibition of Art. 101, 1 TFEU. For that reason, they are assumed not to affect trade between Member States and do not restrict competition within the Common Market.

7

The following block exemptions are upheld by the EU:

- Vertical agreements (Regulation 2790/1999).
- Horizontal agreements of cooperation (Regulation 2658 + 2659/2000).
- Motor vehicle distribution (Regulation 1400/2002).
- Patent licensing (Regulation 240/1996).
- Insurance (Regulation 3932/1992).
- Aviation industry (Regulation 1617/1993 and 3652/1993).
- Shipping industry (Regulation 870/199).

A *vertical agreement* is an agreement between two or more undertakings that operate within the same line of production or distribution and which applies to the conditions of sale of products or services. If the undertakings involved in the agreement hold less than 30% of the relevant market, a block exemption is granted, unless they resort to fixing either selling prices or the division of the market. If the undertakings involved in the agreement hold a market share of more than 30%, they can only apply to the Commission or the NCAs for an exemption on an individual basis. If this exemption is denied, the agreement is declared void and the undertaking may be fined in the event the agreement is still put into effect.

Horizontal agreements are agreements between undertakings which are competitors. Block exemptions for these agreements are granted for all specialisation and R&D agreements between these undertakings as long as the market share of all the undertakings involved is not more than 20% (specialisation agreements) or i.e. 25% (R&D agreements). If the market share of the undertakings exceeds the percentages mentioned, the question of exemption must be judged individually. A division of the market or an agreement on pricing is not allowed.

The ECN allocates cases to the best placed authority. It is likely to be either a NCA or a national court which determines whether an agreement or practice covered by Art. 101, 1 merits an exemption under Art. 101, 3 or is covered by a block exemption. NCAs and national courts may apply national competition law in parallel with EU competition law, but cannot prohibit an agreement that does not violate Art. 101 or qualifies for an exemption.

7.3 The abuse of a dominant position under Art. 102 TFEU

Dominant position

It is possible that an undertaking has a dominant position within the EU market for a certain type of goods. A dominant position in itself is not a problem, as long as the undertaking in question does not abuse its position. Art. 102 TFEU prohibits *the abuse of a dominant position by one or more undertakings within the common market or a substantial part of it, as this is also incompatible with the principle of a common market*, i.e. a market where goods, persons, services and capital can circulate freely.

7.3.1 What is a dominant position?

The criterion for dominance is found in the case of Hoffman LaRoche Vitamins. Dominance by one undertaking prevents effective competition or has an appreciable effect on the conditions under which that competition will develop. With regard to the question of whether dominance exists, three issues are relevant: the product market, the geographical market and the level of dominance by the undertaking for this product in that area.

7

First it is important to determine what the exact product market for this undertaking is. That will help in deciding whether or not the undertaking has a dominant position in the market. Undertakings are inclined to define the market as widely as possible as it reduces the likelihood of being declared dominant. However, in most cases, the Commission is of the opinion that the relevant market is much smaller and therefore an undertaking may well be found to be in a dominant position.

EXAMPLE 7.2

In the case of Hoffman LaRoche Vitamins, the definition of a relevant market in relation to dominant position is given: the product market covers goods, which are identical or are regarded by customers as similar in relation to use, quality or price.

EXAMPLE 7.3

In the case of Chiquita, the issue at hand is the definition of the exact product market for United Brands Ltd. Is this market 'bananas' (according to the Commission) or 'fresh fruit' (according to United Brands Ltd.)? The undertaking United Brands, which handles 40% of all trade in bananas in the EU, was of the opinion that there was no separate market for bananas. The Commission was of a different opinion and was proved right by the ECJ. There is a separate market for bananas, because the consumption of bananas is not affected by the price or consumption of other fresh fruit.

When it is clear what the product market is, the geographical market should also be determined in order to establish how large the product market is i.e. whether it is *within the common market or a substantial part of it*, as described under Art. 102 TFEU.
After defining dominance and the product market, we have to decide whether the undertaking is dominant with regard to that product in the defined area. This depends on several other circumstances:

1 The market share of the undertaking
A high percentage of market share is proof of the dominant position of an undertaking. In general, a market share of at least 50% is considered a dominant position.

EXAMPLE 7.4

In the Roche vitamins case, as Hoffman LaRoche held an 80% market share for a certain type of vitamin there could be no conclusion other than that the undertaking was in a dominant position.

---

2 The market share of competitors
An undertaking can still be found to be in a dominant position even with a relatively low share of the market, through comparison with the competitors' share of the market.

EXAMPLE 7.5

In the case of Chiquita, United Brands held a market share of only 40–45%, but the next two competitors held only 16% and 10% of the market. Therefore, compared to them, United Brands held a dominant position under Art. 102.

---

3 Financial and technical resources of the undertaking

4 Control of production and distribution
If the undertaking involved has control over production and the distribution of the product in the area mentioned earlier, this could mean a commercial advantage over other competitors which might result in it attaining a dominant position.

EXAMPLE 7.6

In the case of Chiquita, United Brands owned the plantations, the means of transport and also marketed the bananas itself.

EXAMPLE 7.7

In the case of Hoffman LaRoche Vitamins, the existence of a highly developed sales network was one element in proving the existence of a dominant position.

5 Conduct and performance of the undertaking
In this context, the economic performance of the undertaking could also be relevant. If the undertaking retains its market share contrary to the performance of other, major undertakings who are manufacturing the same product in the same area, this could be seen as a circumstance that would contribute to the undertaking's dominance.

7.3.2 When does an undertaking abuse its dominant position?

Abuse its dominant position

Basically, there is nothing wrong with having a dominant position. But when does an undertaking actually abuse its dominant position? Some examples are given in Art. 102, (a) to (d) TFEU inclusive: *imposing unfair purchase or selling prices or other unfair trading conditions, or limiting markets and production and using different conditions in equivalent transactions*, etcetera. In the case of Chiquita, the European Court of Justice came across nearly all forms of abuse of a dominant position by an undertaking. They were: unfair prices, discriminatory prices, unfair trading conditions, a refusal to supply other undertakings (the undertaking United Brands refused to supply a Danish wholesaler who had taken part in a sales campaign by another supplier) and import and export bans.

Bear in mind that in all these examples the Commission, before an infringement of Art 102 TFEU can be established, must prove the effect of such an abuse on trade between Member States. If such an infringement is established, the Commission has several options available, including giving a negative clearance, using an exemption, asking the undertaking to stop infringing Art. 101 or 102 TFEU or imposing fines or penalties.

Commission officers are entitled to enter premises and inspect and copy documents. The Commission has the power to impose fines of up to 10% of turnover on undertakings which it finds have infringed Art. 101 or 102 TFEU. The Commission may also order undertakings to cease such behaviour. The Commission has the power to grant block exemptions in respect of sets of agreements. Such block exemptions provide that the set of agreements concerned satisfy the requirements of Art. 101 TFEU. For example, there are block exemptions for vertical agreements such as those concerning motor vehicle distribution and technology transfer.
If the abuse of a dominant position by an undertaking established in a Member State occurs outside the EU, Art. 102 TFEU applies nevertheless.

7.4 Mergers

Mergers

The EU competition rules contain no specific provisions dealing with mergers within the Community. It is widely recognised, though, that merger control is an essential element of competition policy. Should a large scale

merger take place within the EU, competition within the EU is likely to be affected.
In the case of Continental Can, the European Court of Justice held that mergers which eliminated competition could infringe Art. 102 TFEU. In the case of Philip Morris, the European Court of Justice appeared to extend merger control by deciding that mergers might also fall within the scope of Art. 101 TFEU, which deals with restrictive arrangements between undertakings. The European Commission proposed, subsequent to the case of Philip Morris, that certain mergers should be subject to Community control.
Under the Merger Regulation (Regulation 139/2004), which came into force 1 May 2004 and which has direct effect, mergers or concentrations with an EU dimension are subject to exclusive examination by the European Commission. The Regulation provides that a concentration is deemed to have a Community dimension where:

a The aggregate worldwide turnover of all the undertakings involved exceeds €5,000m, and
b The aggregate EU wide turnover of each of at least two of the undertakings concerned exceeds €250m, unless each of the undertakings concerned achieves more than two thirds of its Community-wide turnover within one Member State.

Under this Regulation the Commission has the power to investigate mergers and takeovers of a certain size. Moreover, it also has the authority to obtain information regarding future mergers, to block mergers, and to impose fines on those undertakings that act contrary to the Merger Regulation. These fines are a percentage of the turnover of the undertakings involved. The Merger Regulation contains the following procedure:

Stage 1
The undertaking is obliged to notify the Commission. Such notification has to take place within one week of the conclusion of the contract or after a bid has been made for the shares.

Stage 2
Within a month the Commission has to decide if the Treaty covers the intended merger, i.e. whether they will start an investigation into the competitive aspects of the merger.

Stage 3
If there is a great deal of doubt concerning the intention to merge, an investigation will follow and within 4 months should lead to one of the following options:

- a decree of prohibition (the merger affects competition within the common market), or
- an decree of approval (the merger does not affect competition within the EU), or
- a decree of suspended approval (the same, but with extra conditions imposed on the merging companies by the Commission).

Stage 4
If 4 months have passed, then the notification will be automatically approved.

When an undertaking makes no notification or ignores a decree of prohibition, the Commission has the right to cancel the contract, and to impose a fine. The undertaking can appeal against the decision of the Commission at the Court of Justice of the European Communities within two months of its notification.

EXAMPLE 7.8

Alcatel, a French telecommunications company, intended taking over Telettra, a daughter company of Fiat. During its investigation, the Commission had to consider the consequences of the merger for the Spanish market in transmission equipment. Alcatel and Telettra together would hold a market share of 80%. Over and against these two suppliers was Telefonica, the only buyer of this equipment in Spain.

The Commission had no objection to the merger in view of the demand situation, although it did make some conditions. Telefonica owns shares in companies belonging to the Alcatel and Telettra companies. This could lead to a considerable restriction on competition in the marketplace. For this reason negotiations had to take place and Alcatel was obligated to provide all necessary information.

7.5 Cases of the European Court of Justice on cartel law

Notes:

VCH has a system of regulated prices and price agreements with their members

Case Vereeniging van Cementhandelaren

Court of Justice, Case 8/72, 17 October 1972

Facts

The *Vereeniging van Cementhandelaren* (V.C.H.) (Association of Cement Dealers) was founded in Amsterdam in 1928. Only wholesalers established in the Netherlands can be members. In 1971 of all Dutch cement traders 408 were associated with the association and 234 were not. According to its statutes the aim of the association includes the 'promotion of the cement trade of its members' and 'the protection of their interests, in particular as regards the relationship between members and their suppliers'.
By becoming members of an association the members accept its statutes and rules. Members are bound by majority decisions of decisive or executive bodies of an association.
Within the scope of its activities the V.C.H. established general rules on prices and the terms and conditions of sale in the Dutch market which, on the one hand, included a system of 'regulated' prices for sales of cement up to 100 metric tons and on the other hand contained 'recommended' prices for sales of over 100 metric tons. A few days before the Commission's judgement the rule about 'regulated' prices was cancelled.
The price agreements were closely connected with other competitive restrictions whose aim was:

- to frustrate the sale of cement to traders who were not members of the association or were not recognised by the association;

- to prevent the accumulation of cement stocks by a third party not subject to the rules of the association;
- to strictly limit any trading advantages for buyers and to prevent the rendering of services to buyers, which would exceed common practice.

On 30 October 1962 the V.C.H. registered a number of agreements and decisions concerning the sale of cement in the Netherlands. On 17 December 1965 the Commission was given notice of various modifications of and additions to these agreements and decisions.
By order of 16 December 1971 (Pb. L 13 of 17.1.1972) the Commission decided that these modified and new Regulations were in violation of Art. 81 paragraph 1 EEC Treaty (now Article 101 TFEU) and therefore did not qualify for an exemption ex Art. 81 paragraph 3 (now Article 101 TFEU). The Court of Justice dismissed the appeal against this judgement on – among other things – the following grounds:

Grounds

'The trade between Member States is not affected as VCH operates in The Netherlands only', according to VCH

25. Thus an examination of all the rules to which the contested decision relates shows these to be a coherent and strictly organised system the object of which is to restrict competition between the members of the association.

(B) Influence on trade between member states

26. According to the applicant association, the community nonetheless has no jurisdiction to appraise the cartel to which the contested decision relates because it is a purely national cartel, limited to the territory of the Netherlands, which does not apply in any way to imports or exports and which consequently has no influence over the patterns of trade between Member States.

Connection with Art. 81, 1 (now Article 101 TFEU)

27. In this respect, it emphasises more especially the fact that the total production of cement in the Netherlands far from satisfies the needs of the Netherlands economy and leaves a substantial need for imports, that furthermore there is, apart from its members, a large number of cement sellers not affiliated to it and that therefore there is no danger of intra-community trade being affected.

Agreements conflict with the principle of a common market …

28. According to Art. 81 paragraph (1) (now Article 101 TFEU) all agreements, which have as their object or effect the prevention, restriction or distortion of competition, are incompatible with the Treaty once they are in a position to affect trade between Member States.

… and affect trade between Member States as they make it more difficult to enter the Dutch market

29. An agreement extending over the whole of the territory of a member state by its very nature has the effect of reinforcing the compartmentalisation of markets on a national basis, thereby holding up the economic interpenetration which the Treaty is designed to bring about and protecting domestic production.

Conclusion: the acts of VCH conflict with Art. 81, 1 (now Article 101 TFEU)

30. In particular, the provisions of the agreement, which are mutually binding on the members of the applicant association and the prohibition by the association on all sales to resellers who are not authorised by it, make it more difficult for producers or sellers from other member states to be active in or penetrate the Dutch market.

31. It appears therefore that the objection based on the fact that trade between Member States is not capable of being affected by the decision of the applicant association must be rejected.

32. It follows from the foregoing that the complaints based on an alleged infringement of the rules of the treaty must be dismissed.

Notes:

Case ICI

Court of Justice, case 48/69, 14 July 1972

Facts

Facts describe parallel behaviour relating to pricing policy by a number of large chemical multinationals

The principal producers of aniline dyes, large chemical multinationals such as I.C.I., BASF, Hoechst, Geigy, Zandoz and others, more or less simultaneously raised their prices by the same percentage (of non-identical base prices) in 1964, 1965 and 1967 in several EU countries. In 1964 this happened within a period of a few days only (in most of the cases even within hours) by means of telex instructions to take immediate effect, which were sent from head offices to subsidiaries in various countries and the wordings of which showed remarkable similarities. In 1965 and 1967 an initiator repeatedly announced that prices would increase on date X (about one month later), whereupon within a few weeks announcements were made with a similar content that the competitors were to follow suit (in one case one of these competitors in a member state (Italy) did not follow suit, whereupon the others withdrew their announcements). Besides, the increase in 1967 appeared to have been announced beforehand by the initiator during a meeting of the producers in Basel.
The Commission was of the opinion that in this case one could deem it to be a case of 'mutually geared actual actions' and therefore prohibited those actions by order of 24 July 1969 with the threat of a fine of 50,000 ECU per enterprise. The Court dismissed the appeal lodged by different enterprises except for the fact that the fine was somewhat lowered in one case.

Explanation of Art. 81 , 1 (now Article 101 TFEU)

Grounds

A 'concerted practice' under Art. 81, 1 (now Article 101 TFEU) does not require a contract

64. Art. 81 draws a distinction between the concept of 'concerted practices' and that of 'agreements between undertakings' or of 'decisions by associations of undertakings'; the object is, within that article, to prohibit any form of coordination between undertakings which, without having reached the stage where an agreement that was so-called properly concluded, knowingly substitutes practical cooperation between them for the risks of competition.

Parallel behaviour can become a concerted practice: conditions

65. By its very nature, then, a concerted practice does not have all the elements of a contract but may *inter alia* arise out of coordination, which becomes apparent from the behaviour of the participants.

66. Although parallel behaviour may not in itself be identified with concerted practice, it may however amount to strong evidence of such a practice if it leads to conditions of competition which do not correspond to the normal conditions of the market, having regard to the nature of the products, the size and number of the undertakings, and the volume of the said market.

Conditions apply to this case: the parallel behaviour is a concerted practice

67. This is especially the case if the parallel conduct is such as to enable those concerned to attempt to stabilise prices at a level different from that to which competition would have led, and to consolidate established positions to the detriment of effective freedom of movement of the products in the common market and of the freedom of consumers to choose their suppliers.

Final conclusion of the ECJ

Parent – daughter company

119. In these circumstances and taking into account the nature of the market with the products in question, the conduct of the applicant, in conjunction with other undertakings against which proceedings have been taken, was designed to replace the risks of competition and the hazards of competitors' spontaneous reactions by cooperation thereby constituting a concerted practice prohibited by Art. 81 paragraph (1) of the Treaty (now Article 101 TFEU).

134. Where a subsidiary does not enjoy real autonomy in determining its course of action in the market, the prohibitions set out in Art. 81 paragraph (1) (now Article 101 TFEU) may be considered inapplicable in the relationship between it and the parent company with which it forms one economic unit.

135. In view of the unity of the group thus formed, the actions of the subsidiaries may in certain circumstances be attributed to the parent company.

136. It is well known that at the time the applicant held all, or at any rate, the majority of the shares in those subsidiaries.

137. The applicant was able to exercise decisive influence over the policy of the subsidiaries as regards selling prices in the Common Market and in fact used this power on the occasion of the three price increases in question.

Notes:

Case Grundig vs. Consten

Court of Justice, cases 56/64 and 58/64, 13 July 1966

Facts

Contract between Grundig and Consten:
1. Consten is the only distributor in France
2. Consten is not allowed to export Grundig products
3. Grundig's trade mark 'Gint' was registered under Consten's name

Grundig-Verkaufs GmbH and the French enterprise Consten had concluded a so-called exclusivity contract in 1957. In the contract it was agreed that in France Consten was to act as Grundig's sole representative for the sale of equipment manufactured by Grundig including parts and accessories. Grundig committed itself not to deliver either directly or indirectly to any parties other than Consten in the area mentioned in their contract.. Consten committed itself to sell only Grundig and no other competitive articles in this area. An export prohibition was added to the exclusivity contract: Consten committed itself not to deliver Grundig articles either directly or indirectly from the contract area to other countries. Grundig had also imposed a similar prohibition upon all its sole-importers in other countries and upon the German wholesalers too. This protection of the contract area was further increased with the help of patent and trademark law. Through a supplementary agreement Grundig had had its German brand 'Gint' registered in France in Consten's name.

UNEF buys Grundig products in Germany, exports them to France and sells them under the trademark 'Gint' at a lower price than Consten

Consten: 'Infringement on our trade mark right'

In April 1961 the French enterprise UNEF started selling Grundig equipment under the 'Grint' trademark in France, at better prices than Consten charged. UNEF obtained these pieces of equipment from German dealers who were therefore acting in violation of the export prohibition imposed by Grundig. Consten took legal action against UNEF on the basis of unfair competition and infringement of the trademark 'Gint'. The legal proceedings, which in the meantime had arrived at the Court d'Appel, were suspended awaiting a decision of the EU-Commission. Previously, UNEF had lodged a complaint in which it was requested to declare the Grundig-Consten contract to be in violation of Art. 81 paragraph 1 EEC Treaty (now Article 101 TFEU). Meanwhile Grundig and Consten had reported the contract with the request to declare the prohibition in Art. 81 paragraph 1 EEC Treaty (now Article 101 TFEU) not applicable on the grounds of Art. 81 paragraph 3 EEC Treaty (now Article 101 TFEU). The Commission deemed the contract in violation of Art. 81 paragraph 1 EEC Treaty (now Article 101 TFEU) and did not grant exemption on the grounds of Art. 81 paragraph 3 EEC Treaty (now Article 101 TFEU). Grundig and Consten lodged an appeal against this decision with the Court of Justice on the grounds of Art. 230 paragraph 2 EEC Treaty (now Article 263 TFEU) and among other things referred to Art. 30 EEC Treaty (now Article 34 TFEU).

7

UNEF: 'Agreement with Grundig conflicts with Art. 81, 1 (now Article 101 TFEU)

Grounds

The complaints concerning the applicability of Art. 81 paragraph (1) (now Article 101 TFEU) to sole distributorship contracts

Art. 81, 1 (now Article 101 TFEU) is not exhaustive

Art. 81, 1 (now Article 101 TFEU) includes both horizontal and vertical cartels

1. Neither the wording of Art. 81 (now Article 101 TFEU) nor that of Art. 82 (now Article 102 TFEU) gives any ground for holding that distinct areas of application are to be assigned to each of the two articles according to the level in the economy at which the contracting parties operate. Art. 81 (now Article 101 TFEU) refers in a general way to all agreements which distort competition within the common market and does not lay down any distinction between those agreements based on whether they are made between competitors operating at the same level in the economic process or between non-competing persons operating at different levels. In principle, no distinction can be made where the Treaty does not make any distinction.

Art. 81, 1 (now Article 101 TFEU): both horizontal and vertical cartels distort competition

Explanation of the element '... which may affect trade between Member States ...'

2. Competition may be distorted within the meaning of Art. 81 paragraph (1) (now Article 101 TFEU) not only by agreements which limit it such as those between the parties, but also by agreements which prevent or restrict competition which might take place between one of them and third parties. For this purpose, it is irrelevant whether the parties to the agreement are or are not on an equal footing as regards their position and function in the economy. This applies all the more, since, by such an agreement, the parties might seek, by preventing or limiting the competition from third parties in respect of the products, to create or guarantee for their benefit an unjustified advantage at the expense of the consumer or user, contrary to the general aims of Art. 81(now Article 101 TFEU). It is thus possible that, without involving an abuse of a dominant position, an agreement between economic operators at different levels may affect trade between member states and at the same time have as its object or effect the prevention, restriction or distortion of competition, thus falling under the prohibition of Art. 81 paragraph (1) (now Article 101 TFEU).

The complaints relating to the concept of 'agreements... which may affect trade between member states'

'... and have as their object or effect ...'; an agreement in itself is enough; the execution of such an agreement is not necessary!

5. The concept of an agreement 'which may affect trade between Member States' is intended to define, in the law governing cartels, the boundary between the areas respectively covered by Community Law and national law. It is only to the extent to which the agreement may affect trade between Member States that the deterioration in competition caused by the agreement falls under the prohibition of community law contained in Art. 81(now Article 101 TFEU), otherwise it escapes the prohibition. In this connection, what is particularly important is whether the agreement is capable of constituting a threat, either direct or indirect, actual or potential, to freedom of trade between member states in a manner which might harm the attainment of the objectives of a single market between states. Thus the fact that an agreement encourages an increase, even a large one, in the volume of trade between states is not sufficient to exclude the possibility that the agreement may 'affect' such trade in the above mentioned manner.

The complaints concerning the criterion of restriction on competition

6. The principle of freedom of competition concerns the various stages and manifestations of competition. Although competition between producers is generally more noticeable than that between distributors of products of the same make, it does not thereby follow that an agreement tending to restrict the latter kind of competition should escape the prohibition of Art. 81 paragraph (1) (now Article 101 TFEU) merely because it might increase the former.

7. Besides, for the purpose of applying Art. 81 paragraph (1), (now Article 101 TFEU) there is no need to take account of the concrete effects of an agreement once it appears that it has as its object the prevention, restriction or distortion of competition.

8. The defendant properly took into account the whole distribution system thus set up by Grundig. In order to arrive at a true representation of the contractual position the contract must be placed in the economic and legal context in the light of which it was concluded by the parties. Such a procedure is not to be regarded as an unwarrantable interference in legal transactions or circumstances, which were not the subject of the proceedings before the Commission. The situation as ascertained above results in the isolation of the French market and makes it possible to charge for the products in question prices, which are sheltered from all effective competition. In addition, the more producers succeed in their efforts to render their own makes of product individually distinct in the eyes of the consumer, the more the effectiveness of competition between producers tends to diminish. Because of the considerable impact of distribution costs on the aggregate cost price, it seems important that competition between dealers should also be stimulated. The efforts of the dealer are stimulated by competition between distributors of products of the same make. Since the agreement thus aims at isolating the French market for Grundig products and maintaining artificially, for products of a very well known brand, separate national markets within the Community, it is therefore such as to distort competition in the Common Market.

The complaints relating to the extent of the prohibition

Art. 81, 2 (now Article 101 TFEU) only relates to those parts of the agreement that are prohibited under Art. 81, 1 (now Article 101 TFEU)

9. The provision in Art. 81 paragraph (2) that agreements prohibited pursuant to Art. 81 shall be automatically void applies only to those parts of the agreement which are subject to the prohibition, or to the agreement as a whole if those parts do not appear to be separable from the agreement itself. The Commission should, therefore, either have confined itself in the operative part of the contested decision to declaring that an infringement lay in those parts only of the agreement which came within the prohibition, or else it should have set out in the preamble to the decision the reasons why those parts did not appear to it to be severable from the whole agreement.

The submissions concerning the finding of an infringement in respect of the agreement on the GINT trade mark

A trademark right based on national law is not a way of escaping the prohibition under Art. 81, 1 (now Article 101 TFEU)

10. Art. 30 (now Article 34 TFEU), 222 and 234 of the Treaty (now Article 267 TFEU), upon which the applicants based their case, do not exclude any influence whatever of community law on the exercise of national industrial property rights. Art. 30 (now Article 34 TFEU), which limits the scope of the rules on the liberalisation of trade contained in title I, chapter 2, of the Treaty, cannot limit the field of application of Art. 81 (now Article 101 TFEU). Art. 222 confines itself to stating that the 'Treaty shall in no way prejudice the rules in Member States governing the system of property ownership.' The injunction contained in Art. 3 of the operative part of the contested decision to refrain from using rights under national trademark law in order to set an obstacle in the way of parallel imports does not affect the grant of those rights but only limits their exercise to the extent necessary to give effect to the prohibition under Art. 81 paragraph (1) (now Article 101 TFEU). The power of the Commission to issue such an injunction for which provision is made in Art. 3 of Regulation no 17/62 of the Council is in harmony with the nature of the community rules on competition, which have immediate effect and are directly binding on individuals. Such a body of rules, by reason of its nature described above and its function, does not allow the improper use of rights under any national trademark law in order to frustrate the community's law on cartels. Art. 234 (now Article 267 TFEU), which aims to protect the rights of third countries, is not applicable in the present instance.

The complaints concerning the application of Art. 81 paragraph (1) (now Article 101 TFEU)

No reason to grant the agreement between Grundig and Consten an exemption under Art. 81, 3 (now Article 101 TFEU)

11. The undertakings are entitled to an appropriate examination by the Commission of their requests for Art. 81 paragraph (3) (now Article 101 TFEU) to be applied. For this purpose the Commission may not confine itself to requiring from undertakings proof of the fulfilment of the requirements for the grant of the exemption but must, as a matter of good administration, play its part, using the means available to it, in ascertaining the relevant facts and circumstances. Furthermore, the exercise of the Commission's powers necessarily implies complex evaluations on economic matters. A judicial review of these evaluations must take account of their nature by confining itself to an examination of the relevance of the facts and of the legal consequences, which the commission deduces there from. This review must in the first place be carried out in respect of the reasons given for the decisions, which must set out the facts and considerations on which the said evaluations are based. The contested decision states that the principal reason for the refusal of exemption lies in the fact that the requirement contained in Art. 81 paragraph (3)(a) (now Article 101 TFEU) is not satisfied.

Notes:

Case Chiquita

Court of Justice, Case 27/76, 14 February 1978

Facts

According to the Commission United Brands abused their dominant position in the market for bananas in the EU under Art. 82 (now Article 102 TFEU)

United Brands Company (UBC) in New York is the world's largest banana group. It is composed of a large number of subsidiaries all over the world, all of which are managed by central bodies in New York. Its European subsidiary United Brands Continental BV, established in Rotterdam, coordinates the sale of bananas in West Germany, the Benelux countries, Denmark and Ireland. By decree of 17 December the Commission inflicted a 1m ECU fine on UBC owing to the violation of art 82 EEC Treaty (now Article 102 TFEU). According to this decree UBC held a position of power with regard to the supply of bananas in that part of the EU market comprising the member countries mentioned above, which position of power it abused by:

1. forbidding its clients (dealers/ripeners) – in its terms and conditions of sale – to resell bananas in a green condition, which in practice boiled down to an export prohibition;
2. halting supplies to one of these clients, Th. Olesen in Copenhagen, for a period of nearly 18 months;
3. charging clients entirely different prices for similar bananas in one member state or another, without any objective justification for doing so;
4. charging some clients unfair prices by doing so.

United Brands starts a procedure before the ECJ under Art. 230 (now Article 263 TFEU)

On appeal the decree was annulled as regards point 4, but confirmed for the rest; the fine was decreased to 850.000 ECU owing to this partial annulment.

Grounds

Section 1 – the relevant market

Paragraph 1. The product market

Product market: 'bananas' (Commission) or 'fresh fruit' (United Brands)?

12. As far as the product market is concerned it is first of all necessary to ascertain whether, as the applicant maintains, bananas are an integral part of the fresh fruit market, because they are reasonably interchangeable by consumers with other kinds of fresh fruit such as apples, oranges, grapes, peaches, strawberries, etc. Or whether the relevant market consists solely of the banana market that includes both branded bananas and unlabelled bananas and is a market sufficiently homogeneous and distinct from the market of other fresh fruit.

13. The applicant submits in support of its argument that bananas compete with other fresh fruit in the same shops, on the same shelves, at prices which can be compared, satisfying the same needs: consumption as a dessert or between meals.

Product market = bananas = a separate market

34. It follows from all these considerations that a very large number of consumers having a constant need for bananas are not noticeably or even appreciably enticed away from the consumption of this product by the arrival of other fresh fruit on the market and that even the personal peak periods only affect it for a limited period of time and to a very limited extent from the point of view of substitutability.

35. Consequently the banana market is a market which is sufficiently distinct from the other fresh fruit markets.

Dominance of United Brands

65. The dominant position referred to in this article relates to a position of economic strength enjoyed by an undertaking which enables it to prevent effective competition being maintained in the relevant market by giving it the power to behave to an appreciable extent independently of its competitors, customers and ultimately of its consumers.

66. In general a dominant position derives from a combination of several factors which, taken separately, are not necessarily determinative.

Market share: compare the market share of UBC to that of the other competitors in the market

67. In order to find out whether UBC is an undertaking in a dominant position in the relevant market it is necessary first of all to examine its structure and then the situation in the said market as far as competition is concerned.

107. A trader can only be in a dominant position in the market for a product if he has succeeded in winning a large part of this market.

108. Without going into a discussion about percentages, which when fixed are bound to be to some extent approximations, it can be considered to be an established fact that UBC's share of the relevant market is always more than 40% and nearly 45%.

109. This percentage does not however permit the conclusion that UBC automatically controls the market.

110. It must be determined having regard to the strength and number of the competitors.

111. It is necessary first of all to establish that in the whole of the relevant market the said percentage represents *grosso modo* a share several times greater than that of its competitor Castle and Cooke which is the best placed of all the competitors, the others coming far behind.

Abuse of a dominant position

112. This fact together with the others to which attention has already been drawn may be regarded as a factor, which affords evidence of UBC's preponderant strength.

Abuse of a dominant position

Prohibition of sale of green bananas ...

158. Although it is commendable and lawful to pursue a policy of quality, especially by choosing sellers according to objective criteria relating to the qualifications of the seller, his staff and his facilities, such a practice can only be justified if it does not raise obstacles, the effect of which goes beyond the objective to be attained.

... is an abuse of a dominant position

Refusal to supply Mr Olesen

159. In this case, although these conditions for selection have been laid down in a way which is objective and not discriminatory, the prohibition on resale imposed upon duly appointed Chiquita ripeners and the prohibition of the resale of unbranded bananas - even if the perishable nature of the banana in practice restricted the opportunities of reselling to the duration of a specific period of time - was without any doubt an abuse of the dominant position since they limit markets to the prejudice of consumers and affects trade between Member States, in particular by partitioning national markets.

160. Thus UBC's organisation of the market confined the ripeners to the role of suppliers of the local market and prevented them from developing their capacity to trade vis-à-vis UBC, which moreover tightened its economic hold on them by supplying fewer goods than they ordered.

161. It follows from all these considerations that the clause at issue forbidding the sale of green bananas infringes Art. 82 of the Treaty (now Article 102 TFEU).

191. The sanction consisting of a refusal to supply by an undertaking in a dominant position was in excess of what might, if such a situation were to arise, reasonably be contemplated as a sanction for conduct similar to that for which UBC blamed Olesen.

This refusal boils down to eliminating a competitor which conflicts with the principle of a common market (Art. 82) (now Article 102 TFEU)

192. In fact UBC could not be unaware of that fact that by acting in this way it would discourage its other ripeners/distributors from supporting the advertising of other brand names and that the deterrent effect of the sanction imposed upon one of them would make its position of strength in the relevant market that much more effective.

193. Such a course of conduct amounts therefore to a serious interference with the independence of small and medium sized firms in their commercial relations with the undertaking in a dominant position and this independence implies the right to give preference to competitors' goods.

Discriminatory pricing

194. In this case the adoption of such a course of conduct is designed to have a serious adverse effect on competition in the relevant banana market by only allowing firms dependant upon the dominant undertaking to stay in business.

201. Furthermore, if the occupier of a dominant position, established in the common market, aims at eliminating a competitor who is also established in the common market, it is immaterial whether this behaviour relates to trade between Member States once it has been shown that such elimination will have repercussions on the patterns of competition in the common market.

Section 2 – the pricing practice

Paragraph 1. Discriminatory prices

UBC calculates very different prices for the same bananas

223. UBC's answers to the Commission's requests for particulars (the letters of 14 May, 13 September, 10 and 11 December 1974 and 13 February 1975) show that UBC charges its customers each week for its bananas sold under the Chiquita brand name a different selling price depending on the Member State where the latter carry on their business as ripeners/ distributors according to the ratios to which the commission has drawn attention.

224. These price differences can reach 30 to 50% in some weeks, even though products supplied under the transactions are equivalent (with the exception of the Scipio group, subject to this observation that the bananas from Scipio's ripening installations are sold at the same price as those sold by independent ripeners).

225. In fact the bananas sold by UBC are all freighted in the same ships, are unloaded at the same cost in Rotterdam or Bremerhaven and the price differences relate to substantially similar quantities of bananas of the same variety, which have been brought to the same degree of ripening, are of similar quality and sold under the same 'Chiquita' brand name under the same conditions of sale and payment for loading on to the purchaser's own means of transport. The latter have to pay customs duties, taxes and transport costs from these ports.

Discriminatory prices and the prohibition on reselling green bananas conflict with the free movement of goods and lead to distortion of competition and to an abuse of a dominant position under Art. 82 (now Article 102 TFEU)

227. Although the responsibility for establishing the single banana market does not lie with the applicant, it can only endeavour to take 'what the market can bear' provided that it complies with the rules for the regulation and coordination of the market laid down by the Treaty.

228. Once it can be grasped that differences in transport costs, taxation, customs duties, the wages of the labour force, the conditions of marketing, the differences in the parity of currencies, the density of competition may eventually culminate in different retail selling price levels according to the Member States, then it follows those differences are factors which UBC only has to take into account to a limited extent since it sells a product which is always the same and at the same place to ripeners/distributors who – alone – bear the risks of the consumers' market.

229. The interplay of supply and demand should, owing to its nature, only be applied to each stage where it is really manifest.

230. The mechanisms of the market are adversely affected if the price is calculated by leaving out one stage of the market and taking into account the law of supply and demand as between the vendor and the ultimate consumer and not as between the vendor (UBC) and the purchaser (the ripeners/distributors).

...

What are 'unfair prices'

232. These discriminatory prices, which varied according to the circumstances of the Member States, were just so many obstacles to the free movement of goods and their effect was intensified by the clause forbidding the resale of bananas while still green and by reducing the deliveries of the quantities ordered.

Unfair pricing can only be determined if one has analysed the costs structure of UBC (which the Commission has not)

233. A rigid partitioning of national markets was thus created at price levels which were artificially different, placing certain distributor/ripeners at a competitive disadvantage, since compared with what it should have been competition had thereby been distorted.

234. Consequently the policy of differing prices enabling UBC to apply dissimilar conditions to equivalent transactions with other trading parties, thereby placing them at a competitive disadvantage, was an abuse of a dominant position.

No proof of unfair prices

Paragraph 2. Unfair prices

248. The imposition by an undertaking in a dominant position directly or indirectly of unfair purchase or selling prices is an abuse to which exception can be taken under Art. 82 of the Treaty (now Article 102 TFEU).

249. It is advisable therefore to ascertain whether the dominant undertaking has made use of the opportunities arising out of its dominant position in such a way as to reap trading benefits, which it would not have reaped if there had been normal and sufficiently effective competition.

250. In this case charging a price, which is excessive because it has no reasonable relation to the economic value of the product supplied, would be such an abuse.

Conclusion of the ECJ on the issue of unfair prices

251. This excess could, *inter alia*, be determined objectively if it were possible for it to be calculated by making a comparison between the selling price of the product in question and its cost of production, which would disclose the amount of the profit margin; however the Commission has not done this since it has not analysed UBC's costs structure.

252. The questions therefore to be determined are whether the difference between the costs actually incurred and the price actually charged is excessive, and, if the answer to this question is in the affirmative, whether a price has been imposed which is either unfair in itself or when compared to competing products.

253. Other ways may be devised - and economic theorists have not failed to think up several - of selecting the rules for determining whether the price of a product is unfair.

254. While appreciating the considerable and at times very great difficulties in working out production costs which may sometimes include a discretionary apportionment of indirect costs and general expenditure and which may vary significantly according to the size of the undertaking, its object, the complex nature of its set up, its territorial area of operations, whether it manufactures one or several products, the number of its subsidiaries and their relationship with each other, the production costs of the banana do not seem to present any insuperable problems.

...

267. In these circumstances it appears that the Commission has not adduced adequate legal proof of the facts and evaluations which formed the foundation of its finding that UBC had infringed Art. 82 of the Treaty (now Article 102 TFEU) by directly and indirectly imposing unfair selling prices for bananas.

Summary

- Articles 101 and 102 TFEU uphold the principle of the common market within the EU.

- Art. 101, 1 TFEU prohibits all agreements between undertakings, decisions by associations of undertakings and concerted practices, which may effect trade between Member States and which have as their object or effect the prevention, restriction or distortion of competition within the common market.
  Art. 101, 2 TFEU states that if an agreement, decision or practice is prohibited by Art. 101, 1 TFEU, it should be considered null and void from the start.
  Art. 101, 3 TFEU states that Art. 101, 2 TFEU does not have effect in certain situations.

- Art. 102 TFEU prohibits the abuse of a dominant position by one or more undertakings, within the common market or a substantial part of it. Abuse of a dominant position is incompatible with the principle of a common market i.e. the EU market where goods, persons, services and capital can circulate freely. Dominance of an undertaking must be derived from the circumstances of the case:
  - Product market
  - Geographical market
  - The level of dominance in a specific area e.g. the market share of the undertaking

  If an undertaking thus has a dominant position, and displays behaviour that falls within the examples of and the case law based on Art. 102 TFEU, this behaviour is an abuse of a dominant position. The undertaking is liable to fines imposed by the European Commission.

- Art. 103 TFEU prohibits mergers which have an anti-competitive effect. The Merger Regulation provides undertakings which intend to merge with guidelines and procedures on merging within the EU.

Glossary

Abuse of a dominant position	This abuse takes place if an undertaking in a dominant position commits e.g. the acts described in Art. 102 TFEU (e.g. unfair pricing, a refusal to supply another company).
Association of undertakings	Undertakings which set up a form of cooperation between themselves for economic purposes, such as a trade association.
Cartel law	Legislation to uphold the principle of a common market within the EU.
Competition law	Rules on how competition should develop according to the principle of a common European market. Competition law states which acts of undertakings are not permitted, which sanctions may be imposed if they break these rules and the ways of avoiding prohibited competitive practices.
Concerted practices	Parallel behaviour of undertakings (with regard to the type of product, the size and number of undertakings, and the size of the market in question) which results in abnormal competitive advantage.
Dominant position	An undertaking which dominates the market, with regard to the product market (i.e. the appropriate market for the product), the geographical market (i.e. the area where the product is marketed) and the dominance of the undertaking (in that product market within an area of the EU). Under EU law there is nothing wrong with holding a dominant position, as long as the undertaking does not abuse it.
May affect trade	Agreements between undertakings, decisions by associations of undertakings and concerted practices are capable of constituting a threat, direct or indirect, actual or potential, to freedom of trade between member states in a manner detrimental to the attainment of the objectives of a single market between states.
Merger	The combining of two or more undertakings into one.
Undertaking	Any person engaged in economic or commercial activity involving the provision of goods or services.

Exercises

Exercise 7.1
The Bayer Group is one of the main European chemical and pharmaceutical groups, represented in all Member States by national subsidiaries. It produces and markets a range of medicinal products for treating cardio-vascular disease under the trade name 'Adalat' or 'Adalate'. For this product Bayer AG holds a market share of 70% of the total EU market.

In most Member States, the Bayer Group fixes the price of this range of medicinal products, directly or indirectly. Between 1989 and 1993, the price of Adalat in France and Spain was much lower than that in the United Kingdom. The price difference of about 40%, gave Spanish wholesalers (from 1989) and then French wholesalers (from 1991) the opportunity to export that medicinal product in large quantities to the United Kingdom. That practice of parallel imports caused a loss of turnover of DEM 230 million for Bayer's British subsidiary.

The Bayer Group then unilaterally changed its supply policy, fulfilling orders from Spanish and French wholesalers only at the level of their habitual needs. So the Bayer Group delivered just enough to supply the Spanish and French market, but no more. For that reason, parallel exports to the United Kingdom were made almost impossible.

The German and French wholesalers did not agree to this change of policy and asked for the deliveries to be continued as before.

The Commission investigated the Bayer Group and found its conduct to be in conflict with EU competition law.

1 Does the conduct of the Bayer Group conflict with Art. 101 TFEU? Argue your answer well, using all relevant elements of Art. 101 TFEU. Also mention relevant case law in your answer.
2 Does the conduct of the Bayer Group conflict with Art. 102 TFEU? Argue your answer well, using all relevant aspects of this Article. Also mention relevant case law in your answer.

Exercise 7.2
Cars are substantially cheaper in Italy than in Germany and Austria, because of tax differences. According to European Law consumers are allowed to buy their cars anywhere in the EU. Many German consumers made use of this and bought their cars in Italy.

Volkswagen AG is one of the largest automobile manufacturers within the EU. Volkswagen has a large dealer network throughout the European Union, which sells cars under the names Volkswagen and Audi. Volkswagen dealers in every country are independent entrepreneurs who have a contractual relationship with Volkswagen AG in Germany. Under this contract it is prohibited for a dealer to re-export cars to any other country in the EU. Volkswagen also tries to restrict parallel imports from Italy by imposing supply quotas on Italian dealers and a bonus system, discouraging them from selling to non-Italian customers.

Volkswagen dealers in the south of Germany and in Austria started to complain to Volkswagen AG that customers were leaving them for Italian dealers. Volkswagen AG put a great deal of pressure on its Italian dealers. It reminded the dealers of the contents of the dealer contracts and intimidated them or threatened to withdraw their dealership if they sold Volkswagen cars to non-Italians. After an investigation by the Commission it appeared that twelve Italian companies had lost their dealership and that fifty companies had been threatened by Volkswagen AG.

1 Are the contracts and acts of Volkswagen in violation of Art. 101 TFEU? Mention relevant case law in your answer!
2 Is the conduct of Volkswagen AG in violation of Art. 102 TFEU? Mention relevant case law in your answer!

8 Carriage, Incoterms, Payment and Entry modes

Having discussed international contracts of sale and the free movement of goods within the EU, this chapter is concerned with the carriage of goods from one country to another, under the terms agreed by the parties involved. This chapter also deals with the so-called Incoterms, with international payments, and shows several ways in which businesses can enter new, foreign markets and contact, and contract with, new business partners.

International carriage of goods; limitation of risks and international payments

8

Kuznetsov, a Russian firm (the buyer), brings a claim against Baumgartner, a Hungarian firm (the seller). The claim is based on a contract for the international sale of goods which was concluded by the parties. The claim was brought because Kuznetsov, who put down a 100% advance payment for the goods, did not receive them. The goods were to be delivered CIP (Carriage and Insurance Paid) to a place of destination in Russia as required by the contract. The transport was carried out by Schmidt Expedition GmbH, a company established in Germany. The carrier was hired by the seller, Baumgartner. The goods were delayed during transportation and kept at a customs warehouse at a transit point in Russia. The buyer demands a refund of the down payment for the goods, as well as penalties for the delay in delivery. In Kuznetsov's opinion, his claims are reasonable as Baumgartner failed to make the delivery to the place of destination stated in the contract. Baumgartner contests the buyer's claim. The seller claims that he duly fulfilled all the obligations under the contract. This opening case contains examples of the three main topics of this chapter: carriage, incoterms and international payments.

8.1 Carriage

To fulfil an obligation of delivery resulting from an international sales contract, the issue of carriage of the goods, mainly by road, becomes relevant.

8.1.1 Parties in a contract of carriage

There are three parties in a contract of carriage: the sender, the consignee and the carrier. **Carriage**

The sender

The contract of carriage is a contract in which the carrier undertakes to carry goods by road on behalf of the sender. The *sender* is any legal entity, whether a person or a business, that hands over goods to the carrier. If the carrier hires someone else to take care of the transport, then he himself is considered the sender. In other words, with respect to a carrier hired in this way, the position of sender shifts from the seller to the (first) carrier who decided to hire someone else to take care of the carriage for him. **Sender**

The consignee

The *consignee* is the one who is entitled to take delivery of the goods, based on the contract of carriage and the conditions of delivery stated in that contract. Depending on the conditions of delivery in the contract, the goods are transported at the risk of the consignee. This risk lies in the entire consignment (or any part of it) and lasts throughout the whole journey of the goods (or any part of it). Both the sender and the consignee have an interest in the safe and proper carriage of goods. **Consignee**

The carrier

The sender hires a carrier to transport the goods and concludes a contract with him. The sender has the option of letting a third party undertake the loading of the goods. The consignee also has the option of letting another party, other than itself, accept the delivery. If the carrier in turn hires a third party to undertake the transport of the goods, then the carrier itself is considered to be the sender. With regard to contracts of carriage, the freedom of the sender and carrier to make a contract is limited by international treaties concerning the carriage of goods. The contract of carriage can be made between the carrier and either the seller or the buyer. **Carrier**

8

EXAMPLE 8.1

Hensen B.V., a company established in The Netherlands, sells 1,000 kilos of cheese to Freiburger GmbH, a company established in Germany. In order to get the cheese delivered, Hensen concludes a contract of carriage with VandenBroucke SA, a company established in Belgium. In this example, Hensen B.V. is the sender, VandenBroucke SA the carrier and Freiburger GmbH the consignee.

EXAMPLE 8.2

Elaborating on Example 8.1, if VandenBroucke SA in turn contracts with McDonald Ltd., a company established in the UK, to take care of the transport, VandenBroucke SA then becomes the sender of the goods. McDonald Ltd is then regarded as the carrier.

8.1.2 Carrier and shipper

The sender has two options when it comes to the carriage of goods. He can either hire a carrier himself or contact a shipper.

Shipper

Shippers

Shippers are go-betweens who conclude contracts of carriage on behalf of the seller i.e. sender. The shipper represents the sender in such a way that the contract of carriage is in the name of the sender and at the sender's expense. A shipper will ensure the goods are carried in the quickest and most efficient way possible.

Carrier

Sometimes a shipper also acts as a carrier. When dealing with carriage it is necessary to make a distinction between a carrier and a shipper. The liability of carriers is laid down in several binding treaties. However, there are no international rules regarding the liability of shippers. The liability of the shipper is determined by the national laws of the countries involved and by the contract made between the seller i.e. sender and the shipper. The liability of the shipper can also be determined from the general terms of transport and delivery applicable to the contract. See table 8.1.

TABLE 8.1 Carrier and shipper

Carrier	Shipper
A carrier 'carries' goods to the address given to him by the seller i.e. sender of the goods	A shipper can also undertake the carriage of goods as well as arranging: • the correct documents for the carriage of goods, • customs formalities, • storage of goods before or after customs formalities, and • payment of taxes or VAT

8

8.1.3 Carriage and documents

Documents

Depending on the way carriage is organised, different documents are required. These documents have several functions: they are the written proof of both the existence and the content of a contract of carriage and also the written proof of receipt of the goods. See table 8.2.

When goods are being carried by sea, a sea consignment note a.k.a. "bill of lading" is used. This is similar to the consignment note used in case of carriage by road, except for one main difference which is that the "bill of lading" represents the goods. This is not the case with the consignment note. The one who holds a sea consignment note is considered to be the owner of the goods mentioned in that document.

8.1.4 CMR-consignment

Convention on the Contract for the International Carriage of Goods by Road

Application of the CMR Convention

The Convention on the Contract for the International Carriage of Goods by Road (hereafter referred to as CMR) applies to every contract for the carriage of goods by road in commercial vehicles, when the place of loading

TABLE 8.2 Documents and means of transportation

Carriage by road	Carriage by rail	Carriage by air	Carriage by sea
The national consignment note – lists the general terms of transport applicable to the national carriage of goods. Varies from country to country.	CIM Treaty gives general rules on the international carriage of goods by rail.	AWB (Airway Bill, also known as an air consignment note)	B/L (Bill of Lading, also known as a sea consignment note)
CMR-consignment – includes general conditions on the international carriage of goods by road.			
FCT - a statement made by the shipper to the sender that the shipper is responsible for the goods.			
FCR - a statement made by the shipper to the sender that the shipper, by means of an agent, is responsible for the delivery of the goods at the place the sender and shipper have agreed on.			

the goods and the place designated for delivery as specified in the contract are situated in two different countries. One of these two countries has to be a Contracting State of the CMR. Neither the nationality nor the places of residence of the sender or carrier are relevant when it comes to the sphere of application of the CMR (Art. 1 CMR). Nearly all European countries and a number of countries in the Middle East are Contracting States of the CMR. The CMR applies if the conditions in Art. 1 are fulfilled. Parties can neither opt into, nor out of, this Convention.

Art. 2 CMR deals with the application of the Convention if the means of transport is changed e.g. from road to sea, or from road to rail, or from road to air, while a contract is in force. If the vehicle containing the goods is transported over part of the route by rail, sea or inland waterway, or by air and the goods are not unloaded from the road vehicle, the CMR will continue to apply to the entire transit. However, if the goods are lost, damaged, or delayed while the vehicle is being carried by the other mode of transport, by an event which could only occur through use of that other mode, the liability of the road carrier will be determined by any national or international mandatory law applicable to that other mode. If there is no such mandatory law, the terms of the CMR-Convention will continue to apply.

Consignment note
Art. 4 CMR states that the contract of carriage shall be confirmed by a *consignment note*. The carrier, when carrying out a contract of carriage, therefore has to be in possession of such a note, but the absence, irregularity or loss of the consignment note will not prevent the CMR provisions from being applied. The sender and carrier have the option of

settling the matter of liability either in the consignment note or in the contract of carriage. Art. 5 CMR states that two further copies (i.e. three in total) must be made of the consignment note. The first is to be handed to the seller i.e. sender, the second accompanies the goods and the third is retained by the carrier.
Certain information *must* be shown in the consignment note (Art. 6, 1 (a) – (k) CMR) such as the names and addresses of the sender, the carrier and the consignee, the place where and date when the carrier took responsibility for the goods, as well as the place designated for delivery. The gross weight of the goods or their quality must also be shown in the consignment note.
The CMR consignment note is not a document of title, but it has great value in the Contracting States of the CMR as evidence of title. For that reason, copies of the consignment note should ideally be retained for at least one year.

Carrier checks and takes over the goods
Art. 8 CMR states that the carrier, as soon as it takes over the goods for delivery to the consignee, has to check the accuracy of the statements in the consignment note as to the number of packages and their marks and numbers. The carrier should also check the apparent condition of the goods and their packaging. Where the carrier has no reasonable means of checking the accuracy of these statements, it should make its reservations known in the consignment note together with the grounds on which they are based. These reservations are not binding on the sender, unless it has expressly agreed to be bound by them in the consignment note.

The sender hands over the goods
The sender is entitled to require the carrier to check the gross weight of the goods or other expression of their quantity. It can also require the contents of packages to be checked. The carrier, however, is entitled to claim the cost of such checking. The result of the checks should be entered in the consignment note. Art. 9 CMR allows the carrier, if he has no reasonable means of checking, to protect himself by noting reservations on the consignment note. The sender should also note anything which is apparently suspect about the goods. If the carrier fails to note such reservations, then it may be presumed, unless the contrary is actually proved, that the number of packages was accurately stated and that the goods appeared to be in good condition.

Liability of the sender
According to Art. 10 CMR, the sender is liable to the carrier for damage to persons, equipment or other goods, and for any expenses due to defective packing of the goods, unless the defect was apparent or known to the carrier at the time it took over the goods and it made no reservations about it.

Liability of the carrier
Art. 17 CMR states that the carrier is liable for the total or partial loss of the goods and for damage occurring between the time it takes over the goods and the time of delivery, as well as for any delay in delivery.
The carrier, however, would be relieved of liability if the loss, damage or delay was caused:
- by the wrongful act or neglect of the sender or the consignee (or another party acting on their behalf),

- by the instructions of one of them given otherwise than as the result of a wrongful act or neglect on the part of the carrier,
- by inherent defects in the goods, or
- through circumstances which the carrier could not avoid and the consequences of which it was unable to prevent.

The carrier should not be relieved of liability resulting from the defective condition of the vehicle used by it in order to perform the carriage, or resulting from any wrongful act or neglect of the person from whom he may have hired the vehicle or of the agents or servants of the latter.
The carrier should be relieved of liability when the loss or damage arises from the special risks inherent in one or more of the following circumstances:

- the use of open unsheeted vehicles, when their use has been expressly agreed upon and specified in the consignment note,
- where there is insufficient or defective packing of goods which, by their nature, are liable to wastage or damage when not packed or when not properly packed,
- the carriage of livestock, and
- when the handling, loading, stowage or unloading of the goods is carried out by the sender, the consignee or any person acting on behalf of the sender or the consignee.

Art. 17 CMR lists further situations in which either the carrier or the sender is liable for damage to the goods. Art. 18 CMR lays down the rules of proof in matters such as these.

Compensation to be paid by the carrier
According to Art. 23 CMR, if a carrier is liable for compensation in respect of the total or partial loss of goods, such compensation should be calculated by reference to the value of the goods at the place and time at which they were accepted for carriage. The value of the goods should be fixed according to the commodity exchange price or, if there is no such price, according to the current market price or, if there is no current market price either, by reference to the normal value of goods of the same kind and quality. In practice this value of the goods is to be linked to the weight of the goods. A compensation of €11 per kilo of goods lost or damaged is reasonable in most cases. If valuable goods e.g. computer chips or expensive LCD television sets were carried, the level of compensation should be higher and the claimant has another reason to make use of Art. 29 CMR. Art. 29 CMR states that the carrier does not have the right to exclude or limit its liability or shift the burden of proof, if the damage was caused by its own wilful misconduct or acts that according to the court of law in question would be seen as wilful misconduct. The same provision applies if the wilful misconduct or default is committed by the agents or servants of the carrier or by any other persons whose services it makes use of for the performance of the carriage, when such agents, servants or other persons are acting within the scope of their employment.

Application to containers
The CMR applies to carriage by road in 'vehicles'. 'Vehicles' include motor vehicles, articulated vehicles, trailers and semi-trailers, but not containers. A container constitutes 'goods' and not a vehicle, and the CMR will not always apply to the movement of containers. If the container remains 'on wheels' throughout the transit, the CMR will apply, but if it is lifted off, e.g. at a port or rail terminal and carried separately by rail or sea, it no longer

comes within the scope of the CMR. It should be noted, however, that even where there is no legal requirement to apply the CMR parties to a contract can agree to apply its terms as is done by some operators.

8.1.5 Jurisdiction in CMR and under Brussels I Regulation

Art. 31 CMR sets out the rules on jurisdiction of courts of law and enforcement of verdicts, should a legal dispute arise from a contract of carriage under the CMR. Under the CMR the plaintiff has several choices of court of law:
- the court of law parties have agreed on in the contract of carriage, or
- the court of law of the place where the defendant has his place of residence, or
- the court of law of the place where the goods were passed to the carrier, or
- the court of law of the place where the goods were to be delivered.

Even though there are several options, the parties can address only one court of law at a time. When a court of law has given its verdict, which then becomes enforceable under the national law of that country, the verdict is enforceable in all Contracting states of the CMR.
If a signatory to the CMR is also from a Member State of the EU, the use of Brussels I in stead of the CMR becomes an issue. However, in matters of jurisdiction, the ECJ ruled that the rules of the CMR on jurisdiction must be applied instead of Brussels I.

8.1.6 CMR and applicable law according to Rome I

8

In a situation where a contract of carriage meets the requirements of Art. 1 CMR, the CMR sets out the rules for settling the dispute which has arisen between the sender, the carrier and/or the consignee. If the CMR does not provide parties with a solution, the law applicable to the contract of carriage according to Rome I has to be established. The sender and carrier have the opportunity to choose a law applicable to the contract according to Art. 3 Rome I, preferably making their choice in writing. If the CMR does not provide parties with a solution and no choice of law is made under Art. 3 Rome I, the parties then have to resort to Art. 4 Rome I. Art. 5 Rome I determines the law applicable to a contract for the carriage of goods. This contract is governed by the law of country in which, at the moment the contract is concluded, the carrier has its principle place of business. But this is only the case when:
- the place of loading of the goods, or
- the place of discharge of the goods, or
- the place where the sender is situated,

is the same country as the one in which the carrier is established.

8.1.7 Carriage of goods by sea: the Hague Visby Rules (HVR)

There are numerous rules concerning the carriage of goods by sea, as nearly all countries export by sea. The following paragraphs emphasise the fact that the Hague Visby Rules are the best internationally accepted set of rules regarding the carriage of goods by sea.

Hague Visby Rules

The Hague Visby Rules were adopted in 1968 and have been adapted several times over the years to broaden their application and to provide rules that govern all contracts of carriage as well as bills of lading. These rules apply when referred to in contracts of carriage as well as in national legislation.

8.1.8 Application of the Hague Visby Rules (HVR)

Under Article X HVR, the provisions of the HVR apply to every bill of lading relating to the carriage of goods between ports in two different States if:

a the bill of lading is issued in a contracting State, or
b the carriage is from a port in a contracting State, or
c the contract contained in or evidenced by the bill of lading provides that these Rules, or legislation of any State giving effect to them, are to govern the contract of carriage.

The nationality of the ship, the carrier, the shipper, the consignee, or any other party involved is irrelevant.

A bill of lading is not necessarily a contract of carriage, but is usually the best evidence of such a contract. A contract comprises information included in advertising material, the booking note and the freight tariff. On occasions, it will also include certain practices of the carrier known to, and accepted by, the shipper.

Note that the HVR do not apply to:

a contracts of carriage of live animals;
b contracts of carriage of deck cargo which is carried on deck and 'is stated as being carried on deck' in the bill of lading;
c transportation by a charter party, unless a bill of lading is issued and this b/l 'regulates the relations between a carrier and holder of the same'.

8.1.9 Definitions of carrier, contract of carriage, goods, ship, carriage of goods

Carrier
Contract of carriage
Goods
Ship

Article I of HVR defines the *carrier* as the owner or the charterer who enters into a contract of carriage with a shipper. The term *contract of carriage* applies only to contracts of carriage, which are covered by a bill of lading or any similar document of title, in so far as such a document relates to the carriage of goods by sea. The term *goods* includes goods, wares, merchandise, and articles of every kind whatsoever except live animals and cargo which under the contract of carriage is stated as being carried on deck and is so carried. The term *ship* is used to include any vessel used for the carriage of goods by sea. *Carriage of goods* applies between the time when goods are loaded onto the ship until the time they are discharged from it.

8.1.10 Obligations of a carrier under the Hague Visby Rules (HVR)

Article II of the HVR states that under a contract of carriage of goods by sea, the carrier is responsible for the loading, handling, stowage, carriage, custody, care and discharge of the goods.

Article III of the HVR states the obligation of the carrier before and at the beginning of the voyage to exercise the so-called due diligence to make the ship seaworthy and to properly man, equip and supply the ship. This means that the carrier has to make the holds, refrigerating and cool chambers, and all other parts of the ship in which goods are carried, fit and safe for the reception, carriage and preservation of the goods. The carrier shall properly and carefully load, handle, stow, carry, keep, care for, and discharge the goods carried on board the ship.

8.1.11 Content of a bill of lading

Bill of lading

After receiving the goods into his charge, the carrier (or the master or agent of the carrier) shall on demand issue to the shipper a bill of lading. This bill of lading shows:

- that the leading marks necessary for identification of the goods are supplied in writing by the shipper before the loading of such goods starts;
- the number of packages or pieces, or the quantity, or weight, as the case may be, as supplied in writing by the shipper;
- the appearance and condition of the goods.

The carrier is responsible for giving correct information in the bill of lading to the shipper (Article III, paragraph 3 HVR).

The shipper guarantees to the carrier the accuracy, at the time of shipment, of the marks, the number, quantity and weight of the cargo, as indicated in the bill of lading. The shipper shall compensate the carrier for all loss, damages and expenses arising or resulting from inaccuracies in the bill of lading. The right of the carrier to such compensation shall in no way limit his responsibility and liability under the contract of carriage to any person other than the shipper.

8.1.12 Delivery of goods by the carrier

Delivery

The carrier has to carry the goods to their port of destination, that is, where the delivery of the goods has to be made. Delivery includes the removal of the goods from the ship (Article III HVR).
The carrier may be held liable for loss of, or damage to, the goods. First, though, a notice of loss or damage to the goods must be given in writing to the carrier (or his agent) at the port of destination of the goods.
This notice must be given before or at the time of the removal of the goods into the custody of the person entitled to receive them under the contract of carriage. If the loss of, or damage to, the goods is not obvious at the moment of their removal, this notice may also be given within 3 days after the removal i.e. the delivery of the goods. A notice in writing need not be given if the goods have, at the time of their receipt, been the subject of survey or inspection by the carrier and the party taking over the goods.

Liability

The carrier and the ship shall in any event be discharged from all liability whatsoever in respect of the goods, unless a lawsuit (as a result of the above notice being given to the carrier) is brought within 1 year of their delivery or of the date when they should have been delivered.

Where the HVR apply, any agreement in a contract of carriage relieving the carrier or the ship from liability for loss or damage to goods otherwise than as provided in the HVR, shall be null and void (Article III, paragraph 8 HVR).

EXAMPLE 8.3

Brasi Yacht Spa of Genoa (Italy) sells a yacht to Mr. Wang of Hong Kong. The yacht was sold under free on board 'water to water' and arrangements were made for it to be shipped from Genoa to Hong Kong on board of another vessel. During loading operations in Genoa, the yacht was hoisted up on bands, but one of the bands broke before the yacht could be lowered. The yacht fell onto the vessel and consequently suffered serious damage.
Mr. Wang issued proceedings against all parties involved, summoning before the Tribunal of Genoa not only the carrier, but also the freight forwarder, the terminal and the companies, which the terminal employed to handle loading operations.
The tribunal in Genoa found the carrier liable for the damage that had occurred on board, as the yacht had passed the ship's rail when the damage occurred and thus had been delivered to the carrier. Further, the tribunal held that the terminal was liable to compensate the carrier. The court said the Hague Visby Rules apply, as the shipment was intended to be an international carriage of goods between ports in two different states (Article X HVR). The court also stated that the mere fact that the bill of lading had still not been issued was irrelevant with regard to the application of the Hague-Visby rules. The court affirmed that in this respect, it was sufficient that it had been agreed that a bill of lading would be issued on completion of the loading of Mr Wang's yacht. The court further stated that the issuance of a bill of lading was common practice in this particular line of business.

8.1.13 Liability for loss of and damage to goods

In Article IV of the HVR, several situations are mentioned in which neither the carrier nor the ship is responsible for loss of or damage to goods.

Neither the carrier nor the ship shall be liable for loss of, or damage to, goods arising or resulting from unseaworthiness of the ship, unless the unseaworthiness is caused by a lack of due diligence on the part of the carrier to make the ship seaworthy. The same applies when the unseaworthiness is a result of the failure of the carrier to ensure that the ship is properly manned, equipped and supplied, and to make the holds and all other parts of the ship in which goods are carried fit and safe for their reception, carriage and preservation (Article IV, paragraph 1 HVR).

Unseaworthiness

Neither the carrier nor the ship shall be responsible for loss of or damage to, goods as a result of an act or neglect by the carrier in the navigation or in the management of the ship.
In addition, neither the carrier nor the ship is responsible for loss or damage e.g. resulting from danger and accidents at the sea. Insufficient packing of the goods as well as insufficient or inadequate labelling are not the responsibility of the carrier or of the ship (Article IV, paragraph 2 HVR).

Any deviation from the route by the vessel in order to attempt to save life or property at sea shall not be an infringement or breach of these Rules or of the contract of carriage. The carrier shall not be liable for any loss or damage resulting therefrom (Article IV, paragraph 4 HVR).

EXAMPLE 8.4

The Endeavour Ultimate IV is a ship that completed loading a full cargo of diesel oil. Endeavour Inc., a carrier from the United Kingdom, signed and issued the original bill of lading to the shippers, Firezone Oil B.V. of The Netherlands. The carrier ordered an employee, i.e. an experienced seaman, to perform routine checks on the two tanks of the ship. As part of the standard procedure before the ship's departure, the seaman was required to secure both tanks. He secured the lid of the first tank, but in the case of the second he only put the lid in place rather than screwing it on properly. When the vessel reached the open sea, it encountered heavy and on-coming waves. A check of the tanks showed that the air vent to the first was damaged with the result that seawater had entered both tanks.

8

As a result of these events the shipper, Firezone Oil B.V., as holder of the bill of lading, sued Endeavour Inc., claiming compensation up to the value of the damaged cargo.

Endeavour Inc. has the option of stating that the ship was unseaworthy, and it is therefore not liable for the damage to the cargo. The carrier may also use in his defence the requirement that he man the ship with a competent crew. Furthermore, Endeavour Inc. provided the crew with a sufficiently detailed list of procedures, so that neglecting to secure the tanks could be regarded as negligence by the seaman to carry out his duties properly. The carrier can also use the argument of peril on the sea, as no one was allowed to go on deck during rough weather. As a result, the crew could not perform the regular rounds to check the deck equipment and fittings.
Another argument available is that the damage to the air intake was a defect in the tank not discoverable by due diligence. The carrier may also use the exemption of an Act of God in his argument, since remedying the problem cannot take place under such circumstances. As a result, the carrier can claim that he is not liable for the damage to the cargo.

8.1.14 Limitation of liability for loss of or damage to goods

The Hague Visby Rules provide the carrier with several options to limit his liability for loss of or damage to goods.

In addition, the HVR provide several ways of calculating the compensation to be paid by the carrier. These options are mentioned in Article IV, paragraph 5 and 6 HVR.
E.g. the value of the goods shall be fixed according to the commodity exchange price, or, if there be no such price, according to the current market price, or, if there be no commodity exchange price or current market price, by reference to the normal value of goods of the same kind and quality. Any limitation of liability in a contract of carriage governed by the HVR, is null and void if it conflicts with the HVR.

Where a container, pallet or similar article of transport is used to consolidate goods during shipping, the number of packages or units

enumerated in the bill of lading, as packed in, or on, such an article of transport, shall be presumed to be the number of packages or units where liability for damages is concerned, to the extent that those packages or units were damaged during shipment. Also here, the purpose of the bill of lading is obvious, as it states the condition of the goods sent by the shipper.
However under Article V HVR, the carrier has the option of agreeing to (?) and accepting more liability and responsibility than that imposed on him by the HVR.

EXAMPLE 8.5

Timbereast Forest Ltd. were the shippers and consignees of 1.000 packages of lumber, to be carried from Vancouver (Canada) to Antwerp (Belgium). The cargo was comprised of two consignments destined for two different consignees and covered by two separate bills of lading. The carrier, Gearbulk Ltd. of Canada, had the right to stow the entire cargo on deck. However, because there was space available, some of the cargo was stowed below deck. The carrier made no effort to specify which packages were loaded either on or below deck. It only kept track of the amount of lumber loaded in each location. In total, 75% of the entire shipment was loaded on deck and 25% below deck. Bills of lading were issued containing a statement that the cargo was stowed 75% on deck and 25% below deck.

The deck cargo was damaged at the port of destination. Gearbulk Ltd. sought to avoid liability by invoking a clause in the bills of lading, which excluded liability for damage to deck cargo.

Timbereast held that the contracts of carriage were not governed by the HVR, because the cargo was carried on deck. It also held that the clause excluding liability for damage to deck cargo was null and void. Timbereast also argued that the 75%–25% description of the stowage in the bill of lading was neither a sufficient description of the deck cargo, nor accurate in respect of the bills of lading.

The court agreed that the 75%–25% description of the stowage in the bill of lading was insufficient to indicate which consignment belonged to what consignee. The court also stated that as a result of that, and because the specific packages carried on deck were not identified, it was impossible to determine the values of the cargo on deck. The court held that the carriage was governed by the HVR, as it was not clear exactly which cargo was carried on deck. And because the HVR were deemed to apply, the court held that the clause excluding liability for deck cargo was inapplicable and therefore held the carrier liable for the damage to the cargo, suffered by the shipper.

8

8.2 Incoterms

The International Chamber of Commerce (hereafter referred to as ICC) in Paris has established general terms of delivery for use in international sales contracts, whose terms have become well accepted guidelines throughout the world. The terms – represented by abbreviations of 3 letters – describe in detail the conditions of delivery, the passing of risk from seller to buyer, customs affairs and the splitting of costs. Incoterms (INternational COmmercial TERMS) therefore apply to contracts of sale, not

Incoterms

to contracts of carriage. The ICC over the years has issued several versions of the Incoterms. For that reason, it is wise to check which version a contracting party is referring to. The ICC is not a legislative institution: parties are free to use or ignore the Incoterms, the use of which is neither a legal requirement nor in any way a form of legislation.
Incoterms do not concern themselves with inherently important issues such as the transfer of the ownership of goods, the carrying out of obligations according to a contract of sale and liability resulting from a breach of contract. Using Incoterms can prevent unnecessary claims and costs and therefore prevent legal problems from arising between seller and buyer.
Schedule 8.1 displays the relationship between the contract of sale, Incoterms and the contract of carriage.

SCHEDULE 8.1 Relationship between contract of sale, Incoterms and contract of carriage

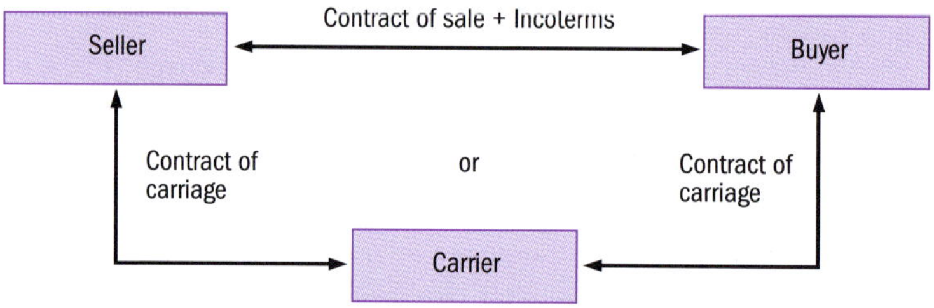

8

8.2.1 Objects of Incoterms

Incoterms deal with the passing of the risk attached to the goods from seller to buyer. Incoterms do not apply to the provision of services or immaterial goods such as computer software. Incoterms can be used when the parties are in different countries, but also when they are domiciled in the same country. In particular, Incoterms deal with:

- the place and time of delivery and the place where, and the moment when, the risk attached to the goods passes from seller to buyer;
- the payment of costs relating to transport, such as those concerning freight, packaging, customs, inspections etcetera;
- determining which of the parties is responsible for customs formalities;
- determining which of the parties deals with the shipping documents.

Incoterms are not concerned with the precise moment the ownership of goods is transferred from seller to buyer. This question is dealt with by the law applicable to the contract of sale based on Rome I. Incoterms do not apply to the contract of carriage between the sender and the carrier or any of the go-betweens involved in that contract.

8.2.2 General set up of Incoterms

The latest version of the Incoterms was issued in the year 2010 and lists 11 Incoterms which are all three-letter abbreviations based on an English phrase. An Incoterm is only applicable when the contracting parties refer to it in their contract of sale. Incoterms divide the responsibility for transport

between seller and buyer. Exactly where this responsibility lies depends on the Incoterm used.
In general Incoterms are divided into four groups.

1 E-group: where do the goods leave the seller
1 EXW: Ex Works (…named place)
Explanation: the seller offers the goods to the buyer at the place they have agreed on which in most cases will be the seller's place of business.

2 F-group: main transport paid for by the buyer
2 FCA: Free Carrier (…named place)
3 FAS: Free Alongside Ship (…named port of shipment)
4 FOB: Free on Board (…named port of shipment)
Explanation: the seller has to hand over the goods to a carrier appointed by the buyer.

3 C-group: main transport not paid for by the buyer
5 CFR: Cost and Freight (…named port of destination)
6 CIF: Cost, Insurance and Freight (…named port of destination)
7 CPT: Carriage Paid (…named place of destination)
8 CIP: Carriage and Insurance Paid to (…named place of destination)
Explanation: the seller draws up a contract of carriage; however, he is not responsible for any loss of or damage to the goods or for extra expenses incurred during the handling or the carriage of the goods.

4 D-group: place of arrival
9 DAT: Delivered at Terminal (… named terminal at port or place of destination)
10 DAP: Delivered at Place (… named place of destination)
11 DDP: Delivered Duty Paid (…named place of destination)
Explanation: the seller pays all costs and bears all risks involved in the carriage of the goods to their place of delivery.

8.2.3 Incoterms 2010

1 EXW (ex works)
The place of delivery of the goods is the seller's place of business. In other words, the seller has to put the goods at the disposal of the buyer at his own business premises. The buyer has to deal with the handling of the goods. Up to this point in time, the seller is responsible for the goods. Where EXW applies, the buyer is obliged to pay the costs of carriage of the goods.

2 FCA (Free Carrier)
The seller has to hand over the goods to a carrier appointed by the buyer. If this takes place at the seller's place of business, the seller is responsible for the loading of the goods. Up to this point in time, the seller is liable for any loss of or damage to the goods and also for all costs relating to the loading of the goods.

3 FAS (Free Alongside Ship)
The seller delivers the goods to the harbour alongside the ship the parties have agreed on; from that moment on the contract of carriage is the

responsibility of the buyer and he is liable for any loss of or damage to the goods. The costs involved in delivering the goods to the ship are borne by the seller.

4 FOB (Free on Board)
The seller has to deliver the goods on board the ship designated by the buyer and agreed on by the parties. Once the goods are within the railings of the ship the seller is no longer responsible for them; at this point the buyer assumes liability for any loss of or damage to the goods. Up to the point the goods are inside the railings, the seller is responsible for the costs of transport. This Incoterm is only used when the means of transport is a ship.

5 CFR (Cost and Freight)
The seller concludes a contract of carriage at his own expense. The seller has to deliver the goods on board the ship designated by the buyer and agreed on by the parties. Once the goods are within the railings of the ship the seller is no longer responsible for them; at this point the buyer assumes liability for any loss of or damage to the goods. Up to the point the goods are inside the railings, the seller is responsible for the costs of transport. This Incoterm is only used when the means of transport is a ship.

6 CIF (Cost, Insurance and Freight)
The seller concludes a contract of carriage and an insurance contract at his own expense. The insurance contract should provide minimal coverage. The seller delivers the goods on board the ship both parties agreed on. At this moment, responsibility for the goods also passes from seller to buyer. Once the goods are within the railings of the ship the seller bears no further risk concerning them and instead the buyer is liable for any loss of or damage to them. The seller has to pay for all transport up to the moment the goods are inside the ship's railings.

7 CPT (Carriage Paid To)
The seller delivers duty free to the place of delivery agreed on by the parties. The seller is responsible for drawing up a contract of carriage. The delivery is deemed to take place at the moment the goods are handed to the carrier, at which point the risk concerning the goods involved passes from seller to buyer If there is more than one carrier involved, the seller has to hand over the goods to the first carrier. The seller pays all costs up to the moment the goods are actually placed at the disposal of the buyer. CPT can be used for all means of carriage, whereas CFR can only be used when carriage is by ship.

8 CIP (Carriage and Insurance Paid to)
The seller concludes a contract of carriage and an insurance contract at his own expense, valid up to the moment the goods reach their destination i.e. the place of delivery the parties have agreed on. Delivery and the passing of risk for the goods from seller to buyer are effected the moment the goods are handed over to the carrier. CIP is similar to CIF, but CIP does not apply when carriage is by ship.

9 DAT (Delivered at Terminal)
The group of 'D' Incoterms comprises those terms, which relate to the place of arrival of the goods. When DAT applies, the seller delivers when

the goods, once unloaded from the arriving means of transport, are placed at the buyer's disposal at a named terminal at the named port or place of destination. "Terminal" includes any place, such as a quay, warehouse, container yard or road, rail or air cargo terminal.
The seller bears all risks involved in bringing the goods to and unloading them at the terminal at the named port or place of destination.

10 DAP (Delivered at Place)
When DAP applies, the seller delivers when the goods are placed at the buyer's disposal on the arriving means of transport ready for unloading at the named place of destination.
The seller bears all risks involved in bringing the goods to the named place.

11 DDP (Delivered Duty Paid)
When DDP applies, the seller delivers the goods – cleared for import – to the buyer at specified destination.
The seller bears all costs and risks of moving the goods to destination, including the payment of customs duties and taxes.

8.2.4 Liability of the seller and buyer in case of damage during carriage

When it comes to the carriage of goods, there is always a risk they will be stolen or damaged. The seller's liability to pay for this can be obviated by choosing the right Incoterm.
By using Incoterms such as EXW, FCA, FAS, FOB, CFR and CPT, any liability during the carriage of goods lies with the buyer. The seller is not obliged to pay for insurance. If there is an insurance contract and the insurance policy contains the provision 'warehouse to warehouse', the carriage of the goods from the place of business of the seller to the place of delivery of the buyer is covered.
If CIF or CIP applies, the seller is obliged to insure himself against the risks associated with the carriage of goods. There is no such obligation if any one of DAT, DAP and DDP applies. In such cases damage to or loss of the goods is at the seller's expense and for that reason insurance is recommended.

8.3 International payments

Payments

Like customs, the way international payments are made varies from country to country. It is wise to use a method of payment which is the most suitable for the country one is dealing with. The decision about suitability is determined by several factors: the market, the amount of money to be paid, the country, the level of understanding and trust between the two parties, the commercial practices associated with a particular line of business, the various restrictions and regulations of the country where the payment has to be made, and the costs involved in selling the goods.
Depending on the level of security the seller or buyer desires, parties can opt for a regular wiring of the money, payment by cheque, or a Letter of Credit (L/C).

There are several methods of payment:
a payment into an open account (paragraph 8.3.1);
b cheque (paragraph 8.3.2);

c draft (paragraph 8.3.3);
d guarantee of payment issued by a bank (paragraph 8.3.4);
e Documentary Collections (paragraph 8.3.5);
f Letter of credit (L/C) (paragraph 8.3.6).

The Letter of Credit (L/C) is the safest method of payment when making an international payment.

8.3.1 Payments in open account or clean payments

Payment into open account is an order given by the buyer to his bank to make a payment to the seller. Payment into an open account is the most basic method of obtaining payment for an export and is used in the majority of export transactions. Goods are despatched in the normal fashion and the export documentation is despatched directly to the buyer.
As there is no third party involvement, this method is relatively cheap and can be quick. As a relationship builds, the buyer may be willing to settle prior to receipt of the goods.
The disadvantage of payments in open account is that the seller loses control over the goods and documentation and is totally reliant on the buyer making payment as agreed. In the event of non-payment the seller may find that he has to mount a costly legal action, in the buyer's country, to obtain his funds or the return of the goods. Payment in open account would, therefore, be recommended for transactions with an established and trusted buyer or for exports of low value where more costly methods of payment are unfeasible.
SWIFT (Society for Worldwide Interbank Financial Telecommunication) is the network for international information on payments issued between banks. This means that local banks, by means of this network, keep in contact with all important banks in the world, in such a way that payments are carried out 'swiftly', efficiently and with a maximum level of safety. Since 1 July 2003 in most countries every bank account is internationally standardised according to the so called IBAN (International Bank Account Number) and BIC (Bank Identification Code = Swift address) of the bank.

8.3.2 Cheque

A *cheque* is a document by which the recipient or the person designated in it is able to draw money from the account of the person who sent it. The type of cheque most often used is the bank cheque. A bank cheque is a written instruction, with no conditions attached, from the person issuing the cheque to the bank to transfer the payment mentioned in it to the recipient. This type of cheque is a common method of payment in countries such as France, the United States and the United Kingdom.

8.3.3 Bills of Exchange (Drafts)

The Bill of Exchange, commonly referred to as a draft or a bill, is an order in writing, with no conditions attached, signed and addressed by the drawer (usually the exporter) to the drawee (usually the confirming bank or the issuing bank used by the buyer), requiring the drawee to pay the drawer a certain sum of money immediately on receipt or at a fixed or determinable future time.

The drawer, usually the seller or exporter, is the party who issues the draft and to whom, as payee, the payment is made. The payee could be another party other than the exporter, or could be the bona fide holder (the bearer) of the draft. The drawee is the party who owes the money or agrees to make the payment and to whom the draft is addressed. The drawee is the buyer or importer and the payer of the draft in a documentary collection. In a letter of credit the drawee is most often the confirming bank or the issuing bank, which is the payer of the draft. The remitting bank is the exporter's bank to whom the exporter sends the draft, the documents and documentary collection instructions, and who subsequently relays them to the collecting bank in a documentary collection.

The term remitting bank as used in a letter of credit may refer to a nominated bank from whom the issuing bank or the confirming bank, if any, receives the shipping documents. The collecting bank (presenting bank) is the bank in the importer's country (the importer's bank usually) involved in processing the collection, which presents the draft to the importer for payment or acceptance, and thereafter releases the documents to the importer in accordance with the instructions of the exporter.
Drafts are a very popular and common method of payment. Drafts represent security for the exporter as the draft documents are drawn up by banks. The draft is widely used in international trade, most frequently as payment against a letter of credit (L/C). It is also used in the open account without any L/C involved.

Drafts can be:
- arranged within the legal systems of most countries;
- transferred to another person;
- avalised by a third party;
- used in case performances under the contract of sale are payable 'after sight' or 'after date'; in the case of 'after date' the bill of exchange is used as an instrument to finance the payment;
- protested.

The sight draft is most commonly used in international trade. In a sight draft, the payment is on demand or on presentation of the negotiation documents to the paying bank or the importer. In practice, the bank may pay within three working days (not necessarily instantly) of receipt and after examination of the negotiation documents and only if they are in order (i.e. as long as the documents comply exactly with the letter of credit (L/C) stipulations).

Sight drafts consist of two types:
- D/P-documents against payment; D/P-drafts are sent by the exporter to the bank which then hands over the documents involved to the importer (buyer) after the bills of exchange have been paid.
- D/A-documents against acceptance; D/A-drafts require the bank to hand over the documents involved to the importer (buyer) after the importer has accepted the bill of exchange and has agreed to make payment within the period of time fixed by the parties.

The term draft (or usance draft) is used in a deferred payment arrangement. Payment is due on a future date determinable in accordance with the stipulations of the letter of credit (L/C). In a term draft the exporter extends credit to the importer.

The future payment date can be at a stated period after sight or after date:
- After sight; the after sight draft is presented to the drawee for acceptance, for example, 'at 90 days sight' and 'at 120 days after sight'.
- After date; the after date draft, for example, 'at 120 days B/L date' (i.e., the future payment date is 120 days after the date of the bill of lading) and 'at 180 days after date' (i.e., the future payment date is 180 days after the date of the draft).

Unless the future payment date is tied to a specific date, the importer may refuse to accept the draft until the goods have arrived; such deferred acceptance can extend the future payment date.

8.3.4 Bank Guarantee

This guarantee ensures that the bank issuing the guarantee will pay a fixed amount of money to a beneficiary, as long as the latter states in writing that his counterpart (who asked the bank to issue the guarantee) has fulfilled his contractual obligations.

8.3.5 Documentary Collections

Every export transaction is accompanied by documents: he who possesses these documents has possession of the goods. After the goods have been shipped the transport documents are presented to either the exporter's own bank or directly to the buyer's bank, along with signed instructions as to the circumstances under which the documents are to be released and payment made.
The collecting bank holds the documents until the exporter's (or more usually, the remitting bank's) instructions have been met and then proceeds to effect payment. Schedule 8.2 points out how documentary collections are effected.
Payment against documents is a method of payment regulated by the International Chamber of Commerce, details of which are published in its Uniform Rules for Collections URC 522.

In the Uniform Rules for Collections URC 522 there are two forms of documentary collections:
1 Documents against Acceptance (D/A);
2 Documents against Payment (Cash against Documents).

Documents against Acceptance (D/A)
In this case documents are only released to the importer, by the collecting bank, against the importer's (drawee) acceptance of a Bill of Exchange for payment at a future date. The advantage of this to the importer is that he does not have to pay for goods until the 'due date'. The exporter, meanwhile, could, should it so wish, have the accepted Bill of Exchange discounted.
The disadvantage to the exporter is that the acceptance of the Bill of Exchange does not ensure payment at a future date. It is only as good as the company that accepted the Bill of Exchange. Reassurance can be obtained by having the Bill of Exchange avalised by the importer's bank.

Documents against Payment (D/P)
Document against Payment is exactly what it says: payment is made in return for the documents. This term is used in both open account

transactions and documentary collections. The advantage to the exporter is that he can receive payment immediately the documents arrive in the importer's country. Nevertheless, it is usual for payment to be made after the arrival of the goods. There is, however, no guarantee of payment but use of a Sight Bill of Exchange does give the option of having the transaction i.e. delivery of the goods protested for non-payment.

SCHEDULE 8.2 Documentary Collections

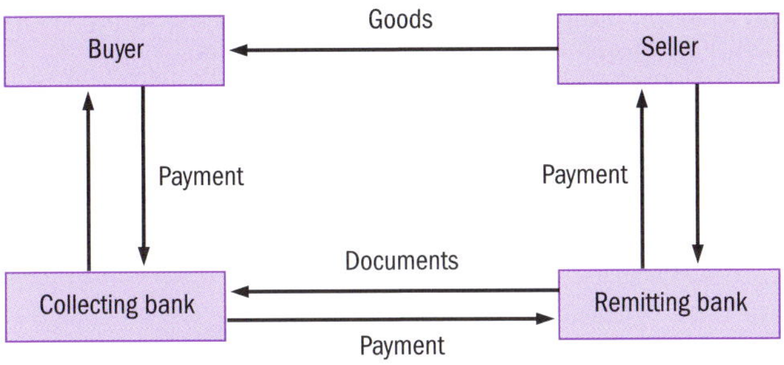

8.3.6 Letter of Credit

Letter of Credit (L/C)

A *Letter of Credit* (L/C) is an agreement between a bank and its client, in which the bank is obliged to pay an amount of money from the account of that client to a third party, provided that the beneficiary (the exporter) proves that it has fulfilled its contractual obligation to make the delivery. In short, this amounts to making the documents required by the L/C speedily available. In general, the issuing bank uses a bank in the exporter's country (the advising bank) to inform the exporter that a L/C has been opened on its behalf. The letter of credit (L/C) is suitable for undertakings that want to limit the financial risks of doing business internationally and maximise the security of international payments. Exporters are assured they will receive full payment rapidly; importers are assured they will receive all relevant documents as agreed on in the contract of sale.

By means of a letter of credit (L/C), the buyer of the goods or services lodges an amount of money with his bank or the bank of the seller. The seller can only collect the money once it hands over those documents required by the L/C and has fulfilled the other obligations imposed on it by the L/C.

Where a L/C applies, the transfer of goods is detached from the transfer of documents. All parties involved in a L/C merely exchange documents (that represent goods or services) and do not exchange goods. The banks involved will thus make payments as long as the correct documents are handed over, even if the importer informs them that the goods delivered are not of the quality required by the contract. Schedule 8.3 illustrates how a L/C works.

The L/C is regulated by the Uniform Customs and Practice for Documentary Credits of the International Chamber of Commerce (ICC). The Uniform Customs and Practice for Documentary Credits are international regulations by which the parties involved (banks and their clients) in a L/C must abide, so that confusion over the terms used in the L/C and differences in interpretation can be avoided. Most banks in the world work according to these rules. For that reason, it is agreed that the application of the Uniform Customs and Practice for Documentary Credits in Letters of Credit should be mandatory.

Parties involved in a L/C
In most cases, four parties are involved in a L/C. The applicant (buyer, importer) is the party that instructs its bank to open a L/C. The issuing bank (opening bank) is the bank that opens the credit and sends it to the advising bank. The advising bank (the notifying bank) is the bank that receives the Letter of Credit from the issuing bank and hands it to the beneficiary under the conditions laid down in the L/C. The beneficiary (seller, exporter) is the party that hands over the required documents and as a result of that receives payment.

SCHEDULE 8.3 Opening a letter of credit

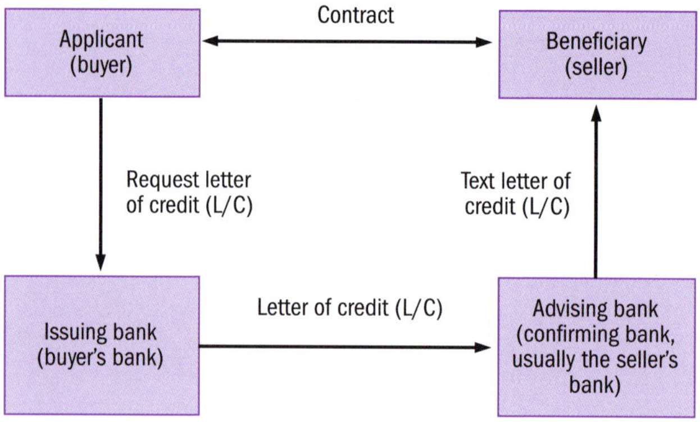

8

I The applicant (the importer)
The applicant is the party who requests and instructs the issuing bank to open a letter of credit (L/C) in favour of the beneficiary. The applicant is usually the importer or the buyer of goods and/or services.

II The issuing bank (the importer's bank)
The L/C contains *inter alia* a list of the documents the importer would like to receive, a description of the goods to be delivered and details of the final date for delivery. The L/C is a document on its own, to be seen as distinct from the contract of sale, and for that reason the issuing bank will want to make certain that the information laid down in the L/C is correct. The importer, therefore, in requesting to open a L/C, has to give detailed information about the goods and the date of delivery. It is preferable that, the importer attaches to his request to open a L/C a copy (of part) of the contract of sale and a copy of the confirmation of the sale of the goods.

III The advising bank (the exporter's bank)
Having received the L/C, the advising bank will advise the exporter of its receipt. In most cases the advising bank is the exporter's usual banker.

However, the issuing bank can also ask a different bank to act as the advising bank e.g. a subsidiary of their own bank in the exporter's country. After receiving the L/C, the advising bank will check the authenticity of the L/C e.g. by means of a signature. The advising bank will also do a quick check for any irregularities in the L/C. Having done this, the advising bank sends a copy of the L/C to the exporter as quickly as possible. The issuing bank will request the advising bank to attach to the L/C its confirmation that the documentation is in order.

IV The beneficiary (the exporter)
After receiving the L/C, the exporter has to check the text of the L/C and compare it with the contract of sale. If it discovers discrepancies between the two, it is required to contact the importer immediately so that they may be amended.
After the exporter agrees to the terms of the L/C, it is required to send the shipment and make delivery of the goods. Subsequently, the exporter makes its documents available to the advising bank in order to receive payment or confirmation that payment will be made.

A short overview of all parties is displayed in Table 8.3.

TABLE 8.3 Parties involved in a Letter of Credit (L/C)

The applicant (the importer, the buyer)	Requests and orders a letter of credit (L/C)
The beneficiary (the exporter, the seller)	Beneficiary of the letter of credit (L/C)
The issuing bank	Opens the letter of credit (L/C) by sending it to a bank in the exporter's country
The advising bank	Advises (i.e. gives word to the exporter of the opening of a documentary credit) and confirms (i.e. establishes the L/C is in order) the documentary credit

Confirmation of the L/C
Through the L/C, the issuing bank has legal ties to both the buyer (the importer) and the seller (exporter). The issuing bank has an irrevocable obligation to pay the seller. For complete assurance regarding the receipt of payment, the seller has the option of having the L/C confirmed by the advising bank. The effect of this is that the advising bank also has an irrevocable obligation to pay the seller (the exporter). This means that the advising bank has to pay the seller, as long as the seller gives the required documents to the advising bank. This payment satisfies the contractual obligation to pay and thus terminates the proceedings. For the L/C to be confirmed, it must be completely in order: there should be no irregularities in the text, the issuing and advising banks should be clearly designated and the payment process must be clearly described and acceptable.

The usual procedure of the L/C
In practice the process involving a L/C requires 11 steps:
1 Seller and buyer conclude a contract of sale and agree that payment should be made by means of a L/C.

2 Buyer requests his bank to open a L/C; this bank will become the issuing bank.
3 The issuing bank opens the L/C and informs the seller's bank of this; this is the advising bank and also the designated bank in case documents have to be handed to that bank.
4 The advising bank advises the extension of credit to the seller and if necessary may also confirm the L/C.
5 The seller sends the goods according to the conditions stated in the L/C.
6 The seller hands the required documents to the advising bank i.e. the designated bank.
7 The advising bank checks the documents and pays the seller according to the terms of the L/C.
8 The advising bank sends the documents to the issuing bank.
9 If the seller is paid by the advising bank, the issuing bank will in turn have to make a payment to the advising bank i.e. the designated bank.
10 The issuing bank checks the documents once again and then internally withdraws the payment from the buyer's account.
11 The buyer, with the documents, is able to gain possession of the goods.

SCHEDULE 8.4 Issuing of a letter of credit

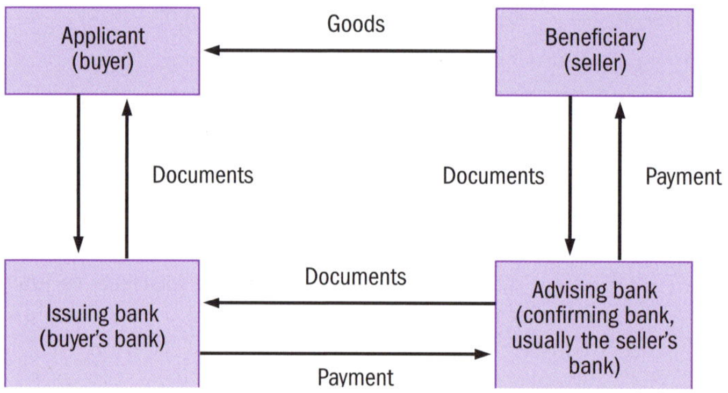

Payment
A payment to the seller may be made by the advising bank:
1 either as soon as the documents required under the L/C are handed to the bank, or
2 at a later date agreed on by the seller and buyer in which case the seller in effect extends extra credit to the buyer by allowing it an additional period of time to make payment.

8.4 Entry modes

Long before an international sale can be agreed, there lies the fundamental question of exactly how one makes inroads into a foreign market. A thorough analysis of potential competitors and possible customers in the potential new market is very important. This would include matters such as trade barriers, localised knowledge, price localisation and export subsidies.

Having decided what new market to enter, the next step is deciding how to proceed. It can be complicated. The company has to decide which of the possibilities would be the most profitable under the prevailing circumstances. It could focus on the export to the new market of goods which are fit for immediate sale. Or it could move actual production to the country where the new market has been identified. This section covers six possible strategies for entry into a new market.

8.4.1 Representative

When a company wants to export goods, there are various ways of making contact with foreign companies. Once a decision has been made, based on e.g. market research, on which markets to enter, the company's representatives can then make contact with future business partners e.g. at trade fairs or by direct mail sent to potential business partners. These future business partners could be e.g. wholesalers, distributors or retailers, depending on the aims of the producer and the product it wants to export. Before representatives can conclude an agreement with new business partners, they should be absolutely clear in advance about several aspects of the concomitant negotiations. As the company i.e. the employer of the representative will be legally bound by the contract, the representative should be fully aware of the scope of the rights and obligations of that future contract. A representative must be equally aware of the content of the terms of sale and delivery. If the company e.g. issues a written mandate or other authorization, it immediately becomes clear what the representative's options are when it comes to e.g. the range of products, prices, discounts, delivery, Incoterms, payment etc. A representative must focus on the opportunities these terms of sale and delivery afford and be aware of the dangers that lie in derogating from such terms of sale.
A contract concluded by a representative within the boundaries fixed by the company, is legally binding on that company. If a representative exceeds his authority to conclude a contract with a foreign business partner, only he is bound to the contract, not his employer. However, in a situation like that, it is possible for the company to confirm the contract thus made and in doing so get the representative off the hook. The objective of correct representation is that a contract becomes final between the producer i.e. the seller and the foreign buyer. All rights and obligations attached to this contract are to be effected between these two parties.

8

EXAMPLE 8.6

Heros B.V., a producer of metal fences and established in the Netherlands, takes part in the annual European Fair to Celebrate the Metal Fence, held in Brussels, Belgium. At the fair, Michielsen, an employee of Heros, encounters Michailov, an employee of Metalski Inc, a company established in Russia. Michailov is interested in buying 2.500 metres of the world famous Big Gate fence at a price of $150 per metre. A contract for the sale and delivery of the fence is concluded in writing at the fair. Heros's terms of sale and delivery are part of the deal. At $150 per metre, Michielsen has given Michailov a small discount, but all within the limits set out by his employer. The contract of sale and delivery is therefore concluded between Heros B.V. and Metalski Inc. and legally binding on both contracting parties.

8.4.2 Agents

In a way, an agent represents a company in much the same way as does a representative. However, there is a difference: an agent is an independent legal entity, either an undertaking or a person, and as such is independent of the producer of the goods. An agent is familiar with the line of business of the producer and acts on its behalf when it wishes to export goods. The producer concludes a contract with an agent in order to be represented in foreign markets; an agent can never be an employee of the producer.
An agent concludes a contract with another company at the expense and at the risk of his client i.e. the producer. The other company is in most cases established in the same country as the agent. The result is a contract between the producer and the other company, both of which could be in different countries. The agent receives payment for his services based on the contract he himself has drawn up with his client i.e. the producer. As a result of an EU Regulation, general rules on contracts with agents are enforced through the legislation of individual EU Member States. For this reason, there are standard rules on e.g. the right of the agent to information from the client, the termination of the contract with an agent, compensation for client and agent, the ways of paying an agent, the exclusivity of an agent, the law applicable to the contract, and the court of law that has jurisdiction in case of a dispute.

EXAMPLE 8.7

In order to attain a larger share of the German market, Beemster Kaas B.V. of The Netherlands concludes a contract with an agent, Mr. Froehlich from Hamburg (Germany). By this contract, Froehlich becomes the sole agent for Beemster Kaas for the whole of Germany. This exclusivity is granted to Froehlich on condition that he will attain an annual turnover of at least €500.000. In his first year, Froehlich achieves sales totalling €500.000, but nevertheless Beemster Kaas B.V. is dissatisfied with the results of its German agent. According to Art. 4 Rome I, their contract is governed by German law, as it is the agent who performs the contract's characteristic performance. German law offers him protection in case Beemster Kaas B.V. intends to nullify the contract contrary to the arrangement made.

8

8.4.3 Distributors

A distributor is a legal entity or person, who acts independently of the producer i.e. the company that exports goods, its representatives or its agents. A distributor concludes a contract of sale with a foreign company at its own risk and expense, with the objective of selling the goods thus imported. So, if a distributor sells the imported goods to a third party, there have to be two separate contracts. The first, a contract of distribution, is between the seller and the distributor; the second, a contract of sale, is between the distributor and the buyer. The contracts are binding only between the contracting parties. The distributor concludes two contracts: a contract of distribution and a contract of sale.
There are no uniform rules or EU Regulations on contracts of distribution. Thus, a contract of distribution is governed by whichever national law is applicable according to Rome I, and by the arrangements made by the

producer and the distributor in the contract itself. A contract of distribution should contain agreements about:
- the sales territory to be covered exclusively by the distributor,
- the investments to be made by the distributor on behalf of the producer of the goods,
- the producer's terms of sale and delivery,
- the trade marks owned by the producer,
- the duration of the contract (definite period, indefinite period, trail period),
- the targets i.e. the quantity of goods the producer should aim at selling,
- the termination of the contract,
- the law applicable to the contract, and
- the court of law that will have jurisdiction or the referral body for arbitration.

EXAMPLE 8.8

Schenk GmbH of Bielefeld (Germany) is the distributor in Germany of the famous Wildeman outdoor gear, produced by John Sheepskin B.V. of Arnhem (The Netherlands). In 2010 Sheepskin and Schenk made a contract of distribution for a period of 5 years, covering the whole area of Germany, Schenk being the sole distributor of the outdoor gear and responsible for all contracts with German sellers of that product. Schenk is to achieve an annual turnover of €450,000.-.
In his first year, Schenk achieves the required turnover, but after that the sales drop and he no longer reaches the required level of turnover. Also, German sellers of the Wildeman outdoor gear complain to Sheepskin about Schenk, because Schenk fails to deliver their orders. In their view, the quality of the outdoor gear also leaves room for improvement.
Sheepskin and Schenk need to deal with the problems relating to the conditions of the contract of distribution. Schenk is to fix problems with his German sellers arising out of their contracts of sale i.e. the delivery of ordered goods. If a problem related to outdoor goods sold to consumers should lead to a case of product liability, then the German consumers should contact Sheepskin. In all other instances, the German sellers should contact Schenk and German consumers should get in touch with their German seller.

8

8.4.4 Licensing

Any company wishing to enter a new market also has the option of permitting a company in the country of the new market to produce goods on its behalf. The company in the latter country will receive a license to produce and market the goods. The word license refers to that permission as well as to the document recording that permission. A licenser grants a license to another party ('licensee') as one element of an agreement between those (private) parties. This license is not the same license that may be requested by public authorities e.g. to allow an import of goods into that country. This license may also serve to keep the authorities informed of a type of activity, and to give them the opportunity to set conditions and limitations.

8.4.5 Franchising

Franchising is the practice of using another firm's successful business model. Goods are produced in the country of the exporting company and marketed in another country using the business model of the producer of the goods i.e. the franchiser. For the producer, a franchise is an alternative to building chain stores to distribute goods, thus avoiding the significant financial investment required in a chain and its associated liabilities. The franchisee can rely on the – successful – business model of the franchiser. The franchisee is said to have a greater incentive to make the business successful than a direct employee of the franchiser, because the franchisee has a direct stake in the business. The franchisee operates independently from the franchisor, though within the framework of the franchise agreement between them.

As there is no EU law on franchising, it is considered a distribution system to which national laws apply. As demonstrated below, franchising and distribution have a lot in common. Specific covenants and treaties cover trademarks and other intellectual property rights.

Franchising contracts cover such aspects as:
- the sales territory to be covered exclusively by the franchisee,
- the investment to be made by the franchisee on behalf of the franchiser,
- the franchiser 's terms of sale and delivery,
- trade marks owned by the franchiser franchisor,
- the duration of the contract (definite period, indefinite period, trail period),
- targets i.e. the quantity of goods the franchisee should aim at selling,
- the termination of the contract,
- the law applicable to the contract, and
- the court of law that will have jurisdiction or the referral body for arbitration.

8

8.4.6 Alliances

It is always open to any company wishing to export goods to another country to set up a new business there, either by itself or together with a company or private parties based in the country where the new market for its products has been identified. This new business will produce or distribute goods for the new market in this country.
There could be several reasons for setting up a new manufacturing business abroad, close to a potential new market, and they include lower costs of production, high costs of transport, expert knowledge available in that country or the wish to produce goods that meet the public's taste. Similarly, potential reasons for setting up a new distribution business abroad include lower costs of distribution, high costs of transport or the inability to find a suitable distributor close to the new market.

Any new business being set up abroad must abide by the law of that state, and if it should be set up in a Member State of the EU, it should honour the principle of free movement of persons, of workers and of establishment.

Summary

- When a contract for the sale of goods is being drawn up between two parties who are established in different countries, several issues need to be looked at.

- A contract of sale on behalf of the producer i.e. the seller of the goods can be concluded by the producer's representative or agent. If either a representative or an agent concludes a contract with a third party within the scope of his authorisation (the extent of which is usually described in the contract with the producer), the contract of sale is final.
A sales contract will thus exist between the producer and either a distributor or a third party i.e. a buyer such as a retailer or wholesaler.

- The CMR Convention governs the carriage of goods by road. The CMR describes the rights and obligations of the sender, the carrier, the shipper and the consignee.

- The Hague Visby Rules govern the carriage of goods by sea. The HVR describe the rights and obligations of the shipper, the carrier and the legal position of the ship.

- Incoterms set up by the ICC are rules governing both the transfer of risk from seller to buyer and the payment of goods.

- International payments can be made in several ways. The Letter of Credit (L/C) is one of the most secure and frequently used methods. With a L/C, the transfer of goods is detached from the payment of goods. Payment is made, as soon as the correct documents have been handed over, through the use of issuing and advising banks, representing the buyer and seller respectively. After that the goods are delivered.

Glossary

Carriage	A contract of carriage sets out the rules governing the (international) transport of goods from seller to buyer.
Carrier	The person or organisation which transports goods.
Consignee	The person receiving the goods, in most cases the buyer himself or, sometimes, a person acting on behalf of the buyer.
Incoterms	INternational COmmercial TERMS: general terms of delivery, used in international sales contracts, concerning the conditions applicable to delivery, the passing of risk from seller to buyer, customs matters and the detailed sharing of costs. The terms are represented by abbreviations of three letters.
Letter of Credit/ definition	A Letter of Credit (L/C) is an agreement between a bank and its client (the importer), by which the bank undertakes to pay an amount of money from the account of that client to a third party provided that the beneficiary (the exporter) proves that it has fulfilled its obligation under the contract to make the delivery.
Letter of Credit/ applicant	The importer or buyer who requests and orders a letter of credit (L/C).
Letter of Credit/ beneficiary	The exporter or seller who is the beneficiary of the letter of credit (L/C).
Letter of Credit/ issuing bank	The bank that opens the letter of credit (L/C) by sending it to a bank in the exporter's country.
Letter of Credit/ advising bank	The bank that advises the exporter that a documentary credit has been opened on behalf of the importer and, having checked it, confirms that it is in order.
Sender	The person or organisation, in most cases also the seller of the goods, responsible for sending the goods to the consignee. The sender draws up a contract of carriage with a carrier.
Shipper	Shippers are go-betweens who conclude contracts of carriage on behalf of the seller i.e. sender; they represent the sender of the goods.

Exercises

Exercise 8.1
Below are the terms and conditions of sale of Slowakia Tobacco, a company established in Brno (Slovakia). The questions in this exercise are based on these terms and conditions.

Terms and conditions of sale

Description
Cigarette
84mm. Class 'A'
Soft/hard pack with 'For export only' label, bar code and health warning
Cut rag
Cut rag packed in plastic bag with 'For export only' printed on case

Packaging and Loading
Cigarette
20cigarettes per pack / 10 packs per carton / 50 cartons per master case
480 master cases per 20 ft. container
Cut Rag
9 kgs cut rag per master case / 480 master cases per 20 ft. container

Minimum Shipment
Cigarette
100 cases per brand / 50 cases per brand (if ordering more than one brand)
Cut Rag
200 kilograms per brand

Manufacturing Time
Manufacturing will begin immediately upon receipt of payment and will be completed in 30 days or sooner

Place of Loading
Brno, Slovakia

Terms INCOTERMS 2000:
EXW Ex Works Brno

Payments Payment prior to manufacture by:
1 Telegraphic Transfer (TT)
2 Demand Draft (D/D)
3 Irrevocable letter of credit in favour of the seller, available by draft at sight for 100% invoice value with a minimum 60 days period of validity.

Note: All foreign bank charges including cost of postage will be borne by the purchaser

Currency of Payment
US Dollar or Euro

Seller's Bank
Deutsche Bank
Av. Novodny 21-28, 2345 Brno, Slowakia

A/C Name
Slowakia Tobacco Monopoly

A/C Number
009-1-10832-2

Documents Provided
Commercial Invoice Packing List Others as requested

1 With reference to the above three Incoterms, describe the differences between them from the point of view of the seller.
2 With reference to the section on payments, what are the implications for the seller if payment is made by a Demand Draft (D/D)?
3 With reference to the letter of credit mentioned in the section on payments what exactly is the buyer's bank required to do?
4 What is the relevance of the above-mentioned 'Documents Provided'?

Slowakia Tobacco Monopoly concludes a contract of sale with Henderson Ltd., a company established in the UK, for the sale and delivery of three 20-foot containers of cigarettes, delivery FCA Brno. Henderson draws up a contract of carriage with Zorba Transport, a company established in Greece, which will undertake the shipping of the goods from Brno to Southampton (UK). Unfortunately, before loading the first container onto one of Zorba Transport's trucks, the container catches fire and is completely burned out. The goods in the container are no longer fit to be sold. On its way to Southampton the second truck carrying a container with cigarettes is stolen at a parking place near Holten (The Netherlands). The third truck, with its container, actually reaches the port in Rotterdam and is loaded onto a ship bound for the UK. However, due to a fierce storm in the North Sea and the fact that the container was not properly secured, this container falls overboard.

5 Who is liable, looking at the specified Incoterm, for the first container?
6 With regard to the second container, is the CMR applicable in this case? If not, is it possible for the contracting parties to opt into the CMR? If you answered yes to this question, who would be liable under the rules of the CMR for the second container?
7 Is the CMR applicable to the carriage of the third container?
8 Is the CISG applicable in this case? If so, what claims can Henderson make against Slovakia Tobacco Monopoly?

Exercise 8.2

Stark Machinery of Belgium sells machinery and equipment to Bejama Inc. of Yemen, for use in the construction of a liquid natural gas facility. The ship Superior Pescadores loaded the cargo at Antwerp, Belgium. Pescadores Inc. of Panama, the ship owners, issued six bills of lading acknowledging that the cargo was shipped in apparent good order and condition.

The terms of these bills of lading contain a provision stating that the liability of the carrier will be judged according to either the Hague Visby Rules or English Law (being the law applicable to the contract of carriage), should English Law prove more favourable to the shipper.

During the voyage, the cargo inside one hold shifted causing damage to part of the cargo. Stark Machinery calculated its claims using the package limits under both the Hague Visby Rules and English law, preferring to use whichever legal system resulted in them being able to claim more damages.

Pescadores Inc. admitted liability, but only to the amount of the package limit under the Hague Visby Rules. Furthermore, Pescadores Inc. felt that the cargo owners could not, on the matter of liability, choose between whatever legal system suited them best.

1 Do the Hague Visby Rules apply to this case?
2 Under the Hague Visby Rules, who in this case is the shipper and who the carrier of the cargo?
3 In this case, under which Article of the Hague Visby Rules can the carrier be held liable for damage to the cargo?
4 If the choice of English Law by Pescadores Inc. were to deprive Stark Machinery of the protection of the Hague Visby Rules, would this choice be valid or not?

Index